The American Revolutionary Series

AMERICAN AND FRENCH ACCOUNTS

OF THE

AMERICAN REVOLUTION

*The American Revolutionary Series
is published in cooperation with
The Boston Public Library*

Kosciuszko in the American Revolution

By
MIECISLAUS HAIMAN

With a New Introduction and Preface by
GEORGE ATHAN BILLIAS

GREGG PRESS
Boston   1972

Library of Congress Cataloging in Publication Data

Haiman, Miecislaus, 1888-1949.
  Kosciuszko in the American Revolution.

  (American Revolutionary series)
  Reprint of the 1943 ed., which was issued as no. 4 of
Polish Institute series.
  Includes bibliography.
  1. Kościuszko, Tadeusz Andrzej Bonawentura, 1746-
1817. 2. United States—History—Revolution.
I. Title. II. Series. III. Series: Polish Insti-
tute of Arts and Sciences in America. Polish Institute
series, no. 4.
E207.K8H3   1972   973.3'3'0924 [B]   72-10782
ISBN 0-8398-0807-0

AMERICAN AND FRENCH ACCOUNTS
OF THE AMERICAN REVOLUTION

W ho shall write the history of the American Revolution?" John Adams once asked. "Who can write it?" "Who will ever be able to write it?" Adams, however, had overlooked one important area. Materials were available for writing the military side of the struggle for independence. There existed many accounts, both primary and secondary, by the two prime protagonists in the war—the Americans and their French allies. This series is devoted to reprinting a selection of such works.

Books within the first category—personal accounts by officers and men who fought in the Continental army—were quite numerous in the historical literature. Although the age of universal public education in this country lay in the future, a surprising number of soldiers could read and write—a fact to which signatures on muster rolls can attest. Conscious that they were involved in an epoch-making event, many men kept a diary or journal in their knapsacks or wrote long letters home. These firsthand records made it possible to visualize the agonies of marching and fighting battles through the eyes of those who endured them. Equally important, these individual accounts often were more revealing than the official records. Such was the case in two of the works in this series—Caleb Stark's, *Memoir and Official Correspondence of General John Stark, with Notices of Several Other Officers of the Revolution,* and

Egbert Benson's, *Vindication of the Captors of Major Andre.*

A second primary source of utmost importance were army orderly books. The official purpose of these journals was to record the orders given by military commanders, the movement of units, and the disposition of forces during battle. Numerous other details of daily army life were also incorporated, such as the rations issued, sanitary measures taken, and the courts-martial conducted. By analyzing their contents carefully, however, one could read between the lines certain attitudes about which nothing had been written—the relations between officers and men, morale of troops, and reactions to recent military developments. From the book of general orders issued by Israel Putnam in the Hudson Highlands during the summer and fall of 1777, for example, one catches the shiver of apprehension that ran through his men as the invasion by General John Burgoyne from Canada got under way.

Among the secondary sources in this series, biographies rank high. The Revolutionary War produced not only a new nation but a host of heroes. From the study of the personal lives of participants, one can gain new insights regarding the struggle for independence. Elbridge H. Goss' two-volume work, *The Life of Colonel Paul Revere,* reveals that the Boston silversmith was a major figure in Massachusetts along with John Hancock and Sam Adams well before he took his famous midnight ride. Hancock himself is portrayed as a master organizer as well' as a colorful political leader in Lorenzo Sears' biography, *John Hancock, the Picturesque Patriot.* George Rogers Clark, a controversial figure in American history has alternately been described as the heroic conqueror of the West and as a guerilla fighter with dubious motives. Clark's contributions as well as his motives are examined in the careful book by Consul W. Butterfield. One of the European military experts who served the American cause in a unique way was Thaddeus Kosciuszko, the Polish patriot, artilleryman, and engineer. His career, studied by Miecislaus Haiman—a scholar with a command of the Polish language—provides information that is not generally known.

The last category in the American secondary sources reprinted in this series represents certain books that have been out-of-print. Although it is an older work, Sydney G. Fisher's *The True History of the American Revolution* is still regarded as indispensable by many scholars because of its treatment of the Loyalists as well as its emphasis on the internal social divisions within the country during the conflict. Paul Allen's *A History of the American Revolution* is of interest because it reflects the attitude toward the Revolution by the generation that fought the so-called "second war for independence"—the War of 1812. The volume by Simon Wolfe, *The Jew as Patriot, Soldier, and Citizen,* is distinctly different; it stresses, among other things, the contribution of Jews to the revolutionary movement in America. Finally, Clarence Bennett's *Advance and Retreat to Saratoga* goes well beyond the limits indicated in its title; it describes the military actions in the Northern theater of operations from Arnold's ill-fated expedition to Quebec in 1775 to the equally disastrous British invasion by Burgoyne in 1777.

Although French military aid is generally conceded to have made America's independence possible, literary accounts of France's involvement in the war have been relatively few in number. For this reason, three works in this series deal with the subject directly or indirectly. Thomas Balch's book, *The French in America During the War of Independence of the United States,* makes a strong case for the traditional position that France's contribution to the American cause made the difference between victory and defeat. William M. Sloane in *The French War and the Revolution,* on the other hand, concludes that the foreign alliance was a mistake and that America might have been better advised to gain her independence by herself. Abbe Raynal, the French writer and historian, examines the question from another point of view in *The Revolution of America*. He contends that the Revolution had a great impact upon European intellectuals, and that America provided a model for the Old World to follow in molding a new and better society.

One common theme runs through most of the volumes reprinted in this series; the participants—American and French—and the commentators—past and present—were agreed that the Revolution was a profound event whose effects were destined to shape the future of world history.

PREFACE

THADDEUS KOSCIUSZCO (1746-1817), famed Continental army officer and Polish patriot, remains one of the more romantic figures of the Revolutionary War. Born in what was to become Poland, he came to America in 1776 because he was stirred by the struggle for liberty and independence. Among the foreign officers who aided the patriots, he was one of the most significant in making an important contribution to the American cause.

Kosciuszco's professional training and education enabled him to assist the Americans in a unique way. As a youth, he was taught drawing, mathematics, and French by one of his relatives. After attending college, he graduated from the Royal School at Warsaw. Receiving the rank of captain, he was sent to the school at Mezieres, France, where he studied military engineering and artillery. Returning to Poland in 1774, he was disappointed in his hopes for a military career. Faced with bankruptcy and heartbroken because of an unsuccessful love affair, he returned to France. News of the American Revolution fired his imagination, and he borrowed money to come to this country. His talents in military engineering were quickly put to good use after he had received a commission as colonel of engineers in the Continental army in October, 1776.

During his first four years of service, Kosciuszco remained in the North. In the spring of 1777, he joined the army under General Gates of Ticonderoga and recommended that the Americans fortify Mount Defiance. Failure to fortify this position and its subsequent occupation by the British resulted in the loss of the key Ticonderoga fortress. Kosciuszco was then engaged in selecting and fortifying the positions taken by Gates' army at Saratoga. His advice contributed greatly to the brilliant American victories which culminated in the surrender of Burgoyne's army. From March, 1778, to June, 1780, he was in charge of building the fortifications at West Point—a location of great strategic significance.

Most of Kosciuszko's remaining service in the Revolutionary War was in the South under General Nathanael Greene. In the winter of 1780-81, he was assigned the mission of exploring the Catawba River. During Greene's dramatic race to the Dan River as he retreated before Lord Cornwallis, Kosciuszko was placed in charge of the transportation. He played an important but costly role in the campaign around Ninety-six, South Carolina in the summer of 1781. In the winter of 1782, he was stationed near Charleston, where he had an opportunity to show his talents as a cavalry officer rather than as a military engineer. He then returned North with Greene in the spring of 1783, and was promoted to brigadier general in the fall of that year.

Kosciuszko left America in July, 1784, returning to Poland by way of France. After four years of retirement, he became a major general in the Polish army. In the spring of 1792, he led his tiny army in a gallant but unsuccessful campaign against the Russians before his king succumbed to Russian intrigue. He went to France to seek the support of the French revolutionary government, but returned to Poland to lead the famous uprising in 1794. Defeated and captured by the Russians in October, 1794, he was freed after two years of imprisonment and returned to America in August, 1797.

He dedicated the rest of his life to one goal—gaining

Poland's freedom. After receiving money and a land grant from Congress for his Continental army services, he secretly left America in May, 1798, and returned to France. There he sought unsuccessfully to get Napoleon's cooperation for the restoration of his country on favorable terms. He continued similar futile efforts until his death in Switzerland in 1817.

This biography, written by an author who had a knowledge of Polish and used sources written in that language, is one of the best works in English on the subject. The book itself was published in honor of the sesquicentennial of the Kosciuszko insurrection in Poland in 1794. Although it over-emphasizes Kosciuszko's achievements in some instances, it contains information about his feats in military engineering that cannot be found elsewhere.

George Athan Billias
Clark University

KOSCIUSZKO
IN THE AMERICAN REVOLUTION

By

MIECISLAUS HAIMAN

POLISH INSTITUTE SERIES No. 4

Joseph Grassi pinx. Polish Embassy, Washington, D. C.
Photo by Lewis P. Woltz

THADDEUS KOSCIUSZKO

KOSCIUSZKO
IN THE AMERICAN REVOLUTION

By

MIECISLAUS HAIMAN

Polish Institute of Arts and Sciences in America

New York City

1943

Printed and manufactured in the United States of America
By HERALD SQUARE PRESS, INC.
233-245 SPRING STREET
NEW YORK, N. Y.

U. S. A.

"O! how happy we think our Self when Conscious of our deeds, that were started from principle of rectitude, from conviction of the goodness of the thing itself, from motive of the good that will Come to Human Kind."

KOSCIUSZKO TO
GEN. OTHO HOLLAND WILLIAMS,
Feb. 11, 1783

PREFACE

Kosciuszko's relations with America may be divided into two periods: the first one comprising his services in the Revolutionary War (1776-1784); and the second one his visit in America in 1797-8 and his subsequent connections with this country, especially his long and intimate correspondence with Thomas Jefferson. This work is intended to cover the first period and is being published to honor the sesquicentennial of the heroic, but unsuccessful Kosciuszko Insurrection in Poland in 1794; this movement, aimed to free the country from foreign domination, was a distant, but a very distinct, echo of the American Revolution and on this account deserves more than a passing notice of American historians.

The author intends to prepare the second part of this biography of Kosciuszko for the bicentennial of his birth in 1946.

Above all, he is most gratefully obliged to Mr. Bernhard Knollenberg, Librarian of the Yale University Library, who encouraged him in his work, revised the manuscript and constantly helped him in his difficulties and doubts; to the Rev. Sister M. Neomisia Rutkowska, C.S.F.N., Ph.D., of Washington, D. C., who contributed much of her time and labor to this work; to Prof. Peter Ostafin of the University of Michigan, and to Mr. Howard Peckham, Curator of Manuscripts, William L. Clements Library, for their many helpful suggestions; to Mr. Harry Emerson Wildes of Valley Forge, Pa.; to Prof. Louis Gottschalk of the University of Chicago; to Mr. Charles H. Wachtl, Ph.D., of Philadelphia, Pa.; to Prof. Samuel White Patterson of the Columbia University; to the Rev. Edward Wołkowski, D.D., of Poland and Chicago; to Mr. Clifford K. Shipton, Librarian, and Miss Viola C. Hamilton of the American Antiquarian Society; to Miss Gertrude D. Hess, Assistant Librarian, American Philosophical Society; to Miss Lillian G. Grant, Librarian's Secretary, Connecticut State Library; to Mr. K. D. Metcalf, Director, and Mr. Edwin E. Williams, General Assistant, Harvard College Library; Mr. William Reitzel, Director, Historical Society of Pennsylvania; Mr. Leslie Edgar Bliss, Librarian, and Miss Norma Cuthbert, Cataloguer, Department of Manuscripts, Henry E. Huntington Library; Dr. St. George L. Sioussat, Chief, Division of Manuscripts, Library of Congress; Mr. Austin K. Gray, Librarian, and

Mr. Barney Chesnick, Assistant Librarian, Ridgway Library; Mr. Raphael Semmes, Librarian, Maryland Historical Society; Mr. Allyn B. Forbes of the Massachusetts Historical Society; Mr. P. M. Hamer, Chief, Division of Reference, the National Archives; Mr. Alexander J. Wall, Director, New York Historical Society; Mr. Robert W. Hill, Keeper of Manuscripts, and Mr. Paul North Rice, Chief, Reference Department, New York Public Library; to Mr. C. C. Crittenden, Secretary, North Carolina Historical Commission; to Mr. Richard G. Hensley, Chief Librarian, Reference Division, Public Library of the City of Boston; Miss Elizabeth H. Jervey, Secretary, South Carolina Historical Society; Lt. Col. E. E. Farman, and Maj. W. J. Morton, Librarians, U. S. Military Academy; Mr. Rittenhouse Neisser, Librarian, Bucknell Library; to Miss Halina Chybowska and Miss Lia Ferrigno of Brooklyn, N. Y., and to all others who extended a helpful hand to the author. A very grateful acknowledgement is also due to the Newberry Library of Chicago which constituted the basic workshop of the author; to Mr. John T. Czech, Director, Youth Department of the Polish Roman Catholic Union of Chicago, whose friendly assistance in arranging the manuscript for publication was of inestimable value to the author; to Mr. William J. Roehrenbeck, Librarian, Fordham University, who was kind enough to peruse the orderly book of Gen. Greene, November 1, 1781, to January 31, 1782, recently acquired by the Library, which, however, contrary to our common expectations, contained no references to Kosciuszko; and to Mr. Harris H. Williams, in Charge of Manuscripts, Alderman Library, who devoted much of his time and efforts to help the author in his research.

Besides the aforementioned the author is indebted to His Excellency John Ciechanowski, the Polish Ambassador, Washington, D. C.; the Hon. Enoch D. Fuller, Secretary of State of New Hampshire; Mr. Otis G. Hammond, Director, New Hampshire Historical Society, and Mr. Fred W. Lamb, Director, Manchester (N. H.) Historic Association, for their kind help in collecting iconographic material for this volume.

The Polish Roman Catholic Union of America helped the author to cover the cost of research and it would be ingratitude on his part not to acknowledge its generous help which made possible the collecting of materials for this volume.

ILLUSTRATIONS AND MAPS

CONTENTS

Chapter I

THE EARLY YEARS

It was the year 1746.

The dusk of political decadence which had come over Poland since the later seventeenth century still enveloped the country. The crown of the Piasts and the Jagiellons now lay on the thoughtless head of Augustus III of the Saxon dynasty. The real force behind the throne was his almighty and dishonest minister Bruehl, whose policy it was to exploit the country for his personal gains. Externally deprived of her former prestige, internally weak, Poland became a "roadway inn" for armies of neighboring countries.

But the dawn of national regeneration was already breaking. Stanislaus Konarski made great strides in reforming the Polish school system and was in the midst of work on his important book *On The Effective Method of Deliberating in the Diet.* The former King Stanislaus Leszczyński, dethroned by the Saxons and now King of Lorraine, wrote his *Free Voice,* by which he became a forerunner of new ideas of political philosophy. The Załuski brothers prepared to open in Warsaw one of the finest and largest public libraries in Europe. Everywhere patriots began to awaken the nation to the need of rebuilding the mouldy ship of state.

At this turning point in her political history Andrew Thaddeus Bonaventure Kosciuszko was born. The exact date and place of his birth as well as many other details of his early years are unknown; so much is certain that he was baptized at the parochial Roman Catholic church at Kossów, County of Słonim, in the Polish eastern province of marshy Polesie, on February 12, 1746.[1] His Polish biographers suppose that he was born on February 4, which is the day of St. Andrew; it was, and still is, a Polish custom to give children the name of the patron saint of the day of their birth. The place of his birth was either Siechnowicze, the old family homestead, or Mereczowszczyzna, which also belonged to his parents. Both were small villages in the vicinity of Kossów.

---

[1] Korzon, *Kościuszko,* 70; on p. 564 he gives the exact text of an extract in Latin from the baptismal books of the church.

His parents were Louis Thaddeus Kosciuszko and Thecla, née Ratomska. The Kosciuszkos were an old Polish noble family of Lithuano-Ruthenian stock.[2] First mentioned in 1509, they received the Polish coat-of-arms Roch III and the estate of Siechnowicze, which gave them their agnomen Siechnowicki. None of Kosciuszko's ancestors reached prominence in the history of Poland; most of them were small landlords, not very active in public affairs, living in the sphere of their homes and immediate vicinity, but keeping strictly to old Polish virtues and customs; they were typical of the Polish gentry which, notwithstanding the decadence of the republic, still formed the morally healthy backbone of the nation. The father had wide family and business connections among the neighbors and was a rather popular figure in the County of Słonim, and even in the whole Palatinate of Brest. He had an official title of Sword Bearer of the Palatinate,—in all an empty decoration. As a man he was honest and humane. Louis Thaddeus died in 1758, leaving, besides the widow, four children of whom Thaddeus was the youngest.

Thecla Kosciuszko was an energetic and industrious woman. She outlived her husband ten years, taking care of the estate and the education of children. It was said, that besides her, one of her relatives who lived with the family after his long and extensive travels, most strongly influenced the early years of Thaddeus. The boy, after some home studies, was sent to college of the Piarist Fathers at Lubieszów, near Pińsk, in 1755, and remained there till 1760. Already in this early youth Timoleon the Corinthian became his favorite hero. Through the influence of Prince Adam Casimir Czartoryski, an old friend and protector of the family, Kosciuszko entered the Corps of Cadets in Warsaw on December 18, 1765. This school founded by the new King Stanislaus Augustus, educated the youth of nobility with emphasis on military art and development of character. Kosciuszko became one of the foremost pupils of the Corps. He is said to have excelled in geometry and drawings and to have displayed great industry together with other high moral qualities.

After a year's course he was commissioned Ensign and became one of the instructors of the Corps. In 1768, still on the staff of its teachers, he advanced to the rank of Captain. The King, who took

---

[2] Sass, "Narodowość Kościuszki", *Przegląd Katolicki*, V (1930), 84-6. Korzon gives an exhaustive genealogy of Kosciuszko, *op. cit.*, 1-24.

great personal interest in the school, liked the youth and offered him a stipend to complete his studies abroad. Prince Czartoryski also promised him financial aid for this purpose. As his mother died in 1768, Kosciuszko left the family estate in the hands of his brother Joseph, borrowed some money from him on account of his share of the inheritance and about the middle of 1769 left for France with his friend, Captain Joseph Orłowski of the Corps of Cadets, another stipendiary of the King.

It is definitely known of his sojourn abroad, that he had studied for a year in the famous Académie Royale de Peinture et de Sculpture at Paris, and associated with many prominent painters. Kosciuszko himself said of this period of his life: "During the five years of my life spent in foreign countries I have endeavored to master those arts which pertain to a solid government, aiming at the happiness of all, also economics and military art; I earnestly tried to learn this, inasmuch as I had a natural passion for these things."[3] Undoubtedly he became thoroughly acquainted with the contemporary French intellectual life. There are traces that he became influenced by Turgot, the economist. He is said to have made the acquaintance of Perronet, the famous engineer. Most probably he served as intermediary in bringing Pierre S. du Pont de Nemours to Poland as instructor under the Commission of Education and as a private tutor for the children of Prince Czartoryski. During this sojourn Kosciuszko also visited Switzerland and probably Italy.

A year before his departure for France the first Polish insurrection against Russian interference in Poland, known as the Confederacy of Bar, broke out. The famous Casimir Pulaski, who later died a hero's death in America, was one of the most picturesque figures of this movement. The Confederation was also directed against Stanislaus Augustus as a puppet imposed and directed by foreign might. Kosciuszko was personally much indebted to the King and that is the reason given by his biographers why he kept himself aloof from the long struggle which ended with the First Partition of Poland.

In the summer of 1774, he returned to Poland and found public, as well as his private affairs in a bad state of things. His brother Joseph is accused by historians of maladministration of the family

---

[3] Kosciuszko to George W. Mniszech, Oct. 19, 1775, Dzwonkowski, "Młode Lata Kościuszki," *Biblioteka Warszawska*, CCLXXXIV (1911). 35.

estate and of wronging Thaddeus. The estate was on the verge of bankruptcy. With the reduction of the Polish army Kosciuszko had no way of getting a commission, except by purchase. For a while he lived with his relatives, especially with his beloved sister Anna, married to Peter Estko, and residing near Kobryń. He visited his neighbors and old friends, among them the family of Joseph Sosnowski, the Lithuanian "hetman." There he met Ludwika Sosnowska, his daughter, and fell in love with her. The affair was an unhappy one. The proud and rich Sosnowski disregarded the poor Captain. With broken heart, with no prospects to serve his country, he decided to leave Poland again. He arranged a loan of 8,820 Polish złotys from Estko for which he pledged his share in the estate of Siechnowicze[4] and immediately set out west through Dukla, in southern Poland, Cracow and Dresden.

His plans for the future were not clear. At first he seems to have intended to enter the Saxon public service. The foremost purpose in his mind, however, was "to be of use to his country at some future period and to repay her the benefits of his citizenship."[5]

---

[4] Kahanowicz, *Memorial Exhibition, Thaddeus Kosciuszko*, 1, No. 1; hereafter referred to as Kahanowicz.

[5] Kościuszko to Mniszech, *loc. cit.*, 53.

Chapter II

PHILADELPHIA

Without doubt the echoes of "the shot that was heard around the world" reached Kosciuszko's ears before he left Poland. It is entirely possible therefore that he prepared for the journey toward Saxony with the ultimate thought of America as his eventual destination.

Perhaps while still in Dresden he met Nicolas Dietrich, Baron de Ottendorf, a nobleman from Lusatia, Saxony, who had served as a Lieutenant in the Prussian army during the Seven Years' War, and together with whom he later sailed for the New World. A Frenchman, Charles Noel Romand, Sieur de Lisle, Captain of Artillery, accompanied them.[1] It is not known, however, when and at what port they embarked.

Lord Stormont, the British Ambassador in Paris, very diligently observed everything bearing on the American Revolution that went on in France. Vergennes, the French Minister of Foreign Affairs, complained that he "had spies in all our ports, even with an ostentation," and "had established a most odious espionage."[2] Though there is no direct mention either of Kosciuszko or of his associates in Stormont's reports to London, one of his remarks may pertain to them. On March 13, 1776, he informed Lord Weymouth, the British Secretary of State, in a letter marked "most secret:"

"I am sorry to say, My Lord, that I have now good Reason to believe that several foreign officers are gone to join the Rebel army. They go under various Pretences to St. Domingo and from thence find their way to North America. I am almost certain that one officer of Cavalry, a German by Birth, who served in the last war under General Seidlitz, and who is reckoned a Man of distinguished Military Talents went to St. Domingo some Months ago with particular Recommendations to Monsieur d'Ennery."[3]

---

[1] *Pennsylvania Archives,* 5, III, 895.

[2] Vergennes to Marquis de Noailles, June 21, 1777, Stevens, *Facsimiles,* XVI, no. 1553, p. 3, and XIX, no. 1737, p. 4.

[3] Comte d'Ennery, Governor of St. Domingo; Stevens, *Facsimiles,* XIII, no. 1317, p. 1.

This description may pertain to Ottendorf. That their route lay through St. Domingo may be surmised from a report on Kosciuszko in a Polish newspaper of 1777, according to which he and his companions met with disaster at sea; their ship sank in a storm, but all were saved and landed on an island whence they reached the American shores.[4]

In any event Kosciuszko left Europe by the end of June, 1776, at the latest. The earliest mention of him in American documents is under the date of August 30, 1776, and it took a sailing vessel two or three months to cross the Atlantic westward. There is little likelihood that he met Silas Deane, the first American agent sent to France, had a chance to lay his plans before him and get a recommendation from him. Deane, arrived at Bordeaux "early in the Month of June" and reached Paris on July 6.[5] There is no mention of Kosciuszko in his papers.[6]

An early historian of Burgoyne's campaign relates of Kosciuszko that "this celebrated engineer came to this country utterly unprovided with letters of recommendation or introduction and nearly penniless and offered himself as a volunteer in the American cause and solicited an interview with Washington."[7] This opinion was heretofore almost generally accepted though Gen. John Armstrong, the son, Kosciuszko's comrade-in-arms, protested against its truthfulness. In his memoir written for Jared Sparks, he asserted: "What can be more incredible, than the story of his coming, not only without money, but without a single professional credential, or letter of even personal introduction?"[8] According to him, Kosciuszko "arrived in this country late in the summer of 1776," and "presented himself and his credentials to the board of war."[9] The Polish historian, W. M. Kozłowski, justly supposed that Kosciuszko might possibly have had a letter of recommendation from Prince Czartory-

---

4 Skałkowski, *Kościuszko w Świetle Nowszych Badań*, 21.

5 Bancroft's Information, Aug. 14, 1776, Stevens, *Facsimiles*, IX, no. 890, p. 3.

6 The Deane Papers, *Coll. N. Y. Hist. Soc.*, XIX (1886), 141. The introduction wrongly gives May 4 as the date of Deane's arrival in France (p. X). In the same volume, p. 141, Deane writes to Robert Morris that he arrived on June 6, 1776.

7 Neilson, *Original Account*, 118.

8 Harvard College Library, Sparks Papers, (hereafter referred to as Sparks Papers), ser. 49, vol. I, f. 72.

9 *Ibid.*, f. 70.

CARICATURE OF GEN. CHARLES LEE
by KOSCIUSZKO

ski to Gen. Charles Lee, now second in command in the American army.[10]

It would be quite natural if Kosciuszko wanted an interview with Washington, but in August, 1776, the Commander-in-Chief was in New York hard pressed by superior British forces. On August 27, the battle of Long Island, unsuccessful for the Americans, was fought.

However, the Continental Congress was sitting in Philadelphia, and Kosciuszko presented it with a memorial which unhappily has been lost. It was read in Congress on Friday, August 30, and referred to the Board of War.[11] The Board returned it with a report on October 18, whereupon Congress "Resolved, that Thaddeus Kosciuszko, Esq., be appointed an engineer in the service of the United States, with the pay of sixty dollars a month, and the rank of colonel."[12]

Kosciuszko appeared in Philadelphia just at the time when the question of strengthening the fortifications of the city, in view of the military situation, became a burning one. Some fortifications had been erected at the expense of Pennsylvania in 1775. These, however, were considered insufficient. On May 16, 1776, the Pennsylvania Council of Safety appointed a Committee to draw up a memorial to Congress respecting the erecting of fortifications at Billingsport, an island on the Delaware River.[13] Congress authorized the project and decided to cover the cost of the works.[14] There was, however, a difficulty in finding a suitable engineer. The Council appealed to Washington.[15] On June 17, the Commander-in-Chief replied from New York "with no small degree of pain" that he could not "spare from hence any person who has the least skill in the business of an

---

10 Kozłowski, "Pierwszy Rok Służby Amerykańskiej Kościuszki," *Przegląd Historyczny*, IV, 310-14. Lee came to Poland in 1765 in order to enter the Polish military service. He became a welcome guest at the home of Prince Czartoryski and at the Warsaw court. The King made him his aide-de-camp and later Major General of the Polish army. Very often they both discussed American matters, the King expressing warm sympathy for the Colonies. With some interruptions, Lee remained in Poland till 1769; cf. "The Lee Papers," *Coll. of the N. Y. Hist. Soc.*, IV-VII (1871-74).

11 *Journals of the Continental Congress*, V, 719; hereafter referred to as *Journals Cont. Cong.*; Force, *American Archives*, ser. 5, vol. I, p. 1625.

12 *Journals Cont. Cong.*, VI, 888; Force, *Archives*, ser. 5, vol. II, p. 1406.

13 Force, *Archives*, ser. 5, vol. III, p. 658.

14 *Ibid.*, ser. 5, vol. III, pp. 1284 and 1293; *Journals Cont. Cong.*, V, 443.

15 Force, *Archives*, ser. 5, vol. III, p. 906.

Engineer."[16] In this difficult situation Kosciuszko who was still waiting for a decision of Congress in respect to his memorial, was engaged to lay out a plan of fortifications at Billingsport.[17] On October 24, the Council of Safety drew "an order on Mr. Nesbit, in favor of Monsieur Thaddeus Kosciuszko for 50 pounds, as a reward for his services" in this connection.[18]

The works at Billingsport were carried on briskly in the fall of 1776, and undoubtedly Kosciuszko was busy, too. On December 5, Congress resolved, that "two months Pay be advanced to Mons. Ramond de Lisle, and to Mons. Kosciuszko,"[19] and most probably it was for his work at the fortifications.

Meanwhile the scene of war shifted from New York to New Jersey. Washington was in full retreat followed by the British. The situation was extremely critical and Washington himself seemed to lose hope. "I think the game is pretty near up," he wrote. "No Man, I believe, ever had a greater choice of difficulties and less means to extricate himself from them."[20] On December 8, he crossed the Delaware. As Philadelphia was in imminent danger, Congress adjourned to meet in Baltimore and Gen. Putnam was sent to the city to "superintend the Works and give the necessary directions."[21]

There was evidently some plan to use Kosciuszko for the purpose of strengthening the new American position on the Delaware. On December 10, Gen. John Armstrong,[22] writing from the headquarters then at Trenton Falls, to the Board of War and warning it of a probable attack of Gen. Howe on Philadelphia, added: "I had without consulting the General written for Colonels Kosciusko

---

16 Fitzpatrick, ed., *Writings of George Washington*, V, 153-4, hereafter referred to as Fitzpatrick.

17 Chevalier de Kermovan, a Frenchman, later commissioned as engineer with the rank of Lieutenant Colonel in the Continental service, was recommended to the Council of Safety of Pennsylvania by the Board of War on June 28, 1776, for the purpose of "planning and laying out the fortifications agreed by Congress, to be erected at Billingsport"; on July 29, he laid a plan and draughts before Congress, who referred them to the Board of War, but evidently these were not acted upon (*Journals Cont. Cong.*, V. 443, 613 and 614).

18 Force, *Archives*, ser. 5, vol. II, p. 92; *Pennsylvania Colonial Records*, X, 764.

19 Force, *Archives*, ser. 5, vol. III, p. 1599; *Journals Cont. Cong.*, VI, 1006. De Lisle, commissioned Major of the Continental Artillery on Nov. 12, 1776, returned to San Domingo April 12, 1777 (Heitman, *Historical Register*, 353).

20 Washington to John Augustine Washington, Dec. 18, 1776, Fitzpatrick, VI, 398.

21 Washington to the Pres. of Cong., Dec. 9, 1776, Fitzpatrick, VI, 340.

22 Father of the then Major John Armstrong.

and Ramond; but as General Putnam is sent down for purposes on their way near town, I suppose they can't be sent here."[23]

By this time Washington evidently also heard of Kosciuszko though he still thought him to be a Frenchman. On December 9, he wrote to John Hancock, then President of Congress: "If the Measure of fortifying the City should be adopted, some skillful persons should immediately view the Grounds and begin to trace out the Lines and Works. I am informed there is a French Engineer of eminence in Philadelphia at this time. If so, he will be the most proper."[24] And again from the "Camp above Trenton" he wrote to the same on December 20, that "none of the French Gentlemen whom I have seen with appointments . . . appear to me to know anything of the Matter. There is one in Philadelphia who I am told is clever, but him I have never seen."[25]

Under Putnam's orders Kosciuszko began to erect new defensive works at Red Bank, on the New Jersey shore of the Delaware, which were named Fort Mercer. It was he who drew the plans and directed the laying of the foundations of this fort during the winter of 1776-7.[26]

Washington's campaign in New Jersey saved Philadelphia for the time being. Nevertheless further work on the fortifications at both points were carried on.[27] In the beginning of February, 1777, Gen. Horatio Gates succeeded Putnam in the command of the city. Between the new commander and the young Polish engineer a warm friendship developed which withstood disagreeable trials during the

---

[23] Force, *Archives*, ser. 5, vol. III, p. 1151.

[24] Fitzpatrick, VI, 340, and note.

[25] *Ibid.*, VI, 405.

[26] Bellas, "The Defences of the Delaware River in the Revolution," *Proceedings and Coll. of the Wyoming Hist. and Geolo. Soc.*, V (1900), 50-1; Kain, "The Military and Naval Operations on the Delaware in 1777," *Publications of the City History Soc. of Philadelphia*, no. 8 (1910), 181.

[27] The works at Billingsport were continued by Robert Smith and those at Fort Mercer by Col. John Bull and Blaithwaite Jones as chief engineer (Bellas, *op. cit.*, 50; Jordan, *A History of Delaware County, Pa.*, I, 217). Du Coudray, French engineer, who made an inspection of the defenses on the Delaware in June, 1777, criticized fortifications at both places as too extensive for proper defense. Washington agreed with his opinion (Fitzpatrick, VII, 411; VIII, 243). Similar objections were raised by Marquis de Chastellux who visited Billingsport in 1780, (*Travels in North America*, I, 252). It is impossible to decide how far Kosciuszko's plans influenced the actual erection of these fortifications. With modifications recommended by Du Coudray the works at Billingsport were ordered by Congress to be carried on in summer of 1777. Lord Howe occupied Billingsport, left nearly unmanned, in October, 1777. Fort Mercer won fame by its brave defense against the Hessian Colonel Donop.

Revolution and the test of time. On March 25, Gates was ordered by Congress to take command of Ticonderoga.[28] On March 31, he received from the same body a permission to take Gen. de Rochefermoy and "such other French officers as he may think proper." Gates invited Kosciuszko to go with him as engineer. To James Wilkinson he offered the post of his aide-de-camp.

---

[28] *Journals Cont. Cong.*, VII, 202.

Chapter III

TICONDEROGA

On April 2,[1] Gates left Philadelphia for the North. On April 7, he and Mrs. Gates passed through Bethlehem.[2] Wilkinson followed them,[3] most probably accompanied by Kosciuszko and by Dr. Jonathan Potts, who was to become chief medical officer in the Northern Department.

Wilkinson reached Albany in the latter part of April and was soon after dispatched by Gates with instructions to examine and regulate the chain of communication with Ticonderoga.[4] It may be assumed that Kosciuszko helped him in this task, though Wilkinson does not mention it in his memoirs. In any event Kosciuszko accompanied Wilkinson on his way from Albany to Ticonderoga. At that time the old fort was under immediate command of Gen. John Paterson, and Col. Jeduthan Baldwin and Lt. Col. Christopher Pelissier supervised the work of strengthening fortifications.

On May 8, Gates wrote to Gen. Paterson:

"Lieut. Col. Kusiusco accompanies Wilkinson, he is an able Engineer, and one of the best and neatest draughtsman I ever saw. I desire he may have a Quarter assigned him, and when he has thoroughly made himself acquainted with the works, have ordered him to point out to you, where and in what manner the best improvements and additions can be made thereto; I expect Col. Baldwin will (give) his countenance and protection to this Gentleman, for he is meant to serve not supersede him.[5]

On May 12, Col. Baldwin noted in his diary: "Doctor (Jonathan) Potts, Colonel Kosciusko and Colonel Wilkinson came in,"[6] and

---

[1] Roger Sherman to Jonathan Trumbull, Apr. 1, 1777, Burnett, *Letters of Members of the Continental Congress*, II, 314, hereafter referred to as Burnett, *Letters*.

[2] Jordan, "Bethlehem during the Revolution," *Pennsylvania Mag. of Hist. and Biogr.*, XIII (1889), 83.

[3] Wilkinson, *Memoirs*, I ,160.

[4] *Ibid.*, I, 162.

[5] N. Y. Public Library, Bancroft's Revolutionary Papers, vol. III, fol. 133.

[6] Baldwin, *The Revolutionary Diary of Col. Jeduthan Baldwin*, 101. Wilkinson wrote to Gates from Ticonderoga, May 16, 1777: "I arrived here on the 13th inst." (*Memoirs*, I, 162), which does not agree with the date given by Baldwin.

a few days later he wrote to his daughter Betsy: "This week Lieut. Col. Kosiosko came to this post, an assistant Engineer, he is from Poland and is a beautiful limner."[7]

Evidently Kosciuszko and Baldwin were on the best terms from the beginning, and the Yankee gladly assumed the functions of host to new arrivals. The next entries in his diary are:

"May 13—Doctor Potts and Colonel Kosciusko Lodged with us.

"May 15—Went around the lines with Lieut. Col. Kosciusko.

"May 16—General Paterson, Colonels Francis, Wilkins, Kosciusko and Major Hull supped with me."[8]

Kosciuszko did not waste time and in a few days after his arrival he sent to Gates a lengthy report in French on the state of fortifications at Ticonderoga and his proposed changes and additions, together with a plan of his own with explanations. "In consequence of your Orders I have visited every part or place, & from My remarks I send you the plan," he wrote. Well satisfied with the reception he met from his immediate superiors, he seemed to be afraid, however, that his project may not have their approval.

"My opinion & advice is asked" he added. "I cannot help giving my sentiments in regard to the Entrenchments. My General, I request the favour you would not give me Orders to proceed, before your arrival. I will give you the reason, I love peace & to be on good terms with all the world if possible; if my opinion or Ideas are adopted, which may be better I should the more so being a stranger, I am convinced how much I ought to be on my Guard, as also have regard to nationality, but our work would not be better.

"I declare sincerely that I am susceptible & love peace. I would chuse rather to leave all, return home & plant Cabbages; as yet my Genl. I have no reason of complaint of any one, I was well

---

[7] "The Baldwin Letters," *The American Monthly*, VI (1895), 196. Martin I. J. Griffin, *Catholics and the American Revolution*, III, 139, most probably errs referring to Kosciuszko the note of Major Kingston, Adjutant General of Gen. Burgoyne, of May 13: "A French officer has lately reached the rebel army, and was appointed engineer-in-chief" (Stone, *Memoirs, Letters and Journals of Riedesel*, I, 295). It is more likely that it pertained to Pelissier who reached Ticonderoga in February and aspired to the post of principal engineer of the fort (Fitzpatrick, VII, 102).

[8] Baldwin, *Diary*, 102. The entry pertains to Col. Ebenezer Francis of the 11th Mass., killed at Hubbardton on July 7, 1777; Wilkinson and Major William Hull of Massachusetts, later Governor of Michigan Territory and the luckless General in the War of 1812.

received by Genl. Paterson who overcome me with politeness, all the Officers are extreamly Friendly."[9]

On the 18th, as reported by Wilkinson, "the General officers," under Schuyler, "made a critical inspection of the fortifications"[10] and on the same day Kosciuszko wrote again to Gates:

"My Opinion may be dangerous. I say if we have time to make an Entrenchment like what I had the honour to send you a Model of; with the addition of a triffling thing towards the Lake to prevent passage of shipping. I say the enemy cannot hurt us; we have an excellent place not only to resist the Enemy, but beat them, but Courage and more artillery men will be necessary, for we have only one Company & that is not enough; we ought to have three.

"The Bridge[11] is not yet finished nevertheless it must be; I say nothing of what unnecessary works have been carried on you will be a Judge yourself my Genl. we are very fond here of making Block houses and they are all erected in the most improper places. Nevertheless Genl. we'll conquer headed by your Excellency, our steady attachment to you, will be a great inducement added to the Sacred Duty which has engaged us to Defend this Country. If we cannot have more artillery men it will be necessary to Draft some soldiers & exercise them having great occasion."[12]

Evidently Kosciuszko's ideas did not meet with the approval of Baldwin, and the former was unwilling to force his opinions by transgressing the rules of discipline and friendship. On May 22, Wilkinson informed Gates:

"I wish to Heaven, either yourself or General St. Clair was here for a few days. Colonel Kosciusko is timidly modest; Baldwin is inclosing the lines on a plan of his own."[13]

Most probably in answer to this Gates wrote from Albany, May 23, to Gen. Paterson:

---

[9] N. Y. Hist. Soc., Gates Papers (hereafter referred to as Gates Papers), box 6, no. 190. Kosciuszko's plan is not among the Gates Papers. The original is in French and has the date May, 1777: contemp. transl.

[10] *Memoirs*, I, 173.

[11] This floating bridge of large logs was to link Ticonderoga with Fort Independence which lay on the other side of the narrow passage connecting Lake George with Lake Champlain.

[12] Gates Papers, box 6, no. 144; the original in French: contemp. transl.

[13] Smith, *The St. Clair Papers*, I, 51; Wilkinson, *Memoirs*, I, 173.

"I entreat, my Dear General, that You will keep every Soul at Work to Strengthen Our posts; perhaps the Enemy may give us Two Months, before they come again to *look* at Ticonderoga; let us regard those two Months, as the most precious Time we have to Live; they may be worth an Age of Droning peace, and, well employ'd may give happiness, and peace to Millions. I earnestly recommend it to You, to order Lieut. Colonel Kosciuszko's plan, to be immediately put in Execution; doing the most defensible parts first. Colonel Baldwin will gain my Affection, and Esteem, by cultivating the Friendship of that Capable Young Man; and he may be assured he can in nothing serve his Country more, than in going hand in hand, with him, in improving the Fortifications of Ticonderoga."[14]

On the same day "General Paterson and Colonel Kosciuszko went to Skenesboro," according to an entry in Baldwin's diary.[15] Hence Kosciuszko passed to Albany for a personal interview with Gen. Gates concerning the situation at Ticonderoga. Wilkinson wrote to Gates on May 28:

"Thinking that Col. Kusiusco would be of more Service by Personally representing to you the Situation of this Place I have obtained leave for His Return."[16]

Sending Kosciuszko to Ticonderoga early in May, Gates gave him orders "to examine and report the condition of that fortress; the extension (if any) to be given to Fort Independence, and lastly, whether Sugar loaf hill could be made practicable to the ascent of guns of large calibre?"[17] The third point of the orders was very important in view of the fact that Sugar Loaf Hill, renamed Mount Defiance, was a key position and its occupation by the British a few months later decided the fate of Ticonderoga.

Armstrong relates the roles of Gates, Kosciuszko and Gen. Schuyler in this regard: "These duties (orders of Gates) were promptly and carefully discharged and the measures recommended by the Engineer entirely approved by the General. The hitherto doubtful and highly interesting question with regard to Sugar Loaf Hill, was fully discussed and the following conclusions arrived at: '1st—That

---

14 Library of Congress, Papers of the Continental Congress (hereafter referred to as Papers Cont. Cong.), ser. 154, vol. I, fol. 222-3.
15 P. 103. Skenesboro now Whitehall, N. Y.
16 Gates Papers, box 6, no. 181.
17 Armstrong memorial, Sparks Papers, ser. 49, vol. I, fol. 70.

the sides of the hill though steep, may, by the labor of strong fatigue parties, be so shaped as to permit the ascent of the heaviest cannon. 2d—That the summit, now sharp and pointed, may by similar means, be quickly reduced to table ground and furnish a good site for a battery, and 3d—that a battery so placed, from elevation and proximity, would completely cover the two forts, the bridge of communication and the adjoining boat-harbor.'

"Unfortunately, about the time these opinions were given by the Engineer and adopted by the General, the latter was recalled and Gen. Schuyler placed in command of the army."[18] Schuyler was highly offended by the nomination of Gates to an independent command at Ticonderoga. He repeatedly complained of it to members of Congress, refusing to serve "unless an absolute command is given him over every part of the army in the Northern department."[19] Ultimately Congress reversed its former decision and reinstated Schuyler. Gates was given the choice "either to continue in command in the Northern Department, under Maj. Gen. Schuyler, or to take upon him the office of Adjutant General in the Grand Army immediately under the Commander in Chief."[20]

This happened on May 15, and the news of the new decision must have reached Albany during Kosciuszko's presence there. It was entirely human that Gates declined to serve under Schuyler and returned to Philadelphia. For the second time in a brief period he felt wronged by Congress for Schuyler's sake. Not fully a year ago Schuyler challenged his right to command troops which returned from the unsuccessful invasion of Canada, and Congress sustained him.[21] Washington himself was annoyed by the irresolution of Congress and undoubtedly it contributed much to the loss of Ticonderoga. "I am too far remov'd from Philadelphia, and have too much business of my own, to know, or enquire into the springs which move Congress to such sudden changes in their Resolutions as have lately appear'd in the Northern department," wrote he to the Rev. William Gordon on June 29, 1777. "It is much to be wished that more stability was observed in a body so respectable, as the Service is really injured by a conduct of this sort."[22]

---

[18] Sparks Papers, ser. 49, vol. I, fol. 70.
[19] Schuyler to Richard Varick, April 26, 1777, Burnett, *Letters*, II, 342.
[20] *Journals Cont. Cong.*, VII, 364.
[21] Cf. Knollenberg, *Washington and the Revolution*, 174.
[22] Fitzpatrick, VIII, 316.

During Kosciuszko's absence at Ticonderoga the works were conducted exclusively under orders of Col. Baldwin, who had no professional schooling. Wilkinson was greatly dissatisfied with him. On May 31, he wrote an urgent letter to Gates, evidently still without knowledge of his having been superseded:

"The works are now pushed on Baldwin's unmeaning plan.— For God's sake, let Kosciusko come back as soon as possible, with proper authority."[23]

Meanwhile Gen. Arthur St. Clair took the immediate command of Ticonderoga. He was an able soldier, but he had to obey orders of Schuyler "who reasoning from the fact that no Engineer hitherto, French, British, or American, had believed in the practicability of placing a battery on Sugar loaf hill, was not disposed to embarrass himself or his means of defence, by making the experiment; and the less so, as he was 'fully convinced, that between two and three thousand men, could effectually maintain Fort Independence and secure the pass.'[24] To this point therefore the General's attention was principally given; no doubt very conscientiously, but very erroneously, as the event proved."[25]

In vain Gates urged St. Clair to occupy Sugar Loaf Hill, in a letter sent after his departure for Philadelphia.[26] St. Clair himself frequently spoke of the importance of this position,[27] but nothing was done in this matter.

Kosciuszko returned to Ticonderoga on June 6[28] and, evidently, immediately thereafter wrote to Gates under the fresh impression of his recall:

"An opportunity now presents to lay before you the real sentiments of my heart Also my present Ideas. If your love for your Country and your easy manner of communicating yourself to every one has attached me to you, among other things, your Great Military knowledge and true merit has so much inspired my confidence in you that I should be happy to be with you every where. Be persuaded General, that I am not actuated by Interest, otherwise than

---

23 Wilkinson, *Memoirs*, I, 171.
24 Schuyler to Congress, June 8, 1777, quoted by Armstrong, Sparks Papers, ser. 49, vol. I, fol. 70.
25 *Ibidem.*
26 Sparks Papers, ser. 49, vol. I, ff. 34 *et seq.*
27 Campbell, *Revolutionary Services of General William Hull*, 74.
28 Baldwin, *Diary*, 104.

the ambition of signalizing myself in this War. And I seek an opportunity, which I am of opinion can never be better, than under your Auspices. If the Works at Ticonderoga, should be any hindrance to my going with you, that will be but triffling, because I can in very short time, do what is necessary for this Campaign. Inform me Genl. if I may prepare to go with you. You know well, that the change of a Commander esteemed by the Troops has considerable effect on their minds.

"I flatter myself, General, that you will grant me my request, which cannot but increase my Attachment to you, and encourage my utmost endeavors to gain your Esteem."[29]

But Gates, divested of command, had nothing to offer to Kosciuszko who had to remain at his post. Col. Baldwin recorded in his diary:

"June 8—Went around among the workmen in the morning & to Crown Point with General Paterson, Colonel Kosciusko, Doctor Craig[30] and Doctor Major Armstrong and 30 Men. Measured the width across to Chimney Point. . . .

"June 14 . . . In the afternoon went with Colonel Kosciusko to advise what works had best be done on the Mount. . ." (Independence).[31]

Major Isaac B. Dunn, aide-de-camp to Gen. St. Clair, arriving at Ticonderoga on June 14, observed that "a day or two after his arrival he went round the lines" and "on Mount Independence he found a party of about one hundred men, under the direction of Colonel Kosciuszko, erecting three redoubts in the rear of the Mount, and forming an abbatis."[32] On June 19, Gen. Schuyler visited Ticonderoga and ordered additional works on Mount Independence. "About five or six hundred men were employed on the batteries on Mount Independence . . . on or about the 23-d day of June," evidently under Kosciuszko, according to his deposition during St. Clair's trial.[33] As ordered by Gen. St. Clair, Kosciuszko also "marked out the lines, and prepared the fascines to improve the redoubt . . .

---

29 Gates Papers, box 6, no. 192; the original in French, contemp. transl.

[30] Dr. James Craik of Virginia, Chief Physician and Surgeon of the Army, 1781-83.

[31] Baldwin, *Diary*, 104-5.

[32] "Proceedings of a General Court Martial, . . . for the Trial of Major General St. Clair," reprinted in the *Coll. N. Y. Hist. Soc.*, XIII (1880), 109.

[33] *Ibid.*, 58.

on the point of Mount Independence,"[34] but found the ground "very stony and rocky" that "would require a great deal of labour to put on the works. A ditch could not be sunk to any proper depth without blowing the rocks."[35]

Also on order of Gen. St. Clair, Kosciuszko built "some additions to the works on the Ticonderoga side . . . between the west end of the French lines and the Lake," though they were "not quite finished at the time of the evacuation."[36]

Lt. Col. Henry B. Livingston, aide-de-camp to Gen. Schuyler, deposed during St. Clair's trial that "no measures were neglected (by Gen. St. Clair) to strengthen the works on both sides of the Lake. Fatigue parties were daily employed in this duty, and the direction of them generally committed to Colonel Kosciuszko, an active officer, who acted as an assistant engineer in the northern department."[37]

On June 30, the army of Burgoyne appeared before Ticonderoga, and on July 5, the besieged saw to their surprise a British battery on the peak of Sugar Loaf Hill, thus completely and unhappily vindicating the opinion of Kosciuszko as to its adaptability for the purpose of fortification.[38] Gen. St. Clair called a council of war composed of general officers and they very wisely decided a quick retreat. "About ten o'clock at night a Speedy retreat was ordered and the main body of the Army got From Ty & Mount Independence a little before Sunrise, followed by the Enemy but did but little damage."[39]

The condition of the retreating army, however, was lamentable. They were "badly armed, and both men and officers half naked, sickly, and destitute of comforts . . . Our troops . . . lost spirit."[40] They were "severely pressed by the enemy" and the retreat "was made with great disorder and its usual accompaniment, frequent desertion."[41] According to still another eyewitness, Col. Udney Hay,

---

[34] *Ibid.*, 60.

[35] Kosciuszko's deposition, *ibid.*, 61.

[36] *Ibid.*, 59.

[37] *Ibid.*, 115.

[38] John Trumbull, the painter, then Lt. Colonel of the Ticonderoga garrison, claims to be the first to call attention to the practicability of fortifying Sugar Loaf Hill (*Autobiography, Reminiscences and Letters of John Trumbull*, 31).

[39] Baldwin, "Diary," *The Bulletin of the Fort Ticonderoga Museum*, IV (1938), 40.

[40] Wilkinson, *Memoirs*, I, 200.

[41] Armstrong memorial, Sparks Papers, ser. 49, vol. I, fol. 70.

Deputy Quarter Master at Ticonderoga, "misfortunes and fatigue have broken down the discipline and spirits of the troops and converted them in a great degree into a rabble. They seem to have lost all confidence in themselves and their leaders. The militia seem to be infected with the same spirit. Such as are with us are good for nothing but to eat and waste and grumble, and those at home think home safest. When I tell you that the sight of twenty or thirty Indians on our flank or rear, fills the whole camp with alarm, and that the act of shooting one from behind the walls of a log cabin has been commemorated in General Orders as a proof of great gallantry, your Excellency (the letter was written to Gov. Geo. Clinton) will be able to judge of what will probably happen, if by any accident we are brought into close contact with Burgoyne's veterans. But of such an event there is little danger. We first collected at Fort Edward, but quickly left that for a strong position on Moses' Creek. The Indians soon made this uncomfortable, when we removed here (Stillwater) and began a fortified camp, but here we are not safe, and I am under orders for another move. Van Schaick's Island is thought to be safe against the attacks of Indians, and there we go. Should he (Gates) not come soon, your Excellency may expect to hear that our Headquarters are removed to Albany."[42]

"In the retreat of the American army Kosciusko was distinguished for activity and courage and upon him devolved the choice of camps and posts and everything connected with fortifications."[43] "The ill-fated Kosciusko was at that time our chief engineer," recalls Wilkinson, "and for months had been companion of my blanket."[44] It was he who directed "placing obstructions in the route, breaking down bridges, rendering Wood Creek unnavigable."[45]

From Fort Edward Gen. Schuyler tried to supply Kosciuszko with carts and oxen;[46] he wrote him on July 16:

"I have sent one of the Quartermasters to Saratoga and the post below to bring up all the Axes which can be collected, and to deliver them to you. Col. Lewis has my orders to send you a horse

[42] Hay to George Clinton, Aug. 13, 1777, Sparks Papers, 49, I, 34; George L. Schuyler, Correspondence and Remarks, 13.

[43] Another memorial on Kosciuszko by John Armstrong, prepared circa 1818, for M. A. Jullien, H. A. Washington, ed., Writings of Jefferson, VIII, 494.

[44] Wilkinson, Memoirs, I, 200.

[45] Smith, St. Clair Papers, I, 82.

[46] Amer. Antiquarian Soc., Orderly book of Henry B. Livingston, July 19, 1777, p. 52.

immediately. I will give the orders for moving General Fermoy's and General Paterson's Brigade to-morrow and dispose of them in the manner you wish."[47]

Overburdened now with work, impeded by the want of tools and men, Kosciuszko nevertheless tried to lift up the spirit of the army. "I met some of the militia on retreat," he himself testified, "and having expressed my surprise at their not staying to fight for their country, they answered, they were willing to stay, but the officers would not."[48]

On July 22, the army moved to camp on Moses Creek, selected by Kosciuszko,[49] where some three hundred men worked hurriedly under him on temporary fortifications.[50] But Schuyler still did not feel safe and soon a further retreat was ordered to Fort Miller, and then successively to Saratoga, Stillwater, and finally to Van Schaick's Island,[51] "by the sprouts of the Mohawk River, nine miles north of Albany."[52] Here Kosciuszko again selected a position for a fortified camp[53] and "threw up numerous fortifications on that and on Hauver Island."[54]

The loss of Ticonderoga was as painful, as it was unexpected to the Americans. The thunders of incriminations for its evacuation fell, above all, on the head of Gen. St. Clair as immediate commander of the place. As formerly in the case of Gates unjustly recalled from the command, Kosciuszko now stood firmly in the defense of St. Clair. Among all the chaos of the retreat he found time to pen him a cheerful note from Fort Edward:

"My General—Be well persuaded that I am wholly attached to you for your peculiar merit and the knowledge of the Military art which you most assuredly possess. If the retreat from Ticonderoga has drawn upon you many Talkers and to some Jealous persons has furnished the occasion of under-mining you, even to the point of saying yesterday at dinner, that it is necessary that someone be sacrificed for the public good, it seems to me rather for their own.

[47] Amer. Antiquarian Soc., Orderly book of Gen. Philip Schuyler, June 26-August 18, 1777, p. 53.
[48] Coll. N. Y. Hist. Soc., XIII, 61.
[49] Sparks, Writings of Washington, IV, 503, n.
[50] Orderly book of Livingston, July 29, p. 72.
[51] Brandow, The Story of old Saratoga, 85-6.
[52] Sparks, Correspondence of the Revolution, I, 427.
[53] Wilkinson, Memoirs, I, 200.
[54] Neilson, Original Account, 60.

Therefore my General it is necessary to take care and to try to shut their mouths. I offer you my services, to reply to give reasons the most convincing with the plan. My General I shall be in despair if we are going to lose you, so I have already Begun to say to Our Generals and Colonels that in losing you we should draw upon ourselves the greatest dishonor; they are convinced of the truth and they will rather quit the service.

"I am well persuaded my General that you are in a position yourself to Give Reasons for the retreat but as it is a matter which touches rather my condition I shall wish to be useful to you here in some way, therefore make use of me."[55]

A court martial under Maj. Gen. Lincoln tried St. Clair for the loss of Ticonderoga and exonerated him entirely. The trial was held at White Plains, N. Y., in August and September, 1778. Kosciuszko, then stationed at West Point, was one of the witnesses and gave testimony favorable to his former commandant.

In his letter to Washington from Fort Edward, July 17, 1777, St. Clair gave the following reasons for abandoning Ticonderoga: "Our force consisted of little more than two thousand effectives, . . . lines and redoubts . . . were very far from being . . . perfected, . . . the enemy had nearly invested us, . . . I had not provision . . . our whole camp on the Ticonderoga side was exposed to fire. . . ."[56]

A very favorable opinion of American fortifications at Ticonderoga, and indirectly of Kosciuszko's work, is given by Du Roi the Elder, Lieutenant and Adjutant in the service of the Duke of Brunswick, who took part in Burgoyne's expedition. He viewed the grounds after their capture by the British and described the fortifications as follows: "Not only the old fortifications of Fort Ticonderoga and the so-called French lines, had been renewed and increased during this time, but the hill just opposite the fort had been cleared of the wood, and a wooden fort been erected there, strengthening the whole with trenches and batteries. They had called this mountain on account of its location and their intentions 'Mount Independence.' The whole was well done and showed no lack of clever engineers among the rebels." In his opinion the bridge between Ticonderoga and Mount Independence which Kosciuszko helped to build, did

---

[55] Library of Congress, Div. of MSS, letter without date; contemp. transl.
[56] Sparks, *Correspondence of the Revolution*, I, 400-2.

"honor to human mind and power" and "it may be compared to the work of Colossus in the fables of the heathen."[57]

Another contemporary witness, Lieut. William Digby of the British 53rd Regiment of Foot, considered the fortifications on Mount Independence "of great strength."[58]

[57] "Journal of Du Roi the Elder," *German American Annals*, XIII (1911), 151-2. Of modern historians Sir George Otto Trevelyan, *The American Revolution*, part 2, vol. I, p. 357; Hoffman Nickerson, *The Turning Point of the Revolution*, 452, and others give a favorable opinion on Kosciuszko's work at Ticonderoga.

[58] Baxter, *The British Invasion*, 204. There is a marker erected in 1929, at the entrance to the Place d'Armes of the Fort, mentioning Kosciuszko as one of "a host of great men of our history" who passed through it. The marker reads: "You who tread in their footsteps remember their glory." The Fort Ticonderoga Museum has an oil portrait of Kosciuszko by an unknown artist. Parts of Kosciuszko's fortifications are still visible on the north side of Haver or Peebles Island (Hayner, *Troy*, I, 76.)

Chapter IV

SARATOGA

In consequence of the evacuation of Ticonderoga, Schuyler was relieved of command and Gates was elected in his place by a nearly unanimous vote of Congress[1] on August 4, 1777.

Gates reached the camp of the Northern Army on Van Schaick's Island on August 19, and almost immediately "things began to wear a new face."[2] "From this miserable state of despondency and terror, Gates' arrival raised us, as if by magic. We began to hope and then to act," reports an eyewitness of these events, Col. Hay.[3]

Still another eyewitness, Major Armstrong, relates of Gates that "having no confidence in the means employed by his predecessor for restoring the morale of his troops, he promptly withdrew them from their insular fortress, and put them in motion, apparently for the camp of their enemy.[4] When their march began, Colonels Kosciuszko and Hay, were sent forward with orders—'to select a position on the western bank of the Hudson, which from its hilly and covered surface, would be best fitted for defence.' This service was performed without loss of time; Bemys' heights were selected and the army quickly brought thither."[5] According to Wilkinson, "Kosciuszko has selected this ground,"[6] generally considered "a very advantageous Post."[7]

"The ground at this place was again examined, a line for entrenchments traced, a fatigue of 1000 men put to work under Colonel Kosciuszko." He "covered its weak point (its right) with redoubts from the hill to the river."[8]

---

[1] *Journals Cont. Cong.*, VIII, 604.

[2] George Clinton to James Duane, August 27, 1777, Sparks Papers, ser. 49, vol. I, fol. 34.

[3] Washington, ed., *Writings of Jefferson*, VIII, 494.

[4] It was on the advice of Kosciuszko that Gates moved the army up the river, according to Upham, *Memoir of Glover*, 30.

[5] Armstrong's memorial, Sparks Papers, ser. 49, vol. I, fol. 71.

[6] *Memoirs*, I, 232.

[7] Dearborn, *Journals*, 105.

[8] Washington, *Writings of Jefferson*, VIII, 494.

One of his faithful assistants in this task was Col. Rufus Putnam of Massachusetts, cousin of Gen. Israel Putnam, who wrote in his memoir: "the worthy Kusesko the famous Polander was at the head of the Engineer department in Gates Army; we advised togather with respects to the works necessery to be thrown up for the defence of the Camp but he had the over Sight in executing them. I therefore have no claim to extra Service this year, nor did I receive any perticuler notice from Genl. Gates."[9]

Unhappily all plans and drawings of Kosciuszko for the fortified camp at Saratoga were lost, as were those pertaining to Ticonderoga.[10]

Marquis de Chastellux who visited the battlefield during the Revolution, describes the fortifications of Kosciuszko at Bemis' Heights as follows: "The eminencies, called Breams Heights, from whence this famous camp is named, are only a part of those high grounds which extend along the right bank of the Hudson, from the river Mohawk to that of Saratoga. At the spot chosen by General Gates for his position, they form, on the side of the river, two different slopes, or terraces. In mounting the first slope, are three redoubts placed in parallel directions. In front of the last, on the north side, is a little hollow, beyond which the ground rises again, on which are three more redoubts, placed nearly in the same direction as the former. In front of them is a deep ravine which runs from the west, in which is a small creek. The ravine takes its rise in the woods; and all the ground on the right of it is extremely thick set with wood. If you will now return upon your steps, place yourself near the first redoubts you spoke of, and mount to the second slope proceeding to the westward, you will find, on the most elevated platform, a large entrenchment which was parallel with the river, and then turns towards the north-west, where it terminates in some pretty steep summits, which were likewise fortified by small redoubts. To the left of these heights, and at a place where the declivity becomes more gentle, begins another entrenchment which turns towards the west, and makes two or three angles, always carried over the tops of the heights to the south-west. Towards the north-west, you come out of the lines to descend another plat-

[9] Buell, ed., *The Memoirs of Rufus Putnam*, 73; cf. Hildreth, *Biographical and Historical Memoirs*, 70.

[10] Walworth, "Value of National Archives," *Annual Report of the Amer. Hist. Association for the Year 1893*, 31.

PLAN OF THE BATTLE OF SARATOGA
by Kosciuszko

27

form, which presents a position the more favourable, as it commands the surrounding woods, and resists every thing which might turn the left flank of the army."[11]

On this ground chosen and fortified by Kosciuszko Burgoyne surrendered to Gates on October 17, 1777. Contemporaries were quick to grasp the importance of the victory. "It is a most brilliant action, and cannot fail of giving our Arms the greatest Eclat," wrote Col. Tench Tilghman, Washington's aid, to Robert Morris.[12] As a direct result of this victory, "the turning point of the Revolution," France signed a treaty of alliance with the United States, on February 6, 1778. Kosciuszko's choice of battlefields and his erection of fortifications contributed greatly to this success.[13]

Gates himself recognized unmistakingly his services. "Doctor R— of Philadelphia,[14] at his first meeting with Gates after Burgoyne's surrender, was somewhat more lavish of his compliments than suited the taste of the old soldier, who exclaimed—'stop, Doctor, stop, let us be honest. In war, as in medicine, natural causes not under our control, do much. In the present case, the great tacticians of the campaign, were hills and forests, which a young Polish Engineer was skilful enough to select for my encampment.' "[15]

Col. Robert Troup of New York, one of Gates' aides-de-camp, remembered as an old man that "during the whole northern cam-

---

[11] Chastellux, *Travels*, I, 410.

[12] Oct. 8, 1777, Henkels, *Confidential Correspondence*, p. 165, no. 337.

[13] According to Woodrow Wilson, it was Kosciuszko who had shown General Gates how to intrench himself upon Bemis' Heights (*A History of the American People*, II, 282). Perhaps the most glowing tribute was paid to Kosciuszko in connection with his work at Saratoga by Trevelyan (*The American Revolution*, part 3, 174). A temporary marker in honor of Kosciuszko was erected at the battlefield of Saratoga in 1930.

[14] Most probably Dr. Benjamin Rush. By 1778, Dr. David Ramsay, historian, had moved to Charleston; Rush was still in Philadelphia at that time.

[15] Armstrong's memorial, Sparks Papers, ser. 49, vol. I, fol. 71. Of the Revolutionary poets Joel Barlow mentions Kosciuszko in his description of the battle of Saratoga, *Columbiad*, London, 1809, p. 202:

> "But on the centre swells the heaviest charge,
> The squares develop and the lines enlarge.
> Here Kosciusko's mantling works conceal'd
> His batteries mute, but soon to scour the field."

The Northern Campaign of 1777 was partly used by Frederick William Thomas as background for his novel *The Polish Chiefs, an Historical Romance*, New York, 1832, 2 vols., woven around Kosciuszko and Pulaski; incidentally Thomas was the first one to introduce Kosciuszko into the American novel. Kosciuszko at Saratoga appears also in Kenneth Roberts' *Rabble in Arms, A Chronicle of Arundel and the Burgoyne Invasion*, New York, 1933.

paign of 1777" Kosciuszko was "constantly about General Gates' person" and that he messed with him, together with the rest of his official family. He described him as a then "rather young man—of unassuming manners—of grave temper."[16]

The knowledge of Kosciuszko's merits reached by this time the ears of Washington. Commenting on a memorial of Col. Duportail for higher ranks for himself and his colleagues, he wrote to Henry Laurens, President of Congress, on November 10, 1777:

"I have inclosed the Memorial of Colo. Portail and the other Engineers for their promotion . . . In respect to their abilities and knowledge in their profession, I must observe, they have had no great Opportunity of proving them since they were in our service . . . While I am on this subject, I would take the liberty to mention, that I have been informed, that the Engineer in the Northern Army (Cosieski, I think his name is) is a Gentleman of science and merit. From the character I have had of him he is deserving of notice too."[17]

Duportail and his French colleagues arrived in America in July 1777. Because they came with the sanction of the French King and his government, Congress immediately gave Duportail the rank of Colonel of Engineers and decided that he is to "take rank and command of all engineers heretofore appointed." Thus Duportail became at once Kosciuszko's superior. This was a purely political move, disregarding the priority of Kosciuszko's nomination and his splendid services at Ticonderoga and during Schuyler's retreat.

---

[16] Troup to Timothy Pickering, Oct. 12, 1824, Mass. Hist. Soc., Pickering Papers, vol. 32, no. 110, pp. 7-8. Troup also said that in contrast with Wilkinson who was "a gross flatterer," Kosciuszko in his relations with Gates "was skilful in the use of delicate flattery where it could be used to advantage." Gates was very susceptible to adulation, Troup continued, and "by the frequent use of it Wilkinson and Kosciuszko got the complete mastery of his mind," in consequence of which he became imbued with the thought that he was the best general in the American army except Charles Lee. Evidently Troup did not understand well Kosciuszko's nature. As a rule, Poles are more sentimental than Americans and the effusion of affection which characterizes Kosciuszko's American correspondence and which might appear as artful and "delicate flattery," was, and still is entirely natural to a Pole. It is difficult to reconcile this critical attitude of the old Troup with his enthusiastic contemporary notes on Kosciuszko. How could one be of "unassuming manners" and a flatterer at the same time? Had later political attitudes anything to do with this change of Troup's heart? By the end of the 18th century Gates and Kosciuszko became very intimately connected with Jefferson; Troup was a staunch Federalist. (Patterson, *Gates*, 378; Troup in the *Dictionary of Am. Biog.*).

[17] Fitzpatrick, X, 35.

COL.ENOCH POOR.

GEN. ENOCH POOR
by U. D. TENNEY
after a miniature by Kosciuszko

In October, 1777, Kosciuszko added Saratoga to his American laurels. Yet, in November, Washington was obliged to state that Duportail had no chance to show his abilities. The only argument of the Frenchman for a new promotion was that "the rank of colonel unless with the command of a regiment is very little respected . . . We suffer very much from this defect."[18] Notwithstanding all this, on November 17, 1777, Congress made Duportail Brigadier General and his colleagues Colonels or Lieutenant Colonels respectively.

The partiality of Congress for the Frenchmen was, to some extent, justified by political reasons. They represented France and the French help indispensible to the American cause. But the effect of such promotions on the army was deplorable. Col. John Laurens wrote to his father:

"It is a pity that Congress should grant any promotion but upon the recommendation of those superior officers, who have known or seen the feats upon which these pretentions are founded. The present way of proceeding is productive of great confusion and much uneasiness. It is complained, that whoever will go to York and speak loudly to members of Congress, of his own abilities and eminent services, will obtain what he intrigues for. One improper promotion induces another, and perhaps several others to silence the murmerers, and rank and Congress, I am sorry to say, but I speak with the bleeding heart of a republican, they are both brought into contempt by it. The august representative body of thirteen free states is said to be bullied by every man who is umpudent enough to make his own panegyrick, and represent his own importance."[19]

As a result of Duportail's promotion some pressure was put upon Congress, evidently by Gates, to advance Kosciuszko in his rank, in view of his services in the North. But to promote Kosciuszko would mean to give Duportail and others a cause for new demands. In view of the state of mind of the army, so strongly described by Laurens, Kosciuszko preferred to renounce all his pretensions to a promotion and he, himself, begged Gates to drop the matter. In a letter to Col. Troup, then accompanying Gates to York, he wrote:

---

[18] Duportail to the Pres. of Cong., no date, read in Congress Nov. 13, 1777, Papers Cont. Cong., no. 41, vol. VIII, ff. 9-10.

[19] John Laurens to Henry Laurens, Feb. 9, 1778, Simms, *Correspondence of Colonel John Laurens*, 121.

"My dear Colonel if you see that my promotion will make a great many Jealous, tell the General that I will not accept of one because I prefer peace more than the greatest Rank in the World."[20]

Thus Kosciuszko's promotion was buried for the duration of war. There was no chance for him unless he molested Congress by his memorials and tried to gain the support of the Commander-in-Chief and other high personages, as the Frenchmen continually did. The whole American career of the Duportail group seems to have been imbued with the supreme thought of gaining personal distinctions.[21] The same may be said of other Frenchmen in the American service, not excepting Lafayette, who also untiringly sought favors for himself or for his countrymen.[22] It may be said for their justification that it was entirely in the spirit of the times. It was one strand of Kosciuszko's greatness that he shunned even deserved recognition; he preferred to serve disinterestingly; the public cause, which he embraced, was always first in his mind.

---

[20] Jan. 17, 1778, Gates Papers, box 9, no. 20.
[21] Cf. Kite, "General Washington and the French engineers," *Records of the Amer. Cath. Hist. Soc.*, XLIII-V (1932-5).
[22] Cf. Gottschalk, *Lafayette joins the American Army*, 106, 119, 131, 140, 154, 234-6 265, etc.

Chapter V

ALBANY AND YORK

After the surrender of Burgoyne, Kosciuszko continued with the headquarters of the Northern Department at Albany. On November 29, 1777, he had a detachment of fifty-seven men working under him.[1] Col. Baldwin still figured as the nominal chief of the group.

On November 27, Gates had been appointed a member and President of the Board of War, newly created by Congress. The victor of Saratoga did not leave his northern command earlier than after the New Year,[2] and so Kosciuszko still had a chance to enjoy the company of his beloved commander. He belonged not only to the official family of the General, but was also on very friendly terms with the whole Gates family. The hardships of the campaign were over, the enemy was not nearer than New York, and the Northern Army could get some respite. The following amusing letter of Kosciuszko to Mrs. Gates, dated Albany, January 17, 1778, and sent after her and her husband's departure, gives a little glimpse of the cordial atmosphere which reigned at Gates' headquarters at Albany.

"Perhaps you are satisfied that you are no longer among the Dutch Society so gloomy and serious but in turn you will now find People who speak solely of politics over a bottle which they embrace strongly from time to time; such reception will not amuse you I am sure; though your French Secretary[3] will always give you cause enough for laughter by his figure, his nose, and his astronomic eye, and Colonel Trop will be the first to help you, but you will not hear the Dutch expression so polite and gallant, in brief, Madam, I suppose that you and I both enjoy the same advantages of good society: I should like to see you, Madam, during the journey taking out biscuits from your portable magazine where they are so neatly stored, and distributing them among your Family and saying: my son, Here, this is for you; come Troup, take this Biscuit, it is very good; and

---

[1] Kozłowski, "Kosciuszko w West Point," *Przegląd Historyczny*, X, 67; researchers working in behalf of this author, were unable to locate this document among the Gates Papers; it may have been lost.

[2] He passed with his family through Bethlehem, Pa., on Jan. 7-9, 1778, on his way to York, *Penna. Mag. of Hist. and Biogr.*, XIII (1899), 79.

[3] William Clajon, a Frenchman, secretary to Gates.

then I should like to see General Gates how he takes one and says, indeed they are good for nothing. O! Madam how I should laugh."[4]

On the same day Kosciuszko wrote to Col. Troup who accompanied the Gates family on their way to York, evidently answering Troup's letter containing expressions of his friendship for the Polish engineer; it is his first known English letter:

"I am very sorry that I am unable to express my sentiments in your Language, so that they would satisfy my desire, and to be sufficiently thankful for your Friendship & good wishes. I am far from possessing such Qualities as you mention—it is true I endeavor to gain Esteem of every Body, and if I succeed I shall be very happy, but it is very difficult.

"For my sincerity, I can assure you, my word always agree with my Heart—but you must not believe me, if you will have me for your Friend; which I should be very glad of; you must be better acquainted with my Character. you cannot loose by, because if you then see in me such as you desire, I get more of your Esteem, and we shall both be very happy take such precaution for every body of your acquaintance."[5]

The above letter to Mrs. Gates included also the following paragraph:

"I rely upon your good Heart that you will not refuse me the favor to remember me to General Gates to whom I write a letter asking his protection and his recommendation before Congress.[6] You may rest assured Madam that my gratitude will be better than that of a Gentleman whom you know."[7]

What was it that Kosciuszko asked Gates, directly and through his wife? It was not the promotion which he had spurned in favor of peace. The only thing he wanted was to be with Gates wherever he went. Just at that time a plan of a new "irruption" of Canada was under discussion. Most probably the subject was often talked over at Gates' headquarters. Naturally, Kosciuszko looked to Gates as the leader of the invasion; he considered him as the only logical choice for a commander of an expedition which could not be regarded otherwise than as an attempt to exploit the success of Saratoga.

---

4 Gates Papers, box 9, no. 19; the original is in French.
5 Gates Papers, box 9, no. 20.
6 The letter to Gates was most probably lost.
7 Most probably an allusion to Wilkinson, Gates Papers, box 9, no. 19.

CAPTAIN JUDAH ALDEN OF MASSACHUSETTS
by Kosciuszko

However, "on General Gates' arrival at Congress the Plan was enlarged . . . and the Command conferred on the Marquis" (Lafayette).[8] The main purpose of the expedition was "to destroy or possess the enemy's vessels and stores of every kind upon Lake Champlain and in the City of Montreal."[9] In preparation for the move Lafayette reached Albany on February 17, and immediately became convinced of the impracticability of the project because of lack of men and material and the end of winter at hand. His own tardiness in reaching the North was partly responsible for the failure of the project. By this time even the Board of War and Congress became doubtful of the success of the undertaking.

The jealousies and ambitions of the army which gave rise to the legend of Conway Cabal, just now reached their culminating point. The only established historical fact is that there were many among the military and civil leaders who were dissatisfied with the "fabian" policies of the Commander-in-Chief. Some were inclined to wish for a change in the supreme command, and Gen. Gates was prominently mentioned as Washington's possible successor. However, there exists no proof of an organized conspiracy.[10] The abortive plan of invasion of Canada added fuel to the tension. On his arrival in Albany Lafayette came to the conclusion that the whole affair was framed purposely to detach him from Washington and to ruin his reputation.

On February 19, he wrote a private and highly excited letter to Henry Laurens in which he described himself as involved in a "hell of Blunders, madness, and deception." He assured Laurens that "I'd loose rather the honor of twenty gatess and twenty boards of wars, than to let my own reputation be hurted in the least thing."[11]

Kosciuszko must have felt confused among all the gossip and ill will. He himself understood that the invasion of Canada could not be undertaken as planned. Probably with the purpose of making a personal inquiry from Gates and of eventually finding another occupation for himself, he left Albany for York on February 19, taking with him the foregoing letter of Lafayette.

A day later, Lafayette wrote another letter to Laurens on the same subject, but strictly official, and most probably, more cautious. This

8 James Duane to George Clinton, March 13, 1778, Burnett, *Letters*, III, 129.
9 Gottschalk, *Lafayette joins*, 202.
10 Cf. Knollenberg, *Washington and the Revolution*, 78, 202, *et seq.*
11 *So. Carolina Hist. and Gen. Mag.*, VII (1906), 189-93

missive was intended by him as subsequent to the one carried by Kosciuszko. The bearer of the latter message was one of his aides-de-camp, who reached York on February 25, a day before Kosciuszko, and left it with other mail at the Board of War. By mistake it was opened by Gen. Gates and there is no reason to doubt that he did it in good faith.[12] As the contents of the letter might well be directed to the Board, he retained it.

Kosciuszko traveled slower and reached York on the 26th. In the afternoon of that day he visited Laurens. "It was then the Colo., introduced by Genl. Gates, did me the honour to call at my little apartment," wrote Laurens to Lafayette.[13] The delay of Kosciuszko and the mixup of the letters caused new irritation to the Marquis. However, he dared not to direct any accusations against him. Writing to Laurens on March 12, he wrongly mentioned Kosciuszko as the bearer of the letter opened by Gates,[14] but most probably soon recognized the mistake, as the matter was never again alluded to in his correspondence.

At York Kosciuszko found an atmosphere far from agreeable. The town still reverberated with gossip and mutual suspicions caused by the "Cabal." The affair was the more unpleasant to him as his beloved former commander was so strongly involved in it through circumstances, mostly outside of his control. Gates must have felt very bitter seeing himself in a turmoil of intrigue through the long tongue of Wilkinson whom he so signally marked out after Saratoga and who repaid his "unbounded friendship" with a base betrayal of confidence. Through Gates' "earnest solicitation" in behalf of Wilkinson, Congress made him brigadier general for the mere bringing of the news of Burgoyne's surrender, and this promotion was so "very injurious and disgustful to the Army," that "to remedy this hasty step, Congress . . . took Mr. W. from the Military line by appointing him Secretary to the Board of War."[15] However, his new position soon became untenable. To save his face he challenged Gates to a duel. Gates accepted the challenge, but instead of dueling with the young scoundrel gave him a fatherly lesson in ethics.[16] This happened on February 23, just a few-days before Kosciuszko's arrival at York.

---

12 Cf. Gottschalk, *Lafayette joins*, 149.
13 March 4, 1778, Burnett, *Letters*, III, 106.
14 *So. Caro. Hist. and Gen. Mag.*, VIII (1907), 9.
15 Abraham Clark to Lord Stirling, Jan. 15, 1778, Burnett, *Letters*, III, 40.
16 Wilkinson, *Memoirs*, I, 386-8.

If there was one thing Gates could never have any doubt of, it was the loyalty of Kosciuszko to himself. But, although he was on such intimate terms with Gates there is no evidence that he participated in any intrigues on behalf of him, if such intrigues existed. The young engineer kept aloof from all excitement, wisely considering that in the situation this was the most proper course for a foreigner. He was ready to defend the honor of Gates to the utmost, as the future soon showed; he wanted to see him the idol of the army and the people, as he was his; yet he understood that above all this, he owed his absolute allegiance to the Commander-in-Chief, in whom he had no cause to lose confidence.

What occupied Kosciuszko's mind, besides these disagreeable occurrences, was the question of his future service. He asked Gates for a new assignment. On March 5, the Board of War, evidently already informed of the difficulties with the engineer in the Highlands, decided "That Col. Kosciuszko be directed to repair to the Army under General Putnam, to be employed as shall be thought proper in his Capacity of an Engineer."[17] At that time Putnam was in charge of fortifying the Hudson and so the assignment meant for Kosciuszko the return to the Northern Department.

This department was still under the nominal command of Gates who hoped to be soon back at his old post, and undoubtedly told Kosciuszko so. It was common knowledge that Gates was "inclined to take the Field"[18] again, and it was "more and more the wish and purpose" of Congress to return him "to his late Command in the Northern department."[19] The plan for an "irruption" into Canada was not yet dead, and Gates still hoped to perfect it. So Kosciuszko had no doubt that he would be in action again under Gates and rejoiced highly at the thought.

It is not known what Kosciuszko did during the next two weeks, for it seems, that he did not return to Albany immediately after the action of Congress. On March 9, Col. Troup wrote to Gen. Gates from Albany, that he would like to go to New Jersey, "and devote a little Time to the arranging of my Private Affairs," but "this tho depends much on the Orders which Col. Kosciuszko brings

17 Clinton, *Public Papers*, II, 848; Gates to Israel Putnam, March 5, 1778, N. Y. Hist. Soc., McDougall Papers (hereafter referred to as McDougall Papers), book III.
18 The Committee of Conference to Washington, March 6, 1778, Burnett, *Letters*, III, 111.
19 Henry Laurens to Lafayette, March 24, 1778, Burnett, *Letters*, III, 142.

me."[20] The main part of the American army still was at its winter quarters at Valley Forge and it is possible that Kosciuszko visited there his comrades of the last year's campaign. On about March 14, General Casimir Pulaski, Commander of Cavalry, arrived at Valley Forge with a plan of organizing an independent corps of infantry and cavalry under his command. It is very likely that the two heroes met personally at that time though there is no documentary evidence. Having received a letter from Washington to the President of Congress, approving the plan, and a letter of recommendation from John Laurens to Gates,[21] Pulaski hurried to York, where on March 19, he presented Gates with a memorial explaining his plan.[22] Undoubtedly Gates on meeting Pulaski, told him some details about Kosciuszko, but the engineer was already gone. He must have left York about March 18 at the latest, for on March 23 he was back at Albany, and on his way to his new destination. On March 26, Troup informed Gen. Gates:

"Kosiuszko left this, for West-Point, on Monday.[23] When I cease to love this young Man, I must cease to love those Qualities which form the brightest & completest of characters."[24]

On his way to West Point Kosciuszko stopped at Poughkeepsie where on March 26, he paid a visit to Gov. George Clinton who gave him the following letter of recommendation to Gen. Parsons, temporarily acting as commandant of the Highlands in absence of Gen. Putnam:

"Colo. Kuziazke who by a Resolve of Congress is directed to act as an Ingeneer at the Works for the Security of the River will deliver you this: I believe you will find him an Ingenous Young Man and disposed to do every thing he can in the most agreeable Manner."[25]

Gen. Alexander McDougall appointed by Washington to take charge of the Highlands arrived at West Point two days later.[26] It was with him that Kosciuszko was to spend most of his long service of over two years, at this important post.

---

20 Gates Papers, box 9, no. 63.
21 Simms, *Correspondence of John Laurens*, 141-3.
22 Sparks Papers, ser. 49, vol. III, f. 16.
23 March 26th, 1778, was Thursday, so the preceding Monday was March 23rd.
24 Gates Papers, box 9, no. 73.
25 Clinton, *Public Papers*, III, 85; Cf. Hall, *Life and Letters of Samuel Holden Parsons*, 161.
26 Geo. Clinton to Conway, March 30, 1778, Clinton, *Public Papers*, III, 101.

Chapter VI

FIRST MONTHS AT WEST POINT

The Hudson River was of primary importance to both sides in the Revolutionary War. "The importance of the North River in the present contest and the necessity of defending it, are Subjects which have been frequently and so fully discussed and are so well understood, that it is unnecessary to enlarge upon them," wrote Washington to Gen. Putnam.[1] "These facts at once appear, when it is considered that it runs thro' a whole State; That it is the only passage by which the Enemy from New York or any part of our Coast, can ever hope to Cooperate with an Army that may come from Canada; That the possession of it is indispensibly essential to preserve the Communication between the Eastern, Middle and Southern States; And further, that upon its security, in a great measure, depend our chief supplies of Flour for the subsistence of such Forces as we may have occasion for, in the course of the War, either in the Eastern or Northern Departments, or in the Country lying high up on the west side of it. These facts are familiar to all." On many other occasions he stressed this view. The Highlands were the backbone of his strategy.

Already early in October, 1777, Lt. Col. Louis de la Radière was sent to the Highlands with an order to direct the erection of necessary works. He, however, failed completely in his task. One of his first official acts on reaching the Highlands was to ask Congress for promotion. He started a prolonged dispute over the choice of the place with Gen. Putnam and other members of the committee delegated to choose a proper place for fortifications. Putnam, Gov. Clinton and other members of the committee were for West Point; he alone stood by his proposition to rebuild the old Fort Clinton. The quick-tempered Gen. Putnam called him "an excellent paper Engineer." In January, 1778, the committee definitively decided to fortify West Point and, indeed, their choice was the best possible. De la Radière directed some work at this place but soon found himself again in a dispute as to the extent of the fortifications. "Not

---

[1] Dec. 2, 1777, Fitzpatrick, X, 129.

43

choosing to hazard his reputation on Works erected on a different scale," he left for Valley Forge in the beginning of March.[2]

When Kosciuszko and McDougall reached West Point, de la Radière was already gone.[3] He presented himself to Washington on March 17. Not knowing of the decision of the Board of War of March 5, assigning Kosciuszko to the Highlands, Washington almost immediately ordered de la Radière back to his post.[4] So for a while the works on the Hudson were under double supervision of two chief engineers which, of course, did not contribute to harmonious cooperation. According to Gen. McDougall's own testimony, de la Radière refused to take any orders from Kosciuszko although he was his junior in rank.[5] He even considered himself Kosciuszko's superior,[6] thus pursuing the common policy of the Duportail group recognizing only themselves as qualified military engineers.

To all concerned the unassuming manners of Kosciuszko were preferable to the stiff behavior of de la Radière. Their superiors begged that the Pole may remain and that the Frenchman might be transferred to some other post. Gen. Sam H. Parsons wrote to McDougall on March 28:

"Inclosed are the Resolutions of Congress and Board of War respecting this Post and the conduct of the Engineer employed. Col. Kosciuszko sent to this Place is particularly agreable to the Gentlemen of this State and all others concerned at this Post." Explaining that de la Radière is not very suitable, he continued: "As we are desirous of having Col. Kosciuszko continue here and both cannot live upon the Point, I wish your Honor to adopt such Measures as will answer the wishes of the People and Garrison; and best serve the public Good."[7]

Meanwhile the news of Kosciuszko's assignment to the Highlands reached Washington, and he wrote to Gen. McDougall on April 6:

"The presence of Colonel de la Radiere rendering the Services of Mr. Kosciousko, as Engineer at Fishkill, unnecessary, you are to give him orders to join this Army without loss of time."

---

[2] Cf. Kite, Records of the Am. Cath. Hist. Soc., XLIII (1932), 193-205.

[3] Buell, Memoirs of Rufus Putnam, 75.

[4] Washington to McDougall, March 21, 1778, Fitzpatrick, XI, 119.

[5] McDougall to Washington, April 13, 1778, Library of Congress, Washington Papers (hereafter referred to as Washington Papers), vol. LXXII.

[6] Duportail to the President of Congress, Aug. 27, 1778, Papers Cont. Congress, no. 41, vol. VII, f. 55.

[7] McDougall Papers, book III.

PLAN OF WEST POINT
by KOSCIUSZKO

45

In an afterthought the Commander-in-Chief added:

"However desirous I am that Mr. Kosciousko should repair to this Army, if he is specially employed by order of Congress or the Board of War, I would not wish to contravene their Commands."[8]

McDougall answered:

"Mr. Kosciousko is esteemed by those who have attended the works at West Point, to have more practice than Col. Delaradiere, and his manner of treating the people more acceptable, that that of the latter; which induced Genl. Parsons and Governor Clinton to desire the former may be continued at West Point. The first has a Commission as Engineer with the rank of Colonel in October 1776—Colonel Delaradiere's Commission I think is dated in November last, and disputes rank with the former, which obliges me to keep them apart; and avail the services of their assistance in the best manner I can devise. This seems to be the Idea recommended by the Board of War in consequence to a reference of Congress to them, on the subject of Disputes relative to the construction of the works. If your Excellency should think proper in this State of those Gentlemen, to order Mr. Kosciusko to join your army, whenever I am honored with your Commands on this head, I shall despatch him."[9]

McDougall's letter ultimately decided the question which one of the engineers was to remain at West Point. On April 22, Washington wrote to him:

"As Colo. La Radiere and Colo. Kosiusko will never agree, I think it will be best to order La Radiere to return, especially as you say Kosiusko is better adopted to the genius and temper of the people."[10]

Now Kosciuszko as "Chief Engineer in the Middle Department," could freely devote his energy and talents to the task, in which he had the friendly assistance of his old and new comrades, especially Col. Rufus Putnam who came together with Gen. McDougall.[11] Fortifications at West Point were still hardly begun. De la Radière

---

[8] Fitzpatrick, XI, 222: McDougall Papers, book III. A reproduction of this letter with some changes in the text in the *Annual Report of the N. Y. Hist. Soc. for 1941*, 17.

[9] McDougall to Washington, April 13, 1778, Washington Papers, vol. LXXII.

[10] Fitzpatrick, XI, 298; a copy in McDougall Papers.

[11] Buell, *Memoirs of Rufus Putnam*, 75.

himself acknowledged to Washington that till about the middle of March "little or nothing" was done in this regard.[12] Truly, a fort was marked out by him "on the extreme point next the river," but after his departure it was abandoned as impractical; "a Battery at this place to anoy the Shiping in case they should come up & attempt to turn the point & force the Boom was Judged Sufficient."[13] Soon Gov. Clinton was able to inform Washington that "the works . . . are now carried on with a Degree of Spirit that promises their speedy Completion."[14] A few days later McDougall wrote to the Commander-in-Chief that "the Fort is by this time so enclosed as to resist a sudden assault of the Enemy. But the Heights near it are such that the Fort is not tenable if the Enemy possess them. For this reason we are obliged to make some work on them."[15] Further quick progress was reported by Col. Troup to Gen. Gates on April 18:

"I have not seen the Works erecting at West Point, but it is said, They are in great Forwardness. Kosiusko has made many Alterations, which are universally approved of; & I am happy to find he is esteemed as an able Engineer."[16]

Troup added that the large chain which was to close the navigation "will be put across the river this week, and if the enemy let us alone two weeks longer, we shall have reason to rejoice at their moving this way."

This historical chain was drawn across the Hudson on April 30, and Gov. Clinton was satisfied that the "Works for its Defence" already were "in good forwardness."[17] Despite temporary difficulties arising from lack of teams or departure of militia[18] which sometimes suspended the work altogether, West Point and its immediate vicinity were being covered with a chain of forts and redoubts. Fort Arnold defended the spur of land, where the river turned abruptly from its course east to south. The principal fort was being built by

---

12 Washington to Henry Laurens, March 17, 1778, Fitzpatrick XI, 103.
13 Buell, *op. cit.*, 75.
14 Clinton to Washington, April 8, 1778, Clinton, *Public Papers*, III, 151.
15 McDougall to Washington, April 13, 1778, Washington Papers, vol. LXXII.
16 Gates Papers, box 9, no. 85.
17 Clinton to Gov. Trumbull, May 1, 1778, *Public Papers*, III, 246. On April 27, 1778, Kosciuszko had 177 men under his command at West Point, according to his return, McDougall Papers, book III.
18 Geo. Clinton to McDougall, April 15, 1778, *Public Papers*, III, 168; Andrew Taylor to Gov. Clinton, April 17, 1778, *ibid.* III, 180; James Clinton to Gov. Clinton, April 19, 1778, *ibid.*, III, 195.

Putnam's regiment (5th Massachusetts), and was named Fort Putnam by Gen. McDougall. It was on "a high hill, or rather rock, which commands the plane & point. The rock on the Side next the point is not difficult to assend but on the other Side wher the fort Stands the rock is 50 feet perpendiculer."[19] Other smaller forts were under construction.[20] When Dr. James Thacher ascended the summit of Sugar Loaf mountain on June 12, and looked at West Point, he was amazed at "a picturesque scenery of peculiar interest." He saw "Fort Putnam, on its most elevated part, the several redoubts beneath, and the barracks[21] on the plain below, with numerous armed soldiers in active motion, all defended by the most formidable machinery of war."[22]

Notwithstanding all this, Gen. McDougall was not entirely satisfied. He informed Gov. Clinton on May 11: "I am far from being pleased with Mr. Korsuaso's constructing the Batteries, and carrying on the works, and I fear they will not answer the expectation of the Country. I wish therefore to have an Hour conversation with you on this Subject, as soon as you can spare one."[23] His uneasiness, however, was not justified. Kosciuszko's ability was repeatedly attested by highest authorities, not excepting Washington himself. To Col. William Malcolm the Commander-in-Chief wrote: "Colo. Kosiusko was left at the Fort as acting Engineer and I have always understood is fully competent to the Business."[24]

The work on fortifications was interrupted by the arrival of intelligence of the French alliance. It reached the Highlands by the end of April evoking general rejoicing. "A number of the friends to freedom and independence, chiefly New Yorkers, have agreed to spend a day in social festivity on account of the aforesaid intelligence, for which purpose they have provided an ox which is to be

---

[19] Buel, op. cit., 75; Boynton, History of West Point, 63.

[20] There are two entries in the orderly books kept by Nathan Savage of Middletown, Conn., for the "Continental Army, Sherburne's Regiment, 1777-1781" (Connecticut State Library), pertaining to the erecting of these forts by that regiment. In vol. I, p. 35, a brigade order of June 11, 1778, states that officers commanding companies of artillery are not on any pretense to give leave of absence to their men without the directions of Col. Kosciuszko, the Chief Engineer. In vol. I, p. 40, there is another order, directing that one hundred men from Col. Hetherns and Col. Hopkins regiments are to cut wood west of Putnam's Hill and the remainder of the regiments to work on the fort, both parties under the directions of Kosciuszko.

[21] These barracks were built before the arrival of Kosciuszko.

[22] Thacher, Military Journal, 134.

[23] Clinton, Public Papers, III, 294.

[24] July 27, 1778, Fitzpatrick, XII, 239.

roasted whole" in Fishkill on May 2, and Hugh Hughes, a Deputy Quartermaster General, "in particular" begged "that Capt. Machin[25] & Col. Cusyesco may be of the party."[26]

Beside the satisfaction with this happy political event, which Kosciuszko wholeheartedly shared with the nation, he also had reasons for personal joy. On April 15, Congress directed Gates to repair to Fishkill and to take the command of the Northern Department.[27] Accompanied by his wife, Gates passed through Bethlehem on May 13,[28] and reached the Highlands a few days later, establishing his headquarters at Robinson's House. As this was only a short distance from West Point Kosciuszko now had the chance often to enjoy the company of the General, of Mrs. Gates, and of their son, an ambitious young man, full of eagerness to serve his country. Undoubtedly he was one of the guests of the Gateses at a dinner on July 4, 1778, when they "had 13 as Catholick Toasts given them by the Genl. as Men ever drank" and all "were very merry."[29]

Kosciuszko was strongly attached to the Gates family. "You Cannot imagine what plaisure it gives me your letter," wrote he to the General at one occasion. "Yours not forgiting of me shall be always in my memory, and attach me so moch that no time not any Circomstance Can't ever change my sentiments, my obligation and altirat my real Frindship." Concerned about the health of the young Gates he added: "I am very Glad that Mr. Gates recovered, his sickness gave me great pain. permit me Sir to assure him of my real Friendship. It is trou that he is Young but verry prudent. his attachment for you Can do anything. and I love him more for that. We have not any News here but Old things that everybody love you, and speak of you."[30]

During the early summer of 1778, there were some rumors that the British intend to march against the American posts on the Hudson,[31] but these did not materialize. Kosciuszko could conduct his work in comparative quiet. To Gen. John Glover, temporarily

---

25 Thomas Machin, Captain of Artillery.
26 Hughes to Gen. Clinton, May 1, 1778, quoted by Griffin, III, 153, without reference note; this author was unable to trace the original.
27 *Journals Cont. Cong.*, X, 354.
28 *Pennsylvania Mag.*, XIII (1889), 83.
29 Col. Tallmadge to Silas Deane, July 6, 1778, Ford, *Correspondence of S. B. Webb*, II, 115.
30 August 4, 1778, Gates Papers, box 10, no. 56.
31 John Mead and McDougall to Gov. Clinton, May 23, resp. July 5, 1778. Clinton, *Public Papers*, III, 347 and 522.

commanding at West Point, Gates wrote: "In consequence of my earnest Wish, and the General's (Washington's) Recommendation, I must beg you to give your whole Attention to the compleating of, first the Out Works at West Point, and then the Body of the Place; Col. Kosciuszko cannot be too vigilant in this important service."[32] Several companies of artificers were under his orders at that time, namely Captain Ezra Eaton's Company of Blacksmiths and two Companies of Carpenters of Captains Jedediah Thayer and Jacob Low,[33] as well as fatigue parties from different regiments. Already at five in the morning work was started and continued till sunset with a few hours intermittence at midday, during the hottest period of the day.[34] On July 5, a party of forty men "used to boats", started on a two-day expedition, most probably for building materials, under orders of Kosciuszko.[35]

Watching the British forces now concentrated in New York, Washington, after the battle of Monmouth, marched through New Brunswick and Paramus to Haverstraw on the Hudson, and on July 16, "visited West Point, to take a view of the works which are constructing there."[36] Kosciuszko, as chief engineer, was undoubtedly introduced to the Commander-in-Chief at this occasion and personally guided him through the posts and redoubts, explaining what was already done and what he still planned to do, though no record exists of this first historical meeting of the two men.[37] Evidently Washington was entirely satisfied with his work; at least such was the tenor of his several letters written on the subject on later occasions.

Col. de la Radière and Gen. Duportail came together with the main army to the Highlands. This brought Kosciuszko some less pleasant experiences. De la Radière already tried to intrigue against him warning Gates "not to risque his reputation for a gentleman who does not know his duty,"[38] and now, evidently at his instigation,

[32] July 2, Kahanowicz, no. 76A.
[33] National Archives, Muster Rolls, Revolutionary War Papers.
[34] General Orders of June 28 and July 3, 1778, Upham, *Memoir of Glover*, 44-5.
[35] General Order of July 4, 1778, *ibid.*, 45.
[36] Thacher, 139.
[37] Armstrong in his memorial, Sparks Papers, ser. 49, vol. I, fol. 72, says "that the first interview between these distinguished men took place at Frederick, (a straggling village in Westchester County) then the Head Quarters of the main army, whither Kosciuszko was brought as a witness in the trials of Schuyler and St. Clair in September 1778"; but most probably he is mistaken.
[38] Gates Papers; cf. Kozłowski, "Kosciuszko w West Point," *Przegląd Historyczny*, X, 80, n.

/27042

Duportail revived the silly question of priority of rank, formally accusing Kosciuszko before the President of Congress of refusing to recognize de la Radière's imagined superiority in rank. Arguing that all American military engineers commissioned before their arrival, were without professional experience, he demanded a privileged position for all his French colleagues. They should be regarded as superiors to all other engineers without regard to their rank, priority of their commissions or their abilities. Congress, continued Duportail,—resolved that he "was to command all the Engineers employed in the United States, whatever might be their Commission," but made only a vague promise as to officially placing the remaining French engineers above the others. "The difference was that our gent^n. were Called Co, Lt Col or Major of the Engineers whereas the others were called only Col^l Lt. Col^{el} or major Engineer . . . Some time ago there happened some difficulty about it—A Col. Engineer, would not acknowledge Mr. de la Radiere, Col. of the Engineers, for his Superior. It is a matter of importance, Sir, that these things should be determined, and I beg you do your endeavors to have them as soon as possible."[39]

Duportail laid the same subject before Washington and the Commander-in-Chief immediately recognized the injustice of his claim, at least in reference to Kosciuszko. He wrote to Henry Laurens:

"General Du Portail lately delivered me a Memorial, in which among other things he represents that he had made an agreement with Congress, at his first appointment, that neither himself nor the other Gentlemen with him, should ever be commanded by any of the Engineers who had preceded them in our Army. I could not but answer, that the Commissions of Officers were the only rule of precedency & command I had to judge by: . . . It will be for the good & tranquility of the service that the claim be determined as speedily as possible one way or the other. At the same time I think it right to observe, that it cannot be expected that Colo. Cosciusko, who had been a good while in this line and conducted himself with reputation and satisfaction will consent to act in a subordinate capacity to any of the French Gentlemen, except Gen. Portail."[40]

[39] Duportail to the Pres. of Congress, Aug. 27, 1778, Papers Cont. Congress, no. 41, vol. VIII, ff. 54-6.

[40] Washington to the Pres. of Congress, Aug. 31, 1778, Fitzpatrick, XII, 376.

Thus Washington again gave a favorable testimony to Kosciuszko, shielding him, at the same time, against the claims of the Frenchmen and an eventual action of Congress in their favor. Even the "timidly modest" Kosciuszko would otherwise have found himself in a humiliating situation.

On September 7, Washington wrote to Col. William Malcolm, the commandant of West Point:

"Sir: Brigadier General Du Portail Chief Engineer is by my orders on a visit to the posts in the Highlands, to examine into the state of the fortifications carrying on there. It is my wish that Colo. Koshiosko may communicate every thing to this Gentleman, who is at the Head of the Department, which he may find requisite for the purpose he is sent upon. I am persuaded you will show him every proper attention."[41]

On September 7 and 8, Kosciuszko was at White Plains as a witness during the trial of Gen. St. Clair. It was during his absence that Duportail made the inspection of West Point, thus, perhaps purposely, avoiding a meeting with him.[42]

"Cold and reserved towards the other officers," haughty and full of high opinion of his own professional knowledge, Duportail was not popular in the army.[43] He never made any friendly gesture toward Kosciuszko; on the contrary, he rather strove to belittle and to displease him. Undoubtedly, his visit to West Point was made in a state of mind very critically disposed toward Kosciuszko and his work. Nevertheless, he could find only few errors and defects and they were minor. He had to acknowledge that Fort Putnam, "the key of all the others," lacked only a larger bomb-proof and needed the raising of one of its sides, "which looks towards the river" to be made "almost impregnable." He also had to say that Fort Arnold appeared to him "to be pretty well situated and traced," and he found "below Fort Putnam a battery nearly round, which is extremely well placed for battering the Vessels which should approach the Chain." He proposed some changes and additions here and there and recommended some new fortifications on Constitution Island. He was most critical of Fort Wyllys which appeared to him not "well traced" and too extensive; in his opinion "it will be

---

[41] Fitzpatrick, XII, 408.

[42] Duportail mentions the fact of his absence in his report of Sept. 13, 1778.

[43] Cf. Kite, Records of the Am. Cath. Hist. Society, XLIII (1932), 122.

53

best perhaps to rebuild this fort altogether." But, on the whole, he was obliged to admit that "the Works which are in hand at West Point and some inconsiderable ones, which it is necessary to add to them, will, with the help of chain, perfectly fulfill the object which is proposed,—that of hindering the enemy's remounting the North River."[44]

If the works were nearly impregnable, it was indeed a great achievement of Kosciuszko after five months of work.

Meanwhile Washington transferred his headquarters to West Point and made another inspection of fortifications on basis of Duportail's report. He disapproved his suggestion to rebuild Fort Wyllys or to make any other radical changes in Kosciuszko's plans. He only agreed on minor changes and additions, proposed by the Frenchman. He thus wrote to Duportail on September 19:

"Sir: I have perused the memorial, which you delivered relative to the defence of the North River at this place, and upon a view of them highly approve what you have offered upon the Subject, Colo. Kosciousko who was charged by Congress with the direction of the forts and batteries, has already made such a progress in the construction of them as would render any alteration in the general plan a work of too much time, and the favorable testimony which you have given of Colo. Kosciousko's abilities prevents uneasiness on this head; but whatever amendments subordinate to the general disposition shall occur as proper to be made, you will be pleased to point out to Col. Kosciousko that they may be carried into execution.

"The Works proposed on the peninsula not being subject to the above mentioned inconvenience, you will desire Colo. Kosciousko to show you his plan for approbation before he proceeds to the construction or have them traced in the first instance comformably to your own ideas."[45]

Evidently Washington also orally expressed his satisfaction with the state of fortifications, perhaps to Col. Malcolm, for Kosciuszko on his return from White Plains, wrote to Gates on October 6:

---

[44] Washington Papers, vol. LXXI, 1778. The original is wrongly dated August 13. The correct date is Sept. 13, 1778. The report of Duportail is given in full by Kite, *op. cit.,* 211-16.

[45] Fitzpatrick, XII, 469.

"His Excellency was here with General Portail to see the works after all Conclusion was made that I am not the worst of Inginier General Washington told him that he should give me direction about the works, but he givet me any what was not lay before and aprouved all some time against his will. I see planly that was the ven to show me that I have superior and abowe me and indeed Sir I discover in Conversation that this Gentlemen wanted little practice because he believe that is the same thing upon the paper as upon the Ground we most always have the works according to the Ground and Circumstance but not as the paper is level and make the works accordingly. That is between us. . . ."[46]

So Kosciuszko's opinion of Duportail's qualifications was not the highest. He felt hurt in his pride and if that made him a little unjust, the primary fault lay with Duportail and his tactlessness.

---

[46] Gates Papers, box 10, no. 108.

Chapter VII

THE AFFAIR WITH JOHN CARTER

During his stay at White Plains Kosciuszko's loyalty to Gates involved him in an unpleasant affair with John Carter, son-in-law of Gen. Schuyler. The affair was a distant echo of the so-called "Conway Cabal."

Present at White Plains at that time was Wilkinson, now Clothier-General of the army. His meeting with Gates on Friday, September 4, 1778, somehow provoked a sharp controversy as to the correctness of his behavior during their bloodless duel at York earlier in the year. What happened between them at that moment is not known in detail,[1] but perhaps to save his face with the army and to punish Gates for his reprimand, Wilkinson again challenged him to a duel.

Gates accepted the challenge and asked Kosciuszko to be his second. The duel was to be fought an hour later and Kosciuszko, though not well acquainted with the nature of the controversy, was glad to do a favor for his chief. John Carter was the second of Wilkinson. He was an Englishman of whose past these facts are positively known, that his real name was John Barker Church and that he fled his country. Some said it was on account of a duel, but men did not at that time leave England for duelling; they sometimes left to avoid a duel. Under the assumed name he appeared in America, and was introduced to Gen. Schuyler by William Duer who assured that though "young in years," he was "an old-fashioned English Whig." However, Carter never entered the American army. Instead, in the fall of 1777, he ran away with Schuyler's eldest daughter Angelica and married her. The event was "exceedingly disagreeable" to her parents. After the marriage he evidently spent his time in idleness, hanging on Schuyler's sleeve for his livelihood.

The duel took place in the evening. "Gen. Gates and Gen. Wilkenson met, and on the word to fire, being given, Gen. Gates's pistol flashed in the pan, on which Gen. Wilkenson fired in the

---

[1] Wilkinson's *Memoirs* close with his resignation from the secretaryship to the Board of War, and resume with the year of 1806.

air. They charged again and Gen. Wilkenson fired, on which Gen. Gates refused to fire. On the word being given a third time, Gen. Wilkenson's pistol fired and Gen. Gates's flashed in the pan." The "seconds interposed, and the gentlemen shook hands, and Gen. Gates declared that in the rencounter at York-Town, Gen. Wilkenson behaved as gentleman."[2] Undoubtedly something amounting to a reciprocal statement came from Wilkinson.

Carter, as better acquainted with the English language, wrote the protocol of the meeting, read it aloud and asked Kosciuszko to sign it. It was already dark; not suspecting any subterfuge, yet because of his poor English not clearly understanding what was read, Kosciuszko signed the paper. The document contained the apology to Wilkinson by Gates, but said nothing that Gates also behaved as gentleman in the duel at York.

The party dispersed. When Kosciuszko returned to headquarters, Col. Troup called his attention to this omission. On seeing that through his inadvertence the one-sided declaration in the protocol left Gates' behavior questionable and thus exposed him to new importunities by Wilkinson, he immediately made up his mind to take the matter into his hands. Notwithstanding the late hour, he went to Gen. Schuyler's quarter where Carter lodged, and here is what happened there, according to a statement of Major Lansing[3] and Lt. Col. Lewis Morris, who witnessed the scene:

"On Friday evening the 4th. September instant, between 10 and 11 o'clock, Colonel Kosciusko came to General Schuyler's quarters and told Mr. Carter that he proposed to leave camp early next morning, and that he wanted a copy of the paper Mr. Carter and he had signed—Mr. Carter immediately took a paper out of his pocket, and presented it to the Colonel, saying 'their it is, copy and I will sign it.' After having received the paper, he folded it and pocketed it; and upon Mr. Carter's questioning him, respecting his intentions in putting it in his pocket, he answered, that that paper contained a declaration, relative to the propriety of Gen. Wilkenson's conduct; but not a word respecting that of General Gates at their interview at York-Town—that his unacquaintance with the English language, had caused him to misapprehend the

---

[2] Carter's account, (Fishkill) *New York Packet,* Sept. 17, 1778; *Cf.* Thacher, *Military Journal,* 176.

[3] John Lansing (1754-1829), of New York, later a prominent jurist.

terms in which it was conceived—That in being appointed Gen. Gates's second, he looked upon himself, as interested in supporting his honour, and that he would rather loose the last drop of his blood than consent to a measure which would tend to its prejudice, or words to that effect; and unless Mr. Carter would agree to certify, that General Gates's conduct, had been unexceptionable, on the occasion of his and General Wilkenson's meeting at York Town, he must keep the paper. Mr. Carter observed, that the paper was delivered confidentially; urged to him the inconsistency of certifying to a fact, with which he was entirely unacquainted, and requested him to restore the paper—This the Colonel absolutely refused, repeating his former objections; Mr. Carter asked him whether he had not signed the paper, which he had then taken, and whether Gen. Gates had not previously assented to it; to this he applied affirmatively, and upon Mr. Carter's observing that it was in his power to publish it, and that the Colonel could not pretend to deny his signature; he answered, that though he knew it to be true, that he had signed it, he would deny it—that he was unacquainted with the cause of the duel, and unapprized of General Gates's intentions respecting it, till within an hour before it happened; that the shortness of that time had prevented him from receiving the necessary information—that that was another reason of his omitting to require a similar certificate, respecting Gen. Gates's behaviour; that he had since had an opportunity of being undeceived; that Col. Troup had removed his deception; Mr. Carter then requested a copy of the paper contended for, which Col. Kosciusko refused to give—much altercations passed, and after a variety of repetitions of the discourse above related: Mr. Carter proposed that Col. Kosciusko should declare upon his honour, that he would on the morrow at Ten o'clock in the morning, with General Gates, meet General Wilkenson and Mr. Carter at General St. Clair's quarters, and bring with him the paper alluded to—that he would there produce it to Generals Gates and Wilkenson, and that if the former refused to deliver it, the matter was to be on the same footing as before they fought; that if General Gates refused, to appear at the time and place appointed he would himself attend, and return the paper to Mr. Carter; this declaration the Colonel made, without the least hesitation, and then went off with the paper.

"General Schuyler was present at the time the above conversation passed and overheard it.

"John Lansing, Jun.
"Lewis Morris, 3d.
"White Plains, September 7."[4]

"On Saturday morning," as further related by Carter "we all met at Gen. St. Clair's and Gen. Gates refused to deliver up the certificate unless Gen. Wilkenson would consent to give him a similar certificate of his behaviour at York-Town. Gen. Wilkenson told him he could not prostitute his honour, and that he would not, and proposed to Gen. Gates to fight again and desired him to fix a time, which Gen. Gates refused."[5] Wilkinson then became abusive. Again according to Carter, "on Gen. Gates's refusal either to give up the paper or fight, Gen. Wilkenson told him in the presence of Gen. St. Clair, Col. De Hart[6] and Major Dunn, that he was a rascal and a coward,[7] and that he only wanted to shift the quarrel from his own shoulders on those of Col. Kosciuszko; when Major Armstrong, aid-de-camp to General Gates, who was with him, immediately said that was not the case, for that to his knowledge Col. Kosciuszko had offered General Gates to fight for him the day before, but that the General would not suffer him."[8]

Major Armstrong's version of this verbal scuffle differs somewhat. "I perfectly remember my answer to Gen. Wilkenson," he wrote to Kosciuszko, "when he alleged that Gen. Gates wished to draw, not YOU, but Col. TROUP into the dispute: It was thus 'so ' far from that, Sir, I heard the General lay the strongest injunction ' upon Col. Troup not to challenge you, as he, (Gen. Gates) sus-' pecting what has happened, was in that case, determined to fight ' you.' "

According to further testimony of Armstrong, when Wilkinson offered a second challenge to Gates, saying that "as they asserted things so contradictory, one of them should die," Gates replied:

[4] New York Packet, September 17, 1778.
[5] Ibidem.
[6] William De Hart, Lieut. Col., 2nd New Jersey.
[7] John Armstrong, the son, to Kosciuszko, Oct. 10, 1778; "It is probable, he (Carter) fancies, that he has much exalted Gen. Wilkenson's character, by affirming that he applied the words 'rascal and coward' to Gen. Gates. I will not pretend to say that this is not the language of Gen. Wilkenson; but I am certain that he did not use it upon that occasion" (New York Packet, Oct. 29, 1778).
[8] Carter to Samuel Louden, Sept. 26, 1778, New York Packet, Oct. 8, 1778.

"Wilkinson, I am ashamed I fought you."

The General explained that, "considering how apt the world was to censure those who appeared to make evasions in such cases, he had conformed to the prevailing ideas of honour," and then added:

"As to dying, you may well wish to die, but I can yet live with honour and satisfaction."[9]

In any event, the meeting rather deepened the conflict.

Immediately after Gates and his seconds left St. Clair's quarters, Carter in conversation with other officers gravely insulted Kosciuszko, saying "that Col. Kosciuszko had stolen" the certificate, and "that he would prosecute him" as a thief, or "report him to Head Quarters as a thief."[10] This soon reached the ears of Kosciuszko. "Colo. Kosiusko insulted by Mr. Carter," recorded Col. Baldwin in his diary,[11] and this dry remark bears additional evidence that Kosciuszko fell a victim to provocation. Officers eagerly rallied to his defense. Brig. Gen. Lewis Morris, father of the Lieut. Colonel, who was present at the moment, signed for Kosciuszko a certificate describing the event, and "solemny declaring" that the harsh words of Carter were said "not in jest . . . but to all appearance, serious and determined." The certificate was also signed by Dr. James Brown,[12] Surgeon General, as a witness.

Kosciuszko was deeply affected by Carter's remark. On Sunday, September 6, he sent the following note to him by the younger Morris:

"Sir,—As I learn from undoubted authority, that you have spoken in a very disrespectful and ungentlemanly manner of me, by calling me in a public company, a thief, and seriously determining to prosecute me as such, or report me, to Head Quarters: I make no doubt but that you will meet me precisely at six o'clock this evening, at the smith's shop, upon the hill between Schuyler's and Col. Baldwin's quarters, with your second and arms.—I expect a receipt for

---

[9] *Ibid.*, Oct. 29, 1778.

[10] Certificate from Gen. L. Morris, Sept. 5, 1778, *New York Packet*, Oct. 29, 1778.

[11] Baldwin, *Diary*, 134.

[12] Dr. James Brown of South Carolina, later chief physician of the Southern Department.

this by the bearer—if no other answer—a letter sent any time before five o'clock will find me at Gen. Gates's quarters.[13]

"I am, Sir, your most obedient,

"THAD. KOSCIUSKO.

"Mr. Carter.
"Purchase Street),
"Sunday Morning.)"

Carter refused to face Kosciuszko. He answered him by letter:

"Sir,—Until the paper is returned to me of which you requested a copy, and which I delivered to you for that purpose last Friday night, in the presence of Major-Gen. Schuyler, Major Lansing, and Mr. Morris and which in the presence of those gentlemen you not only refused to return to me, but even refused me a copy; I shall not consider myself, either in point of honour or justice bound to make any apologies or to meet you at the time you request."

"I am Sir,
"Your humble Servant,
"John Carter.

"Storm's Sunday)
"Morning Sept. 6).
"Col. Thad. Kosciusko."

In the afternoon Major John Armstrong delivered another letter from Kosciuszko to Carter, insisting that his challenge should be considered entirely separate from the question of certificate pertaining to the Gates-Wilkinson affair:

"Sir,—As in your note of today by Mr. Morris you consider my retaining the certificate an injury to you; I now wait at Col. Baldwin's quarters prepared to redress it with my sword. The injury you wished to do my reputation by the assertion mentioned in my letter this morning, is posterior and entirely distinct from this— Therefore, Sir, I insist upon your meeting at the hour and place appointed, should you refuse I shall take proper steps to get satisfaction.

"I am, Your's
"Thad. Kosciusco, Col.

---

13 This and the next two letters are from the *New York Packet*, Sept. 17, 1778.

"Sunday noon.

"I send this open as it is intrusted to Major Armstrong, who is my second on the occasion.

"Mr. Carter."

To this Carter answered by Armstrong verbally that he "would have nothing to do with Col. Koscisko, until he has returned . . . the Paper." When Armstrong informed him that in such a case Kosciuszko "should publish him as a villain" and treat him as such wherever he would meet him, Carter retorted with a new contemptuous remark on Kosciuszko and added that he would defend himself if attacked and publish the particulars of the affair in newspapers.

Incidentally he tried to hush up the affair. Meeting Lieut. Jedidiah Rogers of the Sheldon Dragoons who accompanied either Morris or Armstrong in their errands, he denied everything. He desired him to "tell Col. Kosciuszko, that he had been much misinformed; that he had never called him a thief, nor ever said he would report him to Head Quarters, or prosecute him as such."[14] A witness to this was Maj. Isaac Pierce, aide-de-camp to Gen. Gates.

With this the affair seemed to be closed. Unhappily Carter transferred it to the press and sent a long letter describing the controversy in a light favorable to himself, to the *New York Packet,* then published at Fishkill. He closed it with these remarks:

"From what passed on Friday night. it is very apparent that Col. Kosciusko forfeited all pretentions to honour by obtaining the certificate of what passed at the duel, from me under false pretences, and openly vowing that on account of Gen. Gates's reputation he would deny what he knew to be true, which undoubtedly puts it out of the power of any gentleman to put himself upon a level with him. The Colonel offers in his letter to redress the injury with his sword,—a midnight robber, who steals a purse, or an assassin, who attempts a gentleman's life might with equal propriety offer to make amends with his sword—but every man of common sense would look upon the person who met him on such terms, as a mad-man.[15]

"White-Plains)   "JOHN CARTER.
"Sept. 8. 1778."

---

[14] *Ibid.,* Oct. 29, 1778.
[15] *Ibid.,* Sept. 17, 1778.

Thus attacked Kosciuszko prepared a statement of his own and wrote to Gates on Sept. 28:

"I have answer to Carter in York Paper if you find good in yours part I am very happy if not, I will publish more in the next as you Judge proper to add. Believe me Sir that I have real attachment for you, and I have nothing so in vews as your reputation which is dearest at present for me than mine.

"Permit me Sir to send my respect to your Lady and Frindly Compliments to Mister Gates I believe he is Litel leasy (lazy) or Cannot find so good Opportunity to rit me as the other Gentelmen of your family."[16]

Kosciuszko's answer appeared in the *New York Packet* of September 24:

"To Mr. John Carter,

"Sir,

"The general voice of the army hath already pronounced you a scoundrel and coward—You are sensible that in Camp, or where your transaction with me is known, you are not considered as a gentleman—if that is the character you are apprehensive that I will take liberty with you are mistaken—Your pusillanimous behaviour, in the course of our late dispute, even according to your *state of facts,* will convince the public as well as me, that you are destitute thereof.

"But it seems you thought it was necessary to fight me some way or other; and wisely judged that types were safe weapons; in this you discover a degree of cowardice, not indeed so great as when you drew your pistol upon me at the Court-Martial, when I was unarmed, and when the appearance of guard (by order of the Court) to apprehend you as an assassin, and the indignant shouts of the spectators, put you to an ignominious flight. I should have treated your publication with contempt, if you had not basely misrepresented my behaviour respecting the certificate. I think it my duty to correct that part of your *state of facts,* in a public manner, and to convince you Sir, that I can defend my reputation with my pen, as well as my sword;—I shall not add to your disgrace by a tedious detail of circumstances, in your own account of the matter you

---

16 Gates Papers, box 10, no. 91.

acknowledge yourself a coward.—Late in the evening after Gen. Gates and Gen. Wilkenson had fought, you produced a paper, which you read, and with much importunity requested me to sign,—and being in haste and so dark that I could not read it, I very inadvertently did so—But I soon discovered that you had ungenerously taken advantage of my inattention, and obtained a certificate in favour of your principal only, and relating to a former affair at York-Town, with which I was totally unacquainted. I therefore came immediately to your quarters, demanded a copy of the paper, and observing that Gen. Gates was not named, and that it only related to Gen. Wilkenson's behaviour on a former occasion; I expostulated with you,—told you that you had taken the advantage of my ignorance of the language and inattention,—that as a second to Gen. Gates I was bound in honour to support his reputation, on this occasion, which I would with my blood,—and that unless you would give me a similar certificate on his part I would retain yours,—this you refused, assigning as a reason that I had not *demanded it on the spot.* You then said you would publish the paper,—I answered I would deny, not my signature, as you have maliciously intimated, but the intention and design of the certificate; and I am persuaded the gentlemen who were present understood me in that sense.

"You also say that Gen. Gates refused to fix a time for a second duel with Gen. Wilkenson,—I am pretty sure that when the altercation on that subject happened,—that you was at such a distance in warm conversation with me, as to make it impossible, for you to hear what passed between Gen. Gates and Gen. Wilkenson,—but supposing it to be true, the General certainly did right,—I had told him that the affair was become mine and not his,—and that if retaining the certificate was a prejudice either to you or Gen. Wilkenson, I only was answerable, and would not permit him to fight for me, and that I would consider myself injured by his interference.

"I have now done with you Sir, unless you intrude among gentlemen where I may happen to be, on such occasions, I shall think myself at liberty to treat you as a scoundrel.

"THAD KOSCIUSZKO.[17]

"Sept. 20."

---

[17] *New York Packet,* Sept. 24, 1778.

Carter replied to this with a new letter to the publisher of the *New York Packet*, full of invectives against Kosciuszko: "In what other light than that of a mercenary bravo can that man be considered, who (by his own confession unacquainted with the circumstances of a quarrel) can offer to fight a person (with whom he has not even the shadow of a dispute) for another man? and his subsequent conduct proves him the needy desperate adventurer, who having nothing to lose, but with a view of pleasing his patron and in hopes of advancing his fortune, is ready to undertake any dirty action, or fight any man for him, and failing in his schemes and detected in his villainy, falsely imagines, that by fighting or sending a challenge, he shall wipe every odium from his character, and re-establish his shattered reputation; and chagrined at being disappointed by a gentleman's refusal to put himself on a levil with him has recourse to scurrility, abuse and falsehood.—Such is his representation of what passed at the Court-Martial a few days after, when meeting me (not unarmed, as he declares, but with his sword on) he became abusive, and kept his hand in his pocket as I supposed handling a pistol: I immediately drew one from my holsters and told him that if he made any attack upon me I would blow his brains out; the Court-Martial was disturbed and ordered out a guard, and as I did not belong to the army preferred riding off rather than be taken into custody by the guard:—this he calls an ignominious flight.

"I shall not trouble the public or you, Sir, any more with this dispute, as I will not be provoked to answer any future publications of so contemptible a being as Col. Kosciusko.

"I am, Sir,

Your humble servant,

JOHN CARTER.[18]

"Sept. 26, 1778."

Kosciuszko did not leave Carter's message unanswered. On October 6, he wrote to Gates:

"The Printer wroat me that he Canot publish this Weak for Want of Paper and place the inclosd in his letter.

---

[18] *Ibid.*, Oct. 8, 1778.

"Your letter mention I have recivd by Capt. D. Elsen[19] in which I found many satisfactory things for me, I winshe you would Come to West Point See the works your aprobation will give me more plaisure then of the others.

"General Washington propose Celebrat the Day of Surrender Burgon I heard so and the Congress—I should be happy if I Could Celebrat with you and ours Yankees.

"My profound respect to your Lady."[20]

The issue of the *New York Packet* of October 29th contained the above mentioned Kosciuszko's reply:

"TO THE PUBLIC

"Reduced by Mr. Carters illiberal attack upon my reputation, in the Fish-Kill paper of the 17th of September last, to the necessity of defending myself with TYPES; I declared in my letter to him, published the following week, and in the same paper, that I had done with him &c.—His publication of last Thursday cannot provoke me to honour him with a continuation of *such* hostilities; and his cowardice as well as my pride perfectly secure him against those of that nature he is most afraid of. But I believe it is my duty to submit to the judgment of the public: sufficient information for preventing Mr. Carter's character from being considered as *equivocal.*

"For this reason a certificate from Gen. Morris is now published, with another from Mr. Rogers, a Liut. in Col. Sheldon's regiment of light dragoon's.[21] It will plainly appear from them that my altercation with Mr. Carter, was occasioned by his invectives and threatnings, thundered against me, in my absence; and that, when he accidentally met Mr. Rogers, by whom I had sent him the letter he published in his *first* sally against me, and in which I demanded satisfaction for those invectives, he *then* denied the fact.

"To these certificates is joined a letter from Major Armstrong, which demonstrates the baseness of my contemptible antagonist, in representing me 'as a bravo,' &c.

---

19 This officer, Captain of the Corps of Engineers, cannot be properly identified. He assisted Kosciuszko throughout the war. Washington called him Dallizen (Fitzpatrick, XIX, 340); Heitman's *Hist. Register* omits him; Kite (*Duportail*, 226) and Lasseray (*Les Français*, II, 648) apparently misspell his name as de Laren or de Lauren.
20 Gates Papers, box 10, no. 109.
21 See *supra.*

66

"He has abused Gen. Gates under the cover of a narrative of fictitious facts, which, he pretends, have happened between Gen. Gates and Gen. Wilkenson.

"Whether the wretch be a mercenary calumniator, in the pay of the understrappers to the principal tools of our enemies, for injuring our cause, by abusing our Generals, I shall not determine; but I firmly believe, with many others, that, should he return to Boston, and visit the Convention troops, they THEMSELVES, would tar and feather him, for having presumed to mention so irreverently the character of Gen. Gates.

"Thaddeus Kosciuszko[22]

"West Point, Oct. 13."

Attached to this letter were the above mentioned enclosures.

The affair became quite notorious. Newspapers reprinted its details.[23] There is no doubt that the opinion of the army was on the side of Kosciuszko as he intimated in his letter. "The papers contain a tolerably good account of the dispute between Kosciuszko and Carter," wrote Major Samuel Shaw of Massachusetts to one of his friends. "Full credit is due to what the former says, so that you cannot be at a loss to form an opinion of the matter."[23a] Armstrong sarcastically recommended Carter to Kosciuszko's mercy: "He has certainly become a much fitter object for compassion, than resentment," he wrote.[24] Morris writing to his father from headquarters on December 7, mentioned that he sent him by Dr. Brown the certificates signed by Lieut. Rogers[25] and a copy of his own letter to Carter pertaining to the affair.[26] "You will there observe," he added, "the Arts Mr. Carter made use of to screen himself from the Resentment of Col. Kosciuszko. Under the influence of Fear and at the expence of his own Veracity he has impeached your's in that publick Manner. The character of the Coward and Lyar is frequently

---

[22] New York Packet, Oct. 29, 1778.
[23] For instance, such was the case with the (Boston) Evening Post and General Advertiser, Oct. 17 and 24, 1778.
[23a] Shaw to the Rev. John Eliot, Nov. 20, 1778, Quincy, Journals of Shaw, 53.
[24] Armstrong to Kosciuszko, Oct. 10, 1778, New York Packet, Oct. 29, 1778.
[25] Morris mentions that the certificate of Rogers was published in the Boston Gazette; a search through files of the Gazette for October and November, 1778, revealed no reference to the Kosciuszko-Carter affair.
[26] Extant files of the (Fishkill) New York Packet of 1778, are broken, and no numbers of it from Oct. 15 to Dec. 10 are known to exist, except for Oct. 29, according to Brigham, "Bibliography of American Newspapers, 1690-1820," Proceedings of the Amer. Antiquarian Soc., new series, XXVII (1917), 235-7.

connected in the same Person, and I think it is conspicuously so in him—A Coward for refusing to give a Gentleman satisfaction for the Injury he had done to his Reputation, and a Lyar for denying such injury when called upon to answer it." He added that he waited for an answer from Carter and having received none, wrote him another letter. "If that does not produce an answer," he concluded, "I shall take the Liberty of caning him whenever I meet him, and will publish him as a Coward and a Lyar."[27]

The episode demonstrated Kosciuszko's unwavering loyalty to Gates. If any of the two adversaries exposed himself as a "mercenary bravo" and a "needy desperate adventurer," it certainly was not Kosciuszko.

The later career of Carter, who subsequently resumed his true name, was illuminating in this regard. He amassed a large fortune as purveyor for Gen. Rochambeau's army. After the Revolution he became prominent in the social life of New York, London and Paris.[28] Truly, he was a pure snob and, in the eyes of history, a total zero, to say the least.

---

[27] "Letters to General Lewis Morris," *Coll. N. Y. Hist. Soc.*, VIII (1875), 456-7.
[28] Blanchard, *Journal*, 50; Humphreys, *Catherine Schuyler*, 191, 201; Jones, "Catherine Schuyler," *Amer. Mo. Mag.*, XIV (1899), 167; Patterson calls him a "bankrupt" who purposely came to this country to fatten himself on the American struggle (*Horatio Gates*, 281).

Chapter VIII

PARTING WITH GATES

In June, 1778, a French fleet under d'Estaing reached the American shores to co-operate with the American army against the British. At the news of its sailings, and in consequence of Lord North's peace proposals, the British evacuated Philadelphia and concentrated their forces around New York. After unsuccessful attempts to attack New York and to occupy Newport, the fleet sailed into the Boston harbor to repair its damages suffered early in August in the storm before Rhode Island.

There was a party in Congress and in the army that urged with renewed strength at this time an invasion of Canada with the help of the French. The chief promoter of the plan became Marquis de Lafayette. Washington appointed a special board of officers under the presidency of Gates to consider what would be the most expedient plan of invasion.

While working on the report, Gates must have discussed the subject with Kosciuszko who was an ardent supporter of the invasion. On August 3, Kosciuszko wrote to him: "You most think Sir to Expedition for Canada which will be Your Consquet not doubt and will add to your Honour, your Reputation and your Habilities of Surrender Borgon.

"Believe me Sir," he reasoned, "if we have not Canada the Bretain will be you verry Trubbelsom. You must not suffer not only them, but any puissance (poison) whatsoever in yours North part of America. Every Preest preach for his Parishoners, and soch interest will never give you Good, but divide your Opinions and unanimity and deslike your on Country, add to this the Gold soch power that hihave upon mind of many Men."[1]

Gates and his colleagues, Gen. Jacob Bailey and Col. Hazen, submitted a report which Washington in turn sent to Congress. The Commander-in-Chief considered it as "liable to fewest objections" and as affording "a reasonable prospect of success."[2]

[1] Gates Papers, box 10, no. 56.
[2] Washington to Henry Laurens, Sept. 12, 1778, Fitzpatrick, XII, 434.

However his chief attention was then directed toward New York where suspicious and large scale embarkations of the enemy were observed. Washington "strongly suspected that the enemy would transport the whole or the greatest part of their force Eastward and combine one great land and sea operation against the French fleet in Boston harbour."[3] He wrote to d'Estaing, September 11, 1778: "Our dispositions must . . . have equal regard to cooperating with you in a defensive plan, and securing the North River."[4]

Accordingly, he moved his army to new positions; part of it was to remain in the vicinity of the Hudson with a view to its defense, and the other was to be pushed towards the Connecticut River, "so as that when occasion may acquire, they may form a junction" to jointly defend either the Hudson or the French "Squadron and the town of Boston."[5] Gen. Gates was to command the left wing movement toward the Connecticut, with temporary headquarters at Danbury, Conn. He received the orders to move eastward on September 11.

Gates sincerely hoped that Kosciuszko would be allowed to accompany him. The Polish engineer had the same hope; he would feel best in his company. The monotony of the garrison life at West Point tired him; he preferred active warfare, especially as the new movement of troops promised to develop into the ardently desired invasion of Canada which was to add new laurels to Gates. The unpleasant affair with Carter strengthened his feelings more in this regard.

Gates tried to win the needed consent of Washington for the transfer of Kosciuszko and wrote to the Commander on September 11:

"I earnestly entreat your Ex — will be pleased to permit Col. Kusiusco to be the engineer to serve with the troops marching under my command if I had not an affectionate regard for this amiable foreighner, I should upon no account have made this my request. The out works at West Point are in a manner finished & the body of the place in such forwardness[6] as to put it in the power of the

---

3 Washington to John Jay, April 14, 1779, Fitzpatrick, XIV, 383.
4 Fitzpatrick, XII, 426.
5 Washington to d'Estaing, Sept. 11, 1778, Fitzpatrick, XII, 427.
6 In fact, toward the end of 1778, the works at West Point were so much advanced that Gérard, the French Minister, considered the place "a considerable fortress." (Gérard to Vergennes, Dec. 19, 1778, Gérard, Despatches, 438).

two Engineers now there to complete the whole with the utmost facility. I am sorry it is not your Ex — pleasure to allow Col. Hay to go with me."[7]

Washington refused the request. In his mind the safety of the Highlands was uppermost. "If they (the British) were able to possess themselves of the Highland passes and interrupt the navigation of the River, the consequences . . . would be terrible."[8] And though he knew of Kosciuszko's attachment to Gates with whom he was on "a direct breach"[9] since the "Conway Cabal," he learned to appreciate Kosciuszko's services and was entirely satisfied with the way he conducted the works at his important post. He, therefore, answered Gates immediately:

"Colo. Kosciusko has had the chief direction and superintendence of the Works at West Point, and it is my desire, that he should remain to carry them on. New plans and alterations at this time, would be attended with many inconveniences, and protract the defences of the River. This possibly in some degree, might take place in case of his absence, under the management of Another Engineer."[10]

Kosciuszko felt very unhappy when he learned of the refusal.

"You cannot Concive," he wrote to Gates on receiving the sad news, "in what passion I am having not plaisure to be under your Command my hapiness is lost, but I hope that you will help me to recover it soon as possible.

"You most remember Sir to have me with you and if you will forget that I beg the faveur of your Lady to have me in her memory.

"Because I have determin tu go with you Sir if not in the other Caracter I must go as Volenter for the next expedition tu Canada."[11]

He poured out his inconsolable and irritable state of mind, two days later in writing to Col. John Taylor:[12] "I am the most enhappy

---

[7] Gates Papers, box 19 c. (this is a copy of the original in Washington Papers).
[8] Washington to Gates, Oct. 7, 1778, Fitzpatrick, XIII, 44.
[9] Washington to John Jay, April 14, 1779, Fitzpatrick, XIV, 383.
[10] Sept. 11, 1778, Fitzpatrick, XII, 419.
[11] Sept. 12, 1778, Gates Papers, box 10, no. 76.
[12] There were two John Taylors with the rank of Colonel, both serving with the New Jersey militia. One, American born and a graduate of Princeton College, was in the Second Middlesex Regiment; the other one, born in England, was in the Fourth Hunterdon Regiment. (Race, *The Two Colonels John Taylor.*)

man in the World, because all my Yankees the best Friends is gone to Whit Plains or to Eastern and Left me with the Skoches or Irishes impolites as the Saviges. The satisfaction that I have at present only is this to go all day upon the Works and the Night to go to bed with the Cross Idea of lost of good Compani. I should go to the Eastern with General Gates but Genl. Washington was obstacle of going me ther and I am verry sorry of it."[13]

But during the next few weeks he slowly regained his composure. When he wrote to Gates on October 6, he still longed to be with him, but the tone of his letter was peaceful. He wrote:

"You should not forget your Good Frind I have not news from you since I lefted Whit Plain. Believe me Sir you Cannot find better frind and more attach to you this Confession I will prouve in every Circumstance whatsoever Will you remember Sir that I want to be with the Army under your Comand . . . I look after happy delivrance from her for northern Expedition & du Dear General Let me remember."[14]

The fate of war soon separated the two friends still farther. On October 20, Washington ordered Gates to proceed toward Hartford.[15] On October 22, Congress ordered him to Boston, to "take command of the continental forces . . . in the eastern district."[16] "Gen. Gates I understand is gone to command at Boston," wrote McDougall with a sneer to George Clinton. "He prefers being the first man of a village, to the second in Rome."[17] Samuel Adams explained the order in a more matter-of-fact way: "When General Gates was ordered to Boston a considerable Embarkation of the Troops had been made at New York and it was apprehended they would attempt a Landing somewhere near that Place. His military Abilities and Experience, his political Principles and Attachments and the Confidence which the Troops and People of Eastern States had in him, were the Considerations which induced his being sent thither."[18]

Still on October 29, Kosciuszko wrote to Gates:

13 Kahanowicz, p. 1, no. 2.
14 Gates Papers, box 10, no. 108.
15 Washington to Gates, Oct. 20, 1778, Fitzpatrick, XIII, 112.
16 *Journals Cont. Cong.*, XII, 1038.
17 Nov. 5, 1778, Clinton, *Public Papers*, IV, 244.
18 Samuel Adams to Dr. Charles Chauncy, Dec. 25, 1778, Burnett, *Letters*, III, 552.

"We have the news that Ten Regiments Embark to West Indiens from New York[19] and many say that all troups Will Soon left this Country I winsh that should be true.

"I am very Enxious to know what is Raison that you is sent so far as to Hatfort. I believe you will go Certainly to Canada if you go to Philadelphia Sir this Whinter I should be glad know because I want to go there my self, and I should stay her so long as to have honour to Accompagn you. My respect to your Lady."[20]

The transfers of Gates came in so quick a succession that Kosciuszko was unable to keep track of him. He wrote him again to Boston on December 28:

"Long ago I looked for oportunity to writ to you. but I was so unhappy that I could not have and after I expected that somebody of your familly will acquiented me with the place where you was, because I knew not that you is in Boston. Be so good Dear General to write me of your health as I am very anxious to know and of your Ladys. For my part I am prety Happy with General Paterson but not so as I should be with you. You promise me Sir if you go to Canada to take me with you will not forget pray your Good Frind who is always with great respect."[21]

The expedition to Canada came to naught and except for a few brief and rather sad meetings, Kosciuszko was destined never to enjoy the presence of his friend till the end of the war.

---

[19] At that time, Sir Henry Clinton, acting on orders from England, sent about 5,000 troops to West Indies and other large detachments to Halifax, Florida and Bermuda for eventual action against the French. Washington and many Americans thought that Clinton intends to evacuate New York.

[20] Gates Papers, box 10, no. 140.

[21] Gates Papers, box 13, no. 387; this letter is wrongly dated 1779; its contents make it clear that it pertains to December, 1778.

Chapter IX

WEST POINT, 1778-9

"West Point is as barren of news as the mountains that surround it," wrote Kosciuszko to Gates in the spring of 1779,[1] and these words might well describe the dullness of the long months which he yet had to spend at that post. Still in the fall of 1778, Col. Baldwin dropped in and lodged with Kosciuszko in his modest quarters several times. He was his guest on October 15, and again on November 23.[2] On December 4, Baldwin came again with Gen. McDougall and dined with "Colo. Kosiusko, Genl. Paterson & others."[3] The engineer always liked a good fun and a company of good friends, and of the latter he had many. If he recently complained of "impolite savages," it was only under the fresh impression of a misfortune of parting with a friend. Sometime he had a chance to enjoy female company and he is said to have been always tender to the graces of the ladies. "My best respect to your Lady and alle Handsom Girlls," he wrote to Col. John Taylor on January 3.[4]

But such friendly visits and meetings were rather rare. The exerting work on fortifications filled up his time. It was constantly handicapped by want of men and tools and, very often of daily necessities. Gen. McDougall was near despair on this account. "I am unhappily left in this Department," he complained to Gov. Clinton, "gleaned of almost every comfort for man and Horse . . . Cattle have been for three Days eating their mangers; others dying for want." As to men, he had "utmost Difficulty to cov~r them, and to provide them for the Winter. . . . My Condition is not much better, than the Israelites in Egypt, who were ordered to make Brick without Straw."[5]

In such conditions work was, indeed, discouraging.

---

[1] March 3, 1779, Gates Papers, box 11, no. 60.

[2] Baldwin, *Diary*, 137 and 139.

[3] *Ibid.*, 140.

[4] Kahanowicz, p. 2, no. 2.

[5] Dec. 15, 1778, Clinton, *Public Papers*, IV, 383-6.

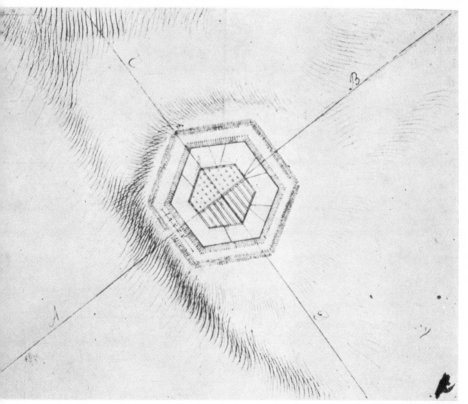

A PLAN OF A REDOUBT AT WEST POINT
by KOSCIUSZKO

75

With the coming winter Kosciuszko's most important task was to bring in the large chain and boom which closed the river.[6] On December 28, he informed McDougall that "the chain is safe and can be very easy taken up when Cold abates. The Boom lies where it was and will be taken up. We shall want I think about 50 Barrels of Tar for the use of the logs of the Chain, Boom and Bumprooves."[7] Evidently the temperature improved and Kosciuszko worked so quickly that on January 2, he already had "taken up and got on Shore three Hundred links of the chain with about one hundred of the Small one where it was fastned to the Skudblock."[8]

During January and February he was busy with tarring and calcimining logs of the chain and replacing the rotten ones, cutting timber for cheveaux-de-frise, bombproofs, parapets and other parts of fortifications, building new barracks as all available were full of sick soldiers, and drawing new plans.[9] Seeing negligence in the furloughing of artificers and in employing masons who were of but little use during the severe weather, he suggested remedies to McDougall, but with due respect: "Those Matter you can Judge better (than) my self you will excuse me in giving my Opinion and Shall perfectly acquess in and execute your Commands."[10] McDougall accepted his suggestion.

Lt. Col. Jean Baptiste Gouvion, a French engineer of the Duportail group, was Kosciuszko's assistant at that time. It seems that he was more accessible than his colleagues, as there is no record of any misunderstanding between them, though both together spent a long time at West Point. Under Kosciuszko's direction Gouvion prepared copies of some plans for Gen. McDougall during the winter.[11] On February 9, Washington wrote to McDougall from his headquarters at Middlebrook:

"From the manner in which you speak of employing Mr. Gouvion in this business (intended survey of the works at West Point),

---

[6] McDougall to Major Dobbs, Dec. 22, 1778, McDougall Papers, book III. For a description of the chain see Heath, *Memoirs*, 277.
[7] *Ibid.*, book III.
[8] Kosciuszko to McDougall, *ibid.*, book V.
[9] McDougall to Gen. Paterson, Dec. 24, 1778, and Feb. 25, 1779; Kosciuszko to McDougall, Jan. 2, Feb. 6 and 24, 1779, McDougall Papers, books III, IV and V; Griffin quotes a pertinent order of McDougall to Kosciuszko, December 30, 1778, the original of which is evidently missing from the collection of the New York Historical Society.
[10] Dec. 28, 1778, McDougall Papers, book III.
[11] McDougall to Gouvion, Dec. 17, 1778, *ibid.*, book III.

I am in doubt whether Col. Koshiosko still remains at West Point, or not. As he has not been removed by my order or permission, I should imagine he is still there. If he is, he will inform you of the plan agreed upon between General Du Portail & myself, which he was instructed in the first place to carry into execution, as might be found necessary to render the plan more perfect.[12] I have spoken to General Du Portail, on your request concerning Col. De la Radière or Gouvion. Whether the former will be sent or the latter continued will depend on circumstances which are not now decided. But if Koshiosko be still at West Point, as he is a senior officer he must of necessity have the chief direction."[13]

To this McDougall replied: "Colo. Kusiasco has been undisturbed in his Line at West Point."[14]

During these labors there happened a minor incident which again manifested the mildness of Kosciuszko's character. Lieut. Timothy Whiting of the Quartermaster Department, committed some breach of discipline and subsequently refused "an arrest from Col. Kusciosko in public Company."[15] He was tried by a court-martial, unanimously found guilty of a breach of the articles of war, and sentenced to be cashiered. Kosciuszko took pity of the man and himself applied to Gen. McDougall to mitigate the harsh sentence. As there also appeared some "ambiguity . . . in the Proceedings relative to the arrest," evidently caused by Kosciuszko's imperfect knowledge of the English language, McDougall reversed the sentence and ordered Whiting to return to his duties. But in his order of the day of January 23, he severely reprimanded the Quartermaster for his "Temper more like a quibbling petty-fogging attoreney than the nice and delicate Principles of Honor which should always govern every Officer connected with the American Army.

---

[12] Among the "Notes of Col. Houskiaso," McDougall Papers, book V, there is an undated one, in Kosciuszko's hand, prepared for McDougall's use and containing instructions of Washington to Kosciuszko:

> "Direction Was given me as I remember is this
> Finisht Fort Putnam with the other Bumprove in it and Chistern.
> Finisht Webs redoubt with the Bumprouve in it. Make ston Wall all around the fort, with the Magasin and Bumprouve.
> Make Small redoubte with the Bumprouve upon the Matters Rock Hill.
> Make small redoubte in the Magasin.
> Finisht the Chain battery over the River
> Finisht small redoubte back Fort Constitution and erect one more."

[13] Fitzpatrick, XIV, 84.
[14] April 15, 1779, Washington Papers, vol. CIII.
[15] Evening order of Dec. 29, 1778, Orderly book no. 95, McDougall Papers.

On the other Hand the General desires Kusciosko and every Officer to be cautious and circumspect in putting officers in arrest on which their Reputations so much depend, and when the Service requires it that it be done in clear and unequivocal Terms."[16]

Kosciuszko's steadfast friendship for Gates is reflected in the following letter of March 3, in which he complained in a very delicate manner that all his letters sent to him after his departure for New England, went unanswered:[17]

"If my friendship is Great for you Person is not less, this will be a perpetual Inducement to me to take every Opportunity of expressing my Sentiments, without any self interest not expecting an Answer having received none in return for four sent you.

"I will Continue to write and if I cannot give you any satisfaction or Pleasure, I shall gratify my own Vanity in expressing my sentiment as an Old woman, who by age expects not a reciprocity of affection or interest to her.

". . . The only piece of news we have here, which I suppose you have heard, is that Col. Putnam with a Detachment from Nixon's Brigade took Eleven Prisoners and killed two of the Enemys at Horse neck, he likwise retook a great number of Cattle they were driving in. I must beg the favour of you to promote the interest of the Yankees at Coast, this request is formed on principles of real Justice as well as because I suppose to be my self at this time more than half a Yankee."[18]

On the same day the "more than half a Yankee" also penned a merry letter addressed to Major Armstrong but referring to several other of his friends, now serving with Gen. Gates:

"I do not tax you with want of Friendships in not writing to me knowing that you have a good Reason to give that the handsome Girls ingross the whole of your Time and attention and realy If I was in your place I should of Choise do the same. But you Col. Clairjon can give me no Reason but your Laziness. I have been told you are about Marying a Young Girl and mean to exert your self that the name of Clairjons may not be extinguished. You Col. Troop as a good Officer of Artillery will make use of your Activity and

---

[16] *Ibid.*
[17] "There is nothing so liable to get lost as letters in this country," Gouvion to de Marbois, Nov. 5, 1779, copy in the MSS Div., Library of Congress.
[18] Gates Papers, box 11, no. 60.

prove the Goodness of your Cannon on the wedding Day of Col. Clairjon. Your help Doctor Brown will be wanted with all your surgical Faculties to promote so laudauble a design for the Interest of Mr. Clairjon and administere such Medicine as will make him Strong and Fameus as Priapus."[19]

Spring was approaching and with it the tempo of labor on fortifications increased. Gen. McDougall asked for new maps of West Point and also ordered a series of minor additions to fortifications.[20] On April 25, Kosciuszko was able to send him "a ruff map" of the place.[21] The chain had to be put in place again,[22] and this was accomplished on April 5. Advising one of his friend of this, Kosciuszko added:

"The Brytains seems to grow more wise, propose the peace to America by influence of Spain, the articles is not yet known but we must supose such as America will chuse.

"Mr. Deane is now out of date and take no more the public notice. However more men is in favour of him against his antagonist; as for Common Sense seem that he have lost his Sense. . . ."

This is another proof that Kosciuszko always took a lively interest not only in public matters pertaining strictly to the war, but also in American domestic affairs. At the end of the letter he stressed again his regional preferences: "My best compliments to all my friends of Yankee speties."[23]

About that time Congress resolved to organize all engineers in the service of the United States into a separate corps headed by a commandant appointed by that body. Duportail was chosen for the post, but Congress delayed his formal nomination. The delay caused his uneasiness. He urged John Jay, then President of Congress, to speed up the appointment. West Point is "the Key of the North River," and notwithstanding his "Directions to the officer entrusted with the fortifications of that Place . . . unhappily, I have lately

19 Kahanowicz, p. 2, no. 3. "Col. Clairjon" refers to William Clajon.

20 McDougall to Kosciuszko, April 17, 1779, McDougall Papers, book IV.

21 *Ibid.*, book IV; the map accompanies the letter and is reproduced here on p. 45.

22 McDougall to Kosciuszko, March 18, and Gen. Paterson to McDougall, March 28, 1779, *ibid.*, book IV.

23 Kosciuszko to Wells, A.D.Q.M.G., May 24, 1779, the original in private possession, quoted by Griffin, III, 166. It alludes to the well known controversy between Silas Deane and Thomas Paine, then at its peak. Rumors of Spain's intervention for peace appeared periodically during the war.

heard, that almost nothing has been done," he argued in his letter using a mere hearsay as his argument. "If the Enemies happen to take possession of West Point, . . . Congress or the Commander-in-Chief will betake themselves to me, and ask of me, why I did not take care that the works at West Point should not be carried on with regularity and dispatch. . . . My answer will be this; 'I had no right to demand the necessary informations from the Engineer entrusted with the fortifications of the Place: When I went there in September by the Commander-in-Chief's order, I requested him to render me an account every month of the Condition of the Works, of the difficulties of every kind that might arise in the Execution:—He has not done it. But that officer is not in any manner to be blamed for he had no orders in writing for that purpose from Congress or the Commander-in-Chief.' " Unless he were given control over the erection of fortifications and engineers at West Point, he disavowed any responsibility "for the neglects or interruptions which may happen in the Works of that Fort."[24]

The tone of Duportail's letter was rather assuming. Nobody ever blamed him for anything pertaining to fortifications at West Point. Washington stressed repeatedly that he relied on Kosciuszko as to the direction of the works, and neither the Commander-in-Chief, nor Congress ever tried to subject him to direct dependence on Duportail. Just about that time, Washington wrote to McDougall: "The completion of the works at West-Point has prudently made a principal part in our system: and I am persuaded every thing has been done by you for this purpose;"[25] which proves that Duportail has been wrongly informed as if nothing were done at the fort during the last several months. Sending the Frenchman for his second inspection to West Point, on June 2, Washington again wrote to McDougall: "It gives me pleasure that the forts at this critical moment are in hands where they may be safely trusted."[26] It is entirely clear that these words referred not to Duportail, but to McDougall and Kosciuszko.

Soon Washington himself followed Duportail to West Point and on June 8, made an inspection of the place in company of Kosciuszko. The next day the following advertising appeared at the post:

---

[24] Dated Philadelphia, May 11, 1779, Papers Cont. Congress, no. 164, ff. 342-5.
[25] May 28, 1779, Fitzpatrick, XV. 167.
[26] Fitzpatrick, XV, 214.

"Lost yesterday, reconnoitering with his Excellency General Washington, a spur, with treble chains on the side, and a single one under foot, all silver, except the tongue of the buckle and the rowel. Whosever has found, or shall find it, and will bring it to Colonel Kosciusko or at head-quarters, shall have ten dollars reward."[27]

The silver spur most probably belonged to Washington and Kosciuszko tried to recover his loss. The purpose of the brief visit of the Commander-in-Chief at the fort was to assure himself personally of its security. He considered West Point "the most important Post in America"[28] and it seemed to be now in great danger. Sir Henry Clinton left New York with strong forces, captured Stony and Verplanck's Points, and hence moved toward Continental Village.[29] His intentions were clear: he was to attack West Point and thus to inflict the rebels a mortal stroke. The Americans, however, were on the alert. Washington transferred his headquarters to New Windsor, near West Point, and to remedy the chronic want of artificers at the stronghold, issued a general order that "all those soldiers who are Masons by trade in the line are immediately to be drawn out & sent to the Fort for a special & temporary service. They are to take their orders from Colonel Kosciuszko."[30]

The garrison worked now days and nights on strengthening the works. All approaches to the forts were closed with felled trees. The British observed diligently all this activity through their spies and reconnaisances. "This Place is a great Object of their Jealosy & Attention, and they have been long labouring to render it as strong as Art can make it," reported the British General Pattison to Lord Townshend.[31] The British were soon convinced of difficulties of the proposed attack, but their forces remained in the vicinity constituting a constant threat.

Notwithstanding Washington's order, no artificers were coming to Kosciuszko. "Thes works want at less six hundret men one hundred & sixty Carpenters twenty Massons, and twelve Miners, ten

27 Johnson, *Traditions and Reminiscences*, 415.

28 Washington to Heath, March 21, 1781, Fitzpatrick, XXI, 344; Heath *Memoirs*, 237.

29 Washington to the President of Congress, June 6, 1779, Clinton, *Public Papers*, V, 21.

30 June 30, 1779, Fitzpatrick, XV, 341; Orderly book no. 99, July 2, 1779, McDougall Papers; the original order in the Kahanowicz Coll., p. 32, no. 75.

31 June 9, 1779, Clinton, *Public Papers*, V, 26.

teams, for two months," he reported to McDougall on July 1.[32] He explained his difficulties to the Commander-in-Chief who removed his quarters to West Point, on July 21:

"I have only two Masons as yet come from the Main Army, and do not expect any more, the Officers being unwilling to part with them. I applyed to the Detachements here who had a number of them, wrote to the Officers in the most pressing terms shewing the necessity of it but got none. I am out of the lime, it is true I have a promise of having some more but when I cannot tell.

"One of the Justice wrote to Mr. Whiting, G.Q.M., that General Green had excused the Inhabitants from sending more Teams than Ten, I suppose he has in view to imploy the Teams of the Brigades, as they do nothing at Present to ease the Burthen of the Inhabitants.

"I have Twenty Carpenters Sick by raison of drinking Water in this hot Weather (as they say) they suppose that one Half Gill added to their daily allowance would remedy the Evil.

"Col. Stewart was so good as to let me have a Stone Cutter from his Regiment for One Week. I wish to have him for a Month having much to do and know not where to find another."[33]

In view of this lack of cooperation on the part of some of the officers, Washington had to resort to the impressment of soldiers for labor under Kosciuszko.[34] To calm his solicitude for carpenters deprived of rum, he ordered the Commissary General to procure a supply. "They must be paid in Rum (if that was the agreement) or an equivalent in Money when they do not get Rum," he wrote to Kosciuszko.[35]

During his stay at West Point, Washington, of course, also orally discussed with Kosciuszko, and probably quite often, matters pertaining to the fortifications.[36] Gen. Heath, who at that time commanded troops on the eastern bank of the Hudson, wrote down in

---

[32] McDougall Papers, book V.

[33] Endorsed July, 1779, Washington Papers, vol. CXIV, 1779. The inclination of officers to shun corvée at West Point is reflected in the act of one Jonathan Blake, commander of a company of artificers, who tore and concealed a letter of Kosciuszko, designating his company to some work, and absented himself from the duty. Blake was court-martialed. (August 21, 1779, Orderly book no. 74, McDougall Papers).

[34] There are several such orders dated Oct. 4, 10 and 22, and Nov. 21, 1779, Orderly book no. 74, McDougall Papers, also Fitzpatrick, XVII, 159.

[35] Sept. 9, 1779, Fitzpatrick, XVI, 255.

[36] Washington to McDougall, Nov. 13, 1779, Fitzpatrick XVII, 102.

his diary on September 9, that at that time there were seven or eight redoubts, built or building, on the western side of the river, besides Fort Clinton and Fort Putnam.[37] A few weeks later Col. Angell of the Second Rhode Island passing through the place, was amazed with the strength of "the American Gibralter." He saw "a fort on Every Emminence Some Distance round."[37a]

The fall of 1779 brought to Kosciuszko some agreeable changes in the daily monotony. Washington remained at West Point till November 28,[38] and on September 30, Chevalier de la Luzerne, the new French Minister, presented himself to him, together with his staff. A few days later the retiring envoy, Gérard, came to take leave. Probably Kosciuszko witnessed honors paid to them and had some occasion for a little amusement. To his delight, his old comrade, Major Armstrong, passed through West Point on November 1, bearing official letters from Gates to Congress announcing the evacuation of Rhode Island by the British.[39] On the same day Clinton evacuated Verplanck's and Stony Points, and the danger to the Highlands passed.

However, there was also some sad news. On November 9, intelligence reached West Point that "Count Pulaski, a remarkably brave and enterprising officer, of Polish descent," died in an unsuccessful attack on Savannah.[40] There is nothing to show what impression the news made on Kosciuszko, but undoubtedly he deeply regretted the untimely end of his famous countryman, who offered his life to the same ideals.

A cause for Kosciuszko's greatest personal satisfaction was a brief visit of Gates with his family on November 23.[41] The General passed from Providence to his Traveller's Rest for a brief respite between the toils of campaigns. On November 28, Gen. Heath took command of all the forts and the troops on the Hudson.[42]

---

37 Heath, *Memoirs*, 229.
37a Angell, *Diary*, 97. Entry of Nov. 28, 1779.
38 Baker, *Itinerary*, 163.
39 Heath, *Memoirs*, 235.
40 *Ibid.*, 236.
41 *Ibid.*, 237.
42 *Ibid.*, 237.

Chapter X

GOING SOUTH

The winter of 1779-80, was the severest in human memory. A violent snowstorm enveloped the whole northeastern part of the country in the first days of January and made the roads impassable. Snow and ice laid for upwards of six weeks.[1] The condition of the American army became deplorable, as the snow cut off the supply of provisions. Hunger was great, but if the whole army suffered much, the situation of the garrison at West Point was still more critical. "The situation of the army at this instant is truly alarming," reported Gen. Heath to Gov. Clinton on January 25. "The garrison of West Point have during the winter been at a scanty allowance of Bread, and often without any at all. This has been the case for these four or five days past. The garrison have been and still are, obliged to be on almost constant fatigue, dragging materials for their Barracks, and all their fuel on hand Sleds more than a mile. Some of the troops are yet in Tents, and during the winter hitherto have been obliged to encounter hunger and cold, performing by hand that business which ought to be done by Teams. These, they have endured and performed with a patience scarcely to be conceived."[2]

The deep snow, "four feet deep on a level," demanded constant work to keep open communications between the forts and redoubts of West Point.[3] At least, if the stomachs were empty, there was plenty of fuel from the virgin forests in the vicinity. The soldiers were not careful enough and in consequence fires broke out several times during the winter. The North Redoubt burned twice during the winter, at one occasion for two days before the fire could be extinguished. Large quantity of stores was consumed at Fort Arnold in another fire.[4]

---

[1] Washington to the President of Congress, Jan. 5; Geo. Clinton to William Floyd, Jan. 6; Du Simitiere to Geo. Clinton, Feb. 16; and Udney Hay to Geo. Clinton, Feb. 5, 1780, Clinton, *Public Papers*, V, 443, 455, 476, 496; Moore, *Diary*, II, 250.
[2] Clinton, *Public Papers*, V, 465.
[3] Heath, *Memoirs*, 239.
[4] *Ibid.*, 240-2; 211, 212; Washington to the President of Congress, Feb. 14, and to Heath, Feb. 16, 1780, Fitzpatrick, XVIII, 8 and 17.

Without doubt Kosciuszko shared all the sufferings and labors of the garrison.[5] Even with the winter at its peak, he did not waste time, but besides his other work, he prepared plans of the forts for Washington and asked Gen. Greene, then Quartermaster General, to give him his opinion about them. "Conscious of your Extensive abilities I am Certain (it) will afford as well to the public good, as to my own improvement," he wrote him modestly. "The desirable qualities which you are parfect Master of will forgive the liberties taken by me," he added, recommending at the same time Captains Wright and Clow of the Artificers and some sergeants as "most active" and "very honest."[6]

On March 23, Kosciuszko wrote to Col. Richard K. Meade, Assistant Adjutant General to Washington:

"I wrote to you the 11th of this instant and send three more Sketches of Plans. I do not know if they are come to hand, I delivered them to General Howe,[7] who promised to forward them. I wrote also to his Excellency respecting teams which I Cannot get by the great scarcity of Forrage and you know I can do nothing without them.

"I beg you would inform him I have but Eighty fatigue men for all the works at West Point and I expect less and less every day; this will be the Cause, that the works will not be Compleated and not to be imputed to my neglect. I wrote to Governor Clinton two days agoe, that he would send some teams with the Fourage of the opulent and rich inhabitants,[8] I have not yet received an answer. I desired General Howe to write him upon the same subject and he did. I have three Masons from the Virginia Line. They are best Masons of few number that I have I should beg to keep them, but as they are in Great want of shoes, I will thank you to procure an order for three pairs of shoes on the Commissary of Cloathing at Newburgh."[9]

---

5 Connecticut State Library, John Fitch Papers, p. 112, contain a letter of Fitch to John Elderkin, dated Fishkill, Jan. 2, 1780, concerning the division of a barrel of sugar of which Col. "Cuskiusko" was to receive a portion.

6 Jan. 28, 1780, Library of the Amer. Philosophical Soc., Correspondence relating to the American Revolution of Maj. Gen. N. Greene, vol. I, no. 55.

7 Gen. Robert Howe of North Carolina substituted for Heath at West Point for a short time early in 1780.

8 The letter to Clinton is quoted by Kozłowski, "Kosciuszko w West Point," *Przegląd Historyczny*, X, 389, as from the Papers of the Cont. Cong., but this author was unable to locate it.

9 Washington Papers, vol. CXXXI (1780, March 21-29).

FACSIMILE OF KOSCIUSZKO'S LETTER TO GEN. HEATH

Meade answered that the maps did not yet reach Washington, but that the General already made dispositions with Gen. Howe as to the augmenting the number of fatigue men.[10] However, lack of material constantly retarded Kosciuszko's work.[11]

Still during the winter Gen. Heath obtained a leave of absence and left West Point for New England[12] to a deep regret of Kosciuszko, who could hardly bear the frequent separation from his best friends. "You have forgot us your Children—," he wrote him anxiously on April 24. "When shall we have the pleasure of seeing you, the uncertainty of time fill our hearts with discontent, and gives us such Glomy and thought full looks, which is tobe seen, only in persons, who have lost the best of friends—Happy should I be to explain those sentiments, which is felt in the breasts of some[13] persons. The object is worth, the cause is just, and the example is noble—

"The Money here is scarce, which oblige the Soldiers going home to give three hundred dollars, which they have due, for half, or one third that Sum in ready money, to Carry them home, I cannot immagin in what maner your Troops will be reinlisted, while they have no prospect of any advantage arrising from it."[14]

He wrote to him again a few days later, urging his return:

"As the Campaign for the insuing year soon Commence; the mouvements and the Arrangement of the Army will immediately take place—In my opinion, it is your own, ours, and the interest of your Country, you should be present to Command us forgive me the truth, which your merit my attachement to you in sincerity extort from my heart.—Flying report says Charlestown is taken by the enemy, but that we have lost our Frigates there is certain."[15]

Meanwhile the hunger in the army became critical again. In a letter to Samuel Huntington, then President of Congress, Washing-

---

[10] Meade to Kosciuszko, March 30, 1780, Fitzpatrick, XVIII, 182.

[11] Morgan Lewis to Col. Yates, Albany, May 17, 1780: "The Officer who was sent here by Colo. Kosciuszko for Saw Logs to lay the Chain with at the Forts is extremely impatient at not being supplied with the Number his orders were for," Kahanowicz, no. 76C.

[12] Heath, *Memoirs*, 246.

[13] Illegible, perhaps "sorry."

[14] Mass. Hist. Soc., Heath Collection, IX, 286.

[15] May 9, 1780, Mass. Hist. Soc. Heath Coll., IX, 389; the letter is wrongly marked as pertaining to the year of 1778. Charleston was captured by Clinton on May 12, 1780.

ton confessed: "There never has been a stage of the War in which the dissatisfaction has been so general or alarming."[16] In answer to Gen. Howe's appeals for help Washington could only offer his sympathy: "The distresses of the Troops under yr Comd give me great pain and what adds to it is, I have not in my power to administer to their relief," he answered.[17] Advising the President of Congress of a mutiny in two regiments of the Connecticut Line and of extreme misery in the army, he added: "They are in as great distress at West Point."[18]

Not only want of provisions, but also want of clothing annoyed Kosciuszko. He himself would have acquiesced in the situation, but his colleagues suffered too. Most probably with their authorization he wrote the following letter to Schuyler, now member of Congress, and this was the only occasion on which he spoke as dean of the Corps of Engineers in the Northern Department.[19]

"As you are the only Person in Congress with whom I have the Honor to be acquainted, that knows the System of the whole Army and it's several departments; you will forgive me the trouble I am about to give you in favour of the Corps of Engineers. We beg that the Honorable Congress would grant us Cloathing in Apointed maner as for the Army. Why should all Departments receive and we be excluded? Justice speek for it's self without farther request from us. If Cloathing could be purchased very easy, in this Country and without injuring the Public service, in the Time which most be necessarily employed for that purpose we should not solicit, but you know how difficult it is to get it, and what inconsistancies it would be, for us to be absent often from Camp. Your remonstrating to Congress in our behalf will I am sure bare great weight, which favour will always be greatfully acknowledged with the greatest Sincerity from us."[20]

In June, after Sir Henry Clinton's return from the South, Washington and Gen. Howe again expected an attack on West Point,

---

16 April 3, 1780, Fitzpatrick, XVIII, 209.

17 May 25, 1780, *ibid.,* XVIII, 413.

18 May 27, 1780, *ibid.,* XVIII, 429.

19 Duportail was sent south and on May 12, was taken prisoner by the British when Charleston capitulated. Carrington, *Battles of the American Revolution,* 527, and some of the Kosciuszko biographers intimate that he succeeded Duportail as chief of the Corps of Engineers after the latter's capture. By justice and seniority the chieftaincy belonged to him, but neither he ever aspired to the position, nor there was any official act in this regard.

20 May 12, 1780, Papers Cont. Cong., series 78, vol. XIII, p. 557.

but their apprehensions did not come true. Meanwhile the long sojourn of Kosciuszko at the fortress was nearing its end.

On June 13, Congress ordered Gen. Gates to take command in the Southern Department,[21] and, in organizing his staff, his first thoughts were of Kosciuszko. He wrote to Washington:

"I could wish your Excellency would somewhat Brighten the Scene, by indulging me in my request, to obtain Colonel Kosciuszko for my Chief Engineer. His Services with me in the Campaign of 77, and the High Opinion I entertain of His Talents, and his Honour, induce me to be thus importunate with your Excellency, to let me have the Colonel for my Chief Engineer."[22]

To Major Armstrong Gates wrote:

"I am destined by the Congress to command in the South. In entering on this new and (as Lee says) most difficult theatre of war, my first thoughts have been turned to the selection of an Engineer, an Adjutant-General and a Quarter-Master-General. Kosciuszko, Hay and yourself if I can prevail upon you all, are to fill these offices, and fill them well. The excellent qualities of the Pole, which no one knows better than yourself, are acknowledged at headquarters, and may induce others to prevent his joining us. But his promise once given, we are sure of him."[23]

Still by the end of July Kosciuszko was uncertain as to his new destination. He aimed at the rapid completing of the fortifications, but after all the difficulties of the winter season, he was again condemned to inactivity. He wrote to Washington on July 30:

"To this day I have not received your Excellencys order respecting my destination, having nothing to do at present as all the artifficers are directed to receive Liut. Colo: Gouvions orders,[24] I beg your Excellency to give me permision to leave the Engeneer Department and direct me a Command in the light Infantry in the Army under your immediate Command or the Army at the Southward agreable to my ranck I now hold. Your Excellency may be certain that I am acquiented with the Tactic & discipline and my

---

[21] Burnett, Letters, V, 213; Journals Cont. Cong., XVII, 508.

[22] June 21, 1780, Kahanowicz, no. 76B.

[23] Washington, ed., Writings of Jefferson, VIII, 496.

[24] After Duportail's departure for the South, Washington ordered Gouvion to his headquarters and he worked on minor fortifications in the lower Highlands.

Conduct joind with a small share of ambition to distinguish myself, I hope will prove not the Contrary."[25]

On August 3, the Commander-in-Chief answered him from his headquarters at Peekskill:

"The Artificers are drawn from the post at West Point for a particular and temporary service only, and as there is a necessity for a Gentleman in the Engineering department to remain constantly at that post, and as you from your long residence there are particularly well acquainted with the nature of the Works and the plans for their completion, it was my intent that you should continue. The Infantry Corps was arranged before the receipt of your letter. The southern Army, by the captivity of Genl. du portail and the other Gentlemen in that branch, is without an Engineer, and as you seem to express a wish of going there rather than remaining at West Point, I shall, if you prefer it to your present appointment, have no objection to your going."[26]

Kosciuszko was elated with joy. Perhaps he did not expect such a satisfactory decision. He replied immediately:

"The Choice your Excellency was pleased to give me in the letter of yesterday is very kind and as the Complition of the works at this place this Campaign as Circumstance are, will be impossible in my opinion, I prefer going to the Southward to Continuing here. I beg you to favor me with your orders, and Letter of recommendation to the Board of War, as I shall pass throw Philadelphia. Shall wait on your Excellency to pay due respects within a few days, but lest the movements of the Army should prevent, beg my request may be granted and sent me at this place."[27]

He still asked another favor and wrote on August 7:

"I beg your Excellency would grant me a request to Carry my boy with me, who since three years wait on me. I have no other at present, and I Cannot get one to go with me so far off. Colo. Sprout is willing if your Excellency will give order for it."[28]

25 Histor. Soc. of Penna., Gratz Collection, case 4, box 12; a copy in Washington Papers, vol. CXLIV, 1780, July 30-August 5.
26 Fitzpatrick, XIX, 316.
27 Washington Papers, vol. CXLIV, 1780, July 30-Aug. 5.
28 Ibid., vol. CXLV, 1780, Aug. 6-11.

FACSIMILE OF KOSCIUSZKO'S LETTER TO WASHINGTON

To which Washington replied: "It is perfectly agreeable to me that You should carry your Servant with you, and so You will inform Colo Sprout."[29]

Gates' letter of June 21, requesting permission for Kosciuszko to go with him South as his Chief Engineer, reached Washington not earlier than August 7, when already the matter was decided in his favor. "A few days since upon Col. Kosciuisco's application for leave to serve to the Southward, he obtained my permission, and I suppose designs setting out immediately. Captn. Dallizen accompanies him,"[30] replied Washington.

Just at that time Benedict Arnold took over the command of West Point. Major Villefranche was directed to take the place of Kosciuszko[31] who, meanwhile left for the South by way of Philadelphia. A few weeks later the dramatic episode of Arnold's treason was unfolded. By pure accident the treason was detected and the fortress was saved. In the confusion, however, which followed the event, a chestfull of plans by Kosciuszko, pertaining to the fortifications, was destroyed. Washington wrote to Gen. Heath, who meanwhile returned to West Point, on October 31:

"There is, I am informed by General Irvine, a Chest belonging to Colonel Koscuiszko, containing principally Papers of a public nature; which General Greene had determined to have removed from Mrs. Warren's to a place of more security; but in the hurry of business might have omitted. If the chest still remains at West Point, you will be pleased to take it into your charge, or have it removed to a place of safety. As the Drafts & Papers are of consequence to the public."[32]

The reminder came entirely too late. Gen. Heath answered on November 6:

"I shall take immediate measures for the security of Colonel Kosciuszko's chest; it—shall be lodged at my own quarters.

"P. S.

"I have just sent for Colᵒ Kosciuszko's chest; it was left without lock. Mrs. Warren saies upon the detection of Arnold she burnt

---

[29] August 8, 1780, Fitzpatrick, XIX, 316.
[30] August 8, 1780, Fitzpatrick, XIX, 339.
[31] Washington to Arnold, Aug. 6, 1780, Fitzpatrick, XIX, 331.
[32] Fitzpatrick, XX, 268; Heath Papers, *Coll. Mass. Hist. Soc.,* ser. 5, vol. IV (1878), p. 168.

the plans lest their being found with her should raise a suspicion to her disadvantage. I shall order a further inquiry into the matter."[33]

If fate hung with heavy hand upon written traces of Kosciuszko's work in the North, neither treason, nor war devastation and time were able to completely destroy West Point which he erected. His name, as no other, became intimately connected with its history. As read from the raw records, this history lacked, perhaps, poetry; if so, it was abundantly supplied by tradition.

Kosciuszko spent over twenty-eight months, almost without interruption, at West Point. When he came there in March, 1778, it was a wilderness, almost uninhabited and almost without any fortifications.

Three months after his departure Marquis de Chastellux visited West Point and he was enraptured with the "beautiful and well contrived works" which he inspected with an eye of an expert.[34] Armstrong most aptly summed up his long services at this post when he added that Kosciuszko "had the credit of giving to it a character of strength which deterred the enemy from any new attempt at gaining the command of the highlands."[35] If West Point was the backbone of Washington's strategy, it was Kosciuszko's merit that this backbone victoriously stood up against British attempts to break it.

Beside his military genius, West Point preserved also touching traces of his human character. In spare moments the great Pole "amused himself in laying out a curious garden in a deep valley, abounding more in rocks than in soil," according to Dr. Thacher, to whom Kosciuszko showed the spot still in 1778. Thacher tells

---

[33] Heath Papers, *ibid.*, ser. 7, vol. V (1905), 126-7.

[34] For the well-known description of West Point by Chastellux see his *Travels*, I, 71-86. However, he closes it with a surprising remark, "that these . . . works, were planned and executed by two French engineers, Mr. du Portail and Mr. Gouvion." Was this a vent of national pride, or ignorance? Most probably both. Chastellux's visit was very brief and it was only natural that on hearing the names of the builders of the fortress, he remembered those of his countrymen, and did not pay attention to that of a Polish engineer, absent from the place and unknown to him. But the facts point out that Duportail's part in erecting West Point was very limited, that it consisted of a few inspections, and even these were in a rather advisory capacity. Though attached to the West Point garrison, Gouvion worked mostly on different fortifications in the Highlands; Armstrong explicitly stated in his memorial that Kosciuszko "superintended" the works, which is fully confirmed by facts.

[35] Sparks Papers, ser. 49, vol. I, p. 71.

of his gratification "in viewing its curious water fountain with spouting jets and cascades."[36] It is said that Kosciuszko himself carried soil in a basket, to cover rocks in this little garden that flowers might have some ground to live on.[37] Often he secluded himself at this spot and, "with Poland's suff'rings rankling in his mind,"[38] dreamed of his beloved and distant land.

With very few exceptions, he was well liked by everyone with whom he came into contact. Though very vigorous in carrying on his tasks, he succeeded in gaining the confidence and sympathy of his superiors and his subordinates.[39] Not only his own letters, but also reminiscences of his comrades preserved traces of his joviality and kind-heartedness. One Col. Van Rensselaer, stationed at Albany, presented Kosciuszko with a bedstead, and the grateful engineer wrote him on November 26, 1779: "I am very much oblige you for Bett that you have send me. I should be glad have opportunity to do some thing for you if I know what and should be in my power. However, before I com to Albany what I expect this winter, I will indeavor to show you my kin feeling and my sentyments."[40] He was full of hospitality and several of his friends claimed to have slept from the necessity of war, in the same bed with him.[41] One of them, Samuel Richards, assured that "his manners were soft and conciliating and, at the same time, elevated. I used to take much pleasure in accompanying him with his theodolite, measuring the heights of the surrounding mountains. He was very ready in mathematics."[42]

Perhaps the most touching West Point tradition is of Kosciuszko feeding British prisoners out of his own, often very meager, allowance. Several decades later, a Polish traveler in Australia would have died of yellow fever were it not for a local merchant who took the best possible care of him, explaining that he thus wished

---

[36] Thacher, *Military Journal*, as quoted in Griffin, III. 154.

[37] Goodrich, *Token*, 342; Harriet Martineau, *Retrospect*, I, 45.

[38] Humphreys, "A poem on the love of country", *Miscellaneous Works*, 146.

[39] Egleston, *Life of John Paterson*, 190.

[40] The original quoted by the American Library Service, New York, as for sale in 1939. The addressee of this letter most probably was Lt. Col. Philip Van Rensselaer of the Ordnance Department, who had charge of armory at Albany during the war. There were eight Colonels Van Rensselaer in the Revolutionary Army (Van Rensselaer, *Annals*, 218).

[41] Egleston, *op. cit.*, 308.

[42] Richards, *Diary*, 55.

to repay the kindness of Kosciuszko who fed his grandfather, a hungry prisoner at West Point, with his own bread.[43]

Gen. Paterson, who belonged to the circle of his bosom friends, still as an old man recalled details of their long common stay at West Point. His most characteristic anecdote pertaining to "Grippy," his black servant, to whom Kosciuszko became much attached and with whom he liked to play jokes,[44] shows that already at that early time the down trodden slaves found sympathy in the heart of the Pole.[45]

---

[43] Korzon, *Kosciuszko,* 601, n. 326.

[44] Egleston, *op. cit.,* 308-10. On his friendship with Major Egleston see: "Major Azariah Egleston," by Thomas Egleston, *N. Y. Gen. and Biogr. Record,* XXIII (1892), 113.

[45] Kosciuszko Garden still exists at West Point; it is one of the most picturesque spots within the U. S. Military Academy. The spring mentioned by Thacher also is still there. Near the Garden there is the Kosciuszko Monument, erected by the Corps of Cadets in 1828 and projected by John H. B. Latrobe. One of the members of the committee entrusted with collecting the fund for the monument, was Robert E. Lee, later Commander-in-Chief of the Confederate States Army (Freeman, *R. E. Lee,* I, 70). There exists a rare pamphlet *An Oration, prepared for delivery on the occasion of laying the corner stone of a monument erected to the memory of Kosciuszko at West Point by the Corps of Cadets, July* 4, 1828 by Cadet Charles Petigru, Newburgh, 1828. Originally the monument consisted only of the base and column; the bronze figure of Kosciuszko, by Anthony Popiel, at the top of the column, was added in 1913, and paid for by popular subscriptions. In the collections of the Academy there is a sword of Kosciuszko, which he presented to Col. John Bayard of Pennsylvania, on leaving America in 1784. Mrs. I. G. Wilson, a Bayard's descendant, donated it to the Academy. It has inscriptions in Spanish on its blade: "Do not draw me out without necessity," and "Do not put me in without honor." (M. Haiman, *Z Przeszłości Polskiej w Ameryce,* 107-112.) References to Kosciuszko in the American poetry pertaining to West Point, are quite numerous. Samuel L. Knapp published *Tales of Garden of Kosciuszko,* New York, 1834. About 1840 there was a steamer Kosciusko plying between the upper Hudson and New York. (Joel Munsell, *The Annals of Albany,* 1859, Feb. 26, 1840).

Chapter XI

WITH THE SOUTHERN ARMY

Kosciuszko left West Point about August 7, and on the 12th, visited Washington at his headquarters at Orange Town.[1] He wished personally to thank the Commander-in-Chief for his permission to join Gates and to take leave of him, and Washington took the occasion to repeat to him his highest satisfaction with his labors in the North and his regret of parting with him. The General was loath to part with the Pole. In a letter to Gates he stressed that only reluctantly he decided to allow him to go, "as I have experienced great satisfaction from his general conduct, and particularly from the attention and zeal with which he has prosecuted the Works committed to his charge at West Point."[2]

In a few days the engineer reached Philadelphia and spent there about a week, meeting his old friends and visiting familiar places. Among the former was Clajon from whom he learned that Bob Gates was sick at home. The Traveller's Rest lay far out of his way, but Kosciuszko decided to visit the young man and Mrs. Gates; perhaps he would be able to bring some consoling news to the General who undoubtedly must have been worried on account of his beloved son's illness.

Still on August 20, Clajon wrote to Gates: "The exhausted State of the Treasury prevents my joining you as yet,[3] or I would set out with Col. Kosciusko . . ." He "intends to visit Traveller's Rest before he joins you, so that you will have by him a more circumstantial Account than you can otherwise have from your Family."[4]

On August 16, Gates fought the unhappy battle of Camden. The sad news of his defeat must have reached Kosciuszko, already on his way.[5] Needless to say, it was a heavy blow to him, the

---

[1] Washington to Gates, August 12, 1780, Fitzpatrick, XIX, 362.

[2] *Ibid.*

[3] Clajon remained in Philadelphia to settle the question of his pay. (*Journals Cont. Cong.*, XVII, 709).

[4] *The State Records of North Carolina*, XIV, 565; hereafter referred to as *Records N. C.*

[5] It first reached Philadelphia on August 31, Pres. of Congress to Washington, Burnett, *Letters*, IV, 106.

heavier as it came so unexpected. It shattered all his joy of the long expected reunion with his old commander and added uncertainty as to his immediate future.

It also brought a new gloom to the Gates' family. It seems that the engineer stayed with them longer than he first intended, to console and to attend them in their hour of trial. To this period belongs Kosciuszko's plan for a new Traveller's Rest. The dwelling of the General seemed too modest to him, so he worked out a detailed plan of a magnificent country residence for the Gateses.[6] He wanted them to live in style and comfort and, though the plan was never carried into execution, it remains an old memento of his friendship for his commander.

On September 21, Clajon, still in Philadelphia, wrote to Gates with expressions of sympathy: "Oh that I were with you! My last was by Col. Kosciusko who is now, as I suppose, at Hillsborough."[7] But Kosciuszko traveled much slower. About the time of this letter he was at Richmond, where he visited Thomas Jefferson, then Governor of Virginia, and deposited with him some money, which officially or privately concerned Gates.[8] It was the first meeting of the two champions of democracy who later became bound together with the strongest attachment.

It is impossible to ascertain when Kosciuszko reached Hillsboro where Gates retreated and now tried to organize the remnants of his army into a new force. The earliest mention of him in the southern documents is on October 20. On that day Gen. Smallwood who retired with a part of the army to Salisbury and intended to cross the Yadkin, asked Gates to send him "Colo. Cuziosco" for the purpose of constructing some defensive works.[9] On October 30, Kosciuszko took part in a council of war called by Gates at Hillsboro to decide "if the Troops . . . should go to West ward, or if they should stay at this Post until further Intelligence from Virginia about the Enemy's being landing there" at Norfolk. Present were Generals Isaac Huger and Edward Stevens, several colonels and majors, and all unanimously decided to await further news at Hillsboro.[10] On the same day the Board of War of North Carolina

---

6 Gates Papers, box 21, no. 81.
7 *Records N. C.*, XIV, 633.
8 Jefferson to Gates, Sept. 23, 1780, Lipscomb, ed., *Writings of Jefferson*, IV, 106.
9 *Records N. C.*, XIV, 704.
10 *Ibid.*, XIV, 719.

PLAN OF TRAVELLER'S REST
by KOSCIUSZKO

issued an order for a pair of shoes "for Colonel Cusiasko's Servant."[11] There is a gap in the documents of nearly a month, during which Kosciuszko was undoubtedly busy helping Gates in whatever he could. While at Hillsboro, he shared quarters, however poor and empty of necessities, with Gen. Huger and Dr. William Read, chief of the hospital service. The condition of the army was so wretched that for more than six weeks all three were without a blanket, their only bedding being the General's cloak, under which they occasionally slept. The weather was very cold, but they bore it without a murmur.[12]

On November 25, Kosciuszko took part in another council of war at New Providence. Besides Gates and himself, there were present also Generals Smallwood, Huger, Morgan and Davidson, Col. Buford and Lt. Colonels Howard and Washington.[13] The question submitted by Gates was whether the army should move to a new camp near Charlotte, or at the Waxhaws, or remain at New Providence where the country was already denuded of provisions and the situation of the camp was unhealthy. All, except Smallwood, declared for Charlotte.

It was there that Gates welcomed Greene sent by Congress to supersede him, on December 2,[14] and two days later the official change of command took place. To all the bitter trials of Gates another cross was added—his only son died. "He was all that you could wish for a Son . . . He was all that I could wish in a friend," wrote Dr. Brown, advising him of Bob's death.[15] The hero returned to his half-empty home doubly broken, without even gaining the gratitude of posterity for his achievements. If anybody among his official family sympathized with him most warmly, it was undoubtedly Kosciuszko.

Sad was their parting, but brief.[16] New duties awaited Kosciuszko. His new commander was well known to him; he felt the greatest respect for his military genius and his human qualities, and

---

11 *Ibid.*, XIV, 438.

12 Gibbes, *Documentary History*, III, 276.

13 *Records N. C.*, XV, 160-1.

14 *The Story of the Revolution*, by Lodge, II, 73, contains a reproduction of a painting by Howard Pyle, showing the meeting of Greene and Gates at Charlotte; Kosciuszko is standing behind Gates, with Generals Davidson and Morgan.

15 Brown to Gates, Nov. 16, 1780, *Records N. C.*, XIV, 740.

16 Gates left Charlotte on Dec. 8, Greene to Washington, Dec. 7, 1780, Sparks, *Correspondence*, III, 168.

considered him "one of the best of American generals."[17] With the same utmost loyalty which he displayed to his former superiors, Kosciuszko now stood with Greene eager to help him in his difficult task. He became at once one of Greene's most important and most faithful collaborators.

Even after the change of command Kosciuszko found some of his old friends in the circle of his new comrades-in-arms. There was Morgan with whom he fought at Saratoga. There were Majors Armstrong[18] and Morris, both friendly and helpful as ever, and Dr. Brown, all of whom supported him in his affair with Carter. There were also a few others. He soon befriended all whom he now met for the first time; none of these became more sincerely connected with him in a friendship than Col. Otho Holland Williams of Maryland, the Adjutant General and the right hand man of Greene.

The utterly lamentable state of the army, which, according to Greene's own expression, was "rather a shadow than a substance," and the overrunning of the South by Cornwallis, demanded prompt decisions and energetic action. His first thoughts were how to solve the problem of transportation and supply for his army which he recognized as the cardinal condition of improving its spirit. Already on his way to the South he wrote to Washington: "On my arrival at Hillsborough, I intend to have all the rivers examined in order to see if I cannot ease this heavy business by water transportation."[19] Accordingly, he assigned Gen. Stevens to survey the Yadkin, Col. Edward Carrington, his new Quartermaster, to explore the Dan, and on December 8, sent Kosciuszko to "explore the navigation of the Catawba river from mill creek below the forks up to Oliphant mill. . . . Report to me," he asked, "its particular situation as to the depth of water, the rapidity of the stream, the rocks, shoals or falls you may meet with and every other information necessary to enable me to form an accurate opinion of the transportation which may be made on the river in the different seasons of the year. It is of the utmost importance that your report to me should be very particular and as early as possible."[20]

---

[17] Kosciuszko to Molineri, March 17, 1809, N. Y. Public Libr., Misc. MSS.

[18] It seems, however, that Kosciuszko did not long enjoy the company of Armstrong who was sick and unfit for duty in Jan., 1781 (Williams Papers, no. 79).

[19] G. W. Greene, *Life of Nathanael Greene*, III, 58.

[20] Huntington Library, Greene Papers, GR 749.

In a canoe Kosciuszko set out into the wilderness, accompanied by a single guide, Capt. Thompson. The country was in a turmoil of civil war. The Tories were "as thick as the trees,"[21] and there was always the danger of being captured. But Kosciuszko executed the order promptly and evidently to Greene's satisfaction. These were the earliest surveys of the western North Carolina rivers, in any event on such a detailed scale, and they were of inestimable value to Greene in his campaign.[22]

Seeing "that the Country around Charlotte was too much exhausted to afford subsistence for the Army at that place for any considerable time," Greene immediately thereafter "dispatched Col. Kosciuszko to look out a position on the Pedee that would afford a healthy camp & provisions in plenty."[23] Greene's order was again very minute as to the survey which had to cover the Pedee "from the mouth of little River twenty or thirty miles down."[24] Major William Polk of the North Carolina Continental Line accompanied Kosciuszko in this venture.[25]

Greene impatiently waited for their return. On December 15, he wrote to Col. Thomas Polk of Charlotte: "I find it impossible to leave camp as early as I intended as Colonel Kosciusko has made no report yet respecting a position on Pedee."[26]

On the next day, however, Kosciuszko returned having selected a very good position at Cheraw Hills, near the junction of Hick's Creek and the Pedee River,[27] and Greene immediately put the army under marching orders; excessive rains, however, prevented their march till December 20.

The new camp was in fertile surroundings and with good water transportation facilities. Here the army reposed for a few weeks. But Greene did not allow Kosciuszko to rest. On January 1, 1781, he ordered him to Cross Creek[28] to canvas the surrounding country

---

[21] Greene to Lafayette, May 23, 1781, G. W. Greene, *op. cit.*, III, 320.

[22] Johnson, *Sketches of the Life of Greene*, I, 336. Most probably the companion of Kosciuszko was William Thompson of South Carolina.

[23] Greene to Washington, Dec. 28, 1780, *Records N. C.*, XV, 184; the original in the Kahanowicz Coll., p. 33, no. 77, but with a different date, of Dec. 29, 1780.

[24] Greene to Kosciuszko, Dec. 8, 1780; the original quoted for sale by C. Tyborowski of New York in 1941; a copy in the Huntington Library, Greene Papers, GR 775.

[25] Polk, *Leonidas Polk*, I, 28.

[26] *Records N. C.*, XV, 179; the original in Kahanowicz, p. 32, no. 76.

[27] Greene to Washington, Dec. 28, 1780, *Records N. C.*, XV, 184; the original in Kahanowicz, p. 33, no. 77.

[28] Now Fayetteville.

for tools and carpenters for "constructing a number of boats, the quantity and kind that will be wanted, you are perfectly acquainted with . . . Confiding in your zeal and activity," wrote Greene with strong assurance, "I persuade myself you will make all the dispatch the business will admit as the safety & support of the Army depend upon your accomplishing this business."[29]

A few days later Greene wrote to Washington from Cheraw: "I am here in my camp of repose, improving the discipline and spirit of my men . . . Kosciusko is employed in building flat-bottomed boats to be transported with the army, if ever I shall be able to command the means of transporting them."[30]

So throughout January Kosciuszko was occupied with building these boats, which gave Greene's army the mobility, now of utmost importance in the forthcoming test of skill between the two adversaries. Cornwallis was on the quick march from the southwest toward the Virginia border in order to cut off Greene's lines of communication. Greene saw through his purpose. Having just received the welcome news of Tarleton's defeat by Morgan at Cowpens, he left Huger in command of the main forces at Cheraw camp, ordered him to move immediately up the Yadkin, and himself, with a handful of men, hurried to Morgan in order to unite both forces and to contest Cornwallis' further progress. Already on his way he summoned Kosciuszko to his side. On February 1, when the army under Huger reached Mark's Ferry, Major Morris, now aide-de-camp to Greene, wrote to Kosciuszko:

"Genl Huger has just received a letter from Genl Greene dated at Olyphant mill on the Catawba. He requests that you would join him there or where ever he may be as soon as possible. You will pass by the way of Salisbury where you will probably hear of him. . .

"You will order such of the boats as are finished to follow the army immediately and such as are not finished you will deliver to the charge of Colonel Wade. Let captain Dellyenn[31] attend to this business. The artificers you will order to join the army as soon as possible, they are much wanted."[32]

---

[29] Library of Congress, Nathanael Greene Letter Book, Jan.-Feb., 1781, pp. 11-12.

[30] Dec. 28, 1780, Greene, *Life of Greene*, III, 131.

[31] Most probably Capt. Dallizen.

[32] Huntington Library, Greene Papers, GR 937 (a copy); the original in Kahanowicz, p. 33, no. 78.

PLAN OF HALIFAX, N. C.
by KOSCIUSZKO

Most probably Kosciuszko found Greene already beyond the Yadkin.[33] The commander dispatched him immediately toward Boyd's Ferry on the Dan with instructions to throw hurriedly some defensive works on the northern bank of the river.

On the 9th, the small armies of Greene united at Guilford and the race for the Dan started. Cornwallis was certain that he had the Americans in his grasp. But when on the 14th, he reached the Dan, he found them all safely posted on the opposite bank. A day before Greene crossed the river, and, "almost fatigued to death, having had a retreat to conduct for upwards of two hundred miles,"[34] he now occupied a safe position behind the earthworks thrown by Kosciuszko.[35] In this masterful manoeuver of Greene and his ragged, barefooted and hungry army, justly considered one of the greatest achievements of the American arms in the Revolution, the Pole played a very important part.

Cornwallis unable to continue his pursuit, rested on the site and made preparations for a new march. His future moves were puzzling to Greene. He thought that the British might move to Halifax, on the Roanoke, so, on the next day he dispatched Kosciuszko to inspect that place, and, if he considers "practicable to fortify it in a short time," to quickly "construct the works . . . As Lord Cornwallis movements are rapid I recommend the greatest dispatch," he added.[36] In this way Greene hoped to prevent the British in establishing a post there that "would greatly awe Virginia, and almost totally subject North Carolina."[37]

Provided by Greene with letters to the North Carolina Board of War and Gen. Casswell, asking them to give him all possible and prompt help,[38] Kosciuszko set out for Halifax. The distance was over eighty miles, over bad roads, infested by Tories, but he managed to reach the place in the afternoon of February 18. "It seems I travaill very slow," he reported to Greene, "but as I Could not get Horses on the road, and was obliged to go foot part of the way, you will be pleased to thing that I have don what I Could."

---

[33] According to Johnson, they met at Guilford (*Sketches,* I, 431).

[34] Greene to Jefferson, G. W. Greene, *op. cit.,* III, 174.

[35] The remains of an enbankment thrown up by Kosciuszko may yet be seen near Halifax, Va. Bryant, "Gen. Stuart," *The Virginia Mag. of History,* XII (1905), 200.

[36] Feb. 16, 1781, Huntington Library, Greene Papers, GR 996 (a copy); the original in Kahanowicz, p. 34, no. 79.

[37] Greene to Washington, Feb. 15, 1781, Sparks, *Correspondence,* III, 235.

[38] Greene to the No. Carolina Board of War, Feb. 15, 1781, Clements Library, Greene Papers.

Immediately the next morning he viewed the ground around the town, accompanied by Col. Nicholas Long.[39] He found the position of Halifax too difficult to be fortified in a short time. It "would require no less than six redoubts to be in tollerable defense." In addition, there was lack of "intrenching tools," as the quartermaster department had not any, and "the inhabitent's Houses afford but very few;" he found no "Militia ready Colected and the number of the negroes is very small to set at Work.

"Nothing Could tempted the Enemys to come her in my opinion but the Stores and Magasines of provision, Should the Enemy Come we will have always the advantage by the Brocking ground, and very thick Bushes." He proposed to remove the stores to the opposite side of the Roanoke, and thought a "Thousend of Good Militia," stationed at Taylor's Ferry, "could cover intirely Halifax and the adjacent Country."

He added with satisfaction: "All Inhabitents with whom only I speak, soon have learn the Circumstances from me and that we have loss not Six pince in our retreat, give Great Credit to you, and have not doubt of successfull Campaign."[40]

In fact, Cornwallis did not try to occupy Halifax. Kosciuszko returned to the main army, perhaps still in time to take part in the battle of Guilford Court House.

Again Washington was very careful not to allow any infringement of Kosciuszko's authority while he was in the South. Just at that time Lafayette joined Steuben in Virginia and asked for the transfer of Lt. Col. Gouvion to his staff. As the army in Virginia was under Greene's orders, Washington declined. Gouvion is needed in the North, he answered, adding: "There is another reason which operates against his going with you, it is, that he would interfere with Colo. Kosciusko who had been considered as the commanding Engineer with the southern Army."[41] Greene's command over Virginia was rather nominal and the attitude of Washington in this instance is characteristic of his most scrupulous observance of official decorum.

---

[39] Long to Greene, Feb. 19, 1781, Kahanowicz, p. 34, no. 80.

[40] Feb. 19, 1781, Huntington Library, Greene Papers, HM 8054. A sketch of Halifax by Kosciuszko is enclosed with the letter. "I send you a Sketch of halifax, the time would not allow me to do better and more particular," he wrote. The drawing is reproduced on p. 107.

[41] Washington to Lafayette, April 8, 1781, Fitzpatrick, XXI, 433.

Chapter XII

NINETY SIX

"We fight, get beat, rise, and fight again,"[1] wrote Greene to Chevalier de la Luzerne, and this was the essence of his success notwithstanding all his adversities. Victory eluded him at Guilford Court House (March 17), and again at Hobkirk's Hill (April 25), but he managed to keep his ragged army intact and full of fighting spirit. Most probably Kosciuszko assisted Greene in carefully choosing positions for both of these battles and he was a member of Greene's reconnoitering party before Camden.

Meanwhile American guerilla leaders were successful in reducing a chain of English posts in the interior of Georgia, and Greene was now ready to strike at Ninety Six, the last remaining stronghold of the enemy in western North Carolina.

On May 22, he reached the place, defended by a strong garrison under Lieut. Col. Cruger. The main body of his army encamped in the wood about half a mile distant.[2] Availing himself of a dark and rainy night, Greene immediately made a reconnaissance of the place. Kosciuszko and Capt. Nathaniel Pendleton, Greene's aide-de-camp, accompanied him. The enemy was on the alert; they were discovered and fired at, but all his shots missed.[3]

"Weuing (viewing) the Enmys Works on every side," according to Kosciuszko's own description of the siege,[4] "it apperd that the Star Redoubt upon our left was the Strongest post, not only by been Complitly finished but that Comanded the others two to our right one in which the Town was inclosed distant at one Hundred and

---

[1] April 28, 1781, Gordon, *History*, IV, 86.

[2] Otho Holland Williams Papers in the Maryland Historical Society contain two documents on the siege of Ninety Six; one is: "Notes and remarks on the History of the War in South Carolina," 2 pp., by Williams, (no. 978), and the other: "Notes by my friend Colo. Kosciuszko relative the siege of 96", a seven page manuscript by Kosciuszko, evidently written in 1783, or 1784 (no. 979). Kosciuszko gives the distance of the camp, "of about one mill," Williams corrects it to half a mile. Contrary to Kosciuszko's usually fine penmanship, this note is written very carelessly, with many corrections, and at places hardly legible.

[3] Johnson, *Sketches*, II, 143.

[4] Williams Papers, no. 979.

fifty yards and situated near the water[5] and the other smal more upon our right at Three Hundred and fifty yards. Thos all three redoubts had Comunication with each other by Coverd way." Being "not strong enogh to capture the trenches to our left and wright at the same time against the Garison of about 500 strong we thought proper to begin against the Star redoubt. . .

"Accordingly the same night the battery was made with two fleches to suport it at one hundred and fifty yard[6] from the Star redoubt, but as the troops were novice to the operation of that kind and begon in the night far advanced it was not Complited at a break day to bring the Canon Pices . . . The Ennemys vigilant took the advantage and in the morning at 9 Clock made in considerable nomber the Sallies suporting it by the musketery and Artillery from the Fort."

The assailants killed some[7] "men of the Guard left in, and demolished the Work."

The next night "was made two Complited Battery but at Three hundred yards[8] to acquiented (acquaint) the men of the proceeding and of the nature of work with less danger—in the morning the Canon was broud (brought) to it and few shot firing to the Town and Star redoubt with great effect, Alarmed the Enemy prodigious(ly).

"On the 27 of May in the night the Battery[9] was made at 220 yards distant with the aproches of Thirty yards farther—her (here) the Workmen began to be exposed to the Continuel of the Enemys fire all night and the suckiding (succeeding) but, more danger forseen, was imediatly conteracted by more Exertions of the Troops. —as the Nature of the Ground was very hard and aproched very much to Soft Stone the Approches Could not be so fast adwancd.

"On the 30th of May the Parallel was half done at one Hundred and fifty yards and her the Second Sallies the Enemys made but with small effect—Three or four men of both side were killed. The militia now began come very fast from the adjacent Countys, which

---

[5] A little stream called Kate Fowler's Branch.

[6] "At 70 paces of the fortifications," according to Stedman, *History*, II, 367, who evidently accepts the version of Mackenzie, *Strictures*, 146. Moultrie, *Memoirs*, II, 285, says of 150 yards.

[7] The number of killed given by Kosciuszko hardly legible.

[8] At 350 yards, according to Williams, *loc. cit.*, and 400 yards, according to Stedman, *op. cit.*, II, 367.

[9] This battery was 20 feet high, Williams, *loc. cit.*

gave oportunity to upon (open) the Trenches against the smal Redoubt mention(ed) upon our right.—and the same day the Battery was made at 250 yards with the aproches of 70 yards more advanced.

"The 4th of the June upon our left the parallel Complited, the Battery was made at 180[10] yards" of the Star Redoubt, "with the fleche 30 yards more adwanced and the same day in the night the Enemys Trow down the roofs of the houses in the Town and in the Star redoubt[11] and made the Sallies suporting with Canon from the work upon our left with no other Sucess then to cut down the mantelet wich there was posted to Cover the workmen from Rifle shot and quited (quiet) them (the British) if possible by ours.

"The Next day upon our left we desmount the Canon in the star Redoubt from the Battery and killed few men in it.

"The 6 we hitned (heightened) our Battery Station to 20 feet which oblidge the Ennemy to intrenche inside half way with the parapet of sixteen feet high.—we adwanced the aproches but very little and Complit the paralell upon our left at 120 yards."

On the 8, Henry Lee arrived "viktorious"[12] with his Legion "and took the Comand of our left." In the night of June 9, the besieged sallied again and a party of them penetrated to "the mouth of the mine intended to be carried under a curtain of the Star, and had nearly taken the chief engineer of the Americans who happened to be viewing it at the time of the sortie."[13] In making his escape Kosciuszko suffered a wound which was slight;[14] he does not even mention it in his notes, though it gave a British officer on occasion to a derisive remark. "Never did luckless wight receive a more inglorious wound," he writes in his reminiscences, "than Count Kozinsco did on this—it was in that part which Hudibras[15] has constituted the seat of honor, and was given just as this engineer was examining the mine which he had projected!"[16] Disregarding the

---

[10] Kosciuszko's manuscript illegible at this place; Williams gives the number of yards, but his ciphers also illegible; according to him, this third battery was of the same height as the second one.

[11] Cruger unroofed the houses to prevent fire from arrows shot by the besiegers and bearing combustible material.

[12] After a successful siege of Augusta, Ga.

[13] Stedman, *History*, II, 369-70.

[14] *Ibid.*; Tarleton, *A History of the Campaign*, 502; Ramsay, *History of the Revolution*, II, 501.

[15] Hero of *Hudibras*, a satire by Samuel Butler, an English poet of the 17th century.

[16] Mackenzie, *Strictures*, 155.

wound, which was attended to by Dr. Read,[17] Kosciuszko remained at his post and on the 10, not only completed the second parallel "at 40 yards distant upon our left," but also began a subterranean gallery which was to serve the mine "to blow the Ennemys Work up."

"The same night," continues Kosciuszko, "The Ennemys made Sallies with prodigous fury and killed 4 or 5 men,—on the 12 upon our left the aproches begon from two places of the Paralell, in side of which the Rifle Battery also begon to stop the Ennemys Riflem(en) who were so industrious and great marksmen that no finger wold be held up half second without been Cut of.

"On the 14th the Rifle Battery Complited 30 feet high, the Gallery adwanced 30 yards[18] and the aproches 20 yards and on our left 40.[19]—on the 16 the Battery was made upon our left.—the Gallery was near to four feet of the Ennemys Dich and the Approches 6 feet.—on the 17th the General reciving the last account of Lord Rawdon coming with 2000 men to relieve the Garison of Ninety Six and been sonear that would oblidge us rise the Siedge the next morning, Thoght prudent to try the ardor and enxiaty of the Troops by the attack upon both redoubts—number of Officers and soldiers hearing the intention of the General present(ed) self as Wolunteers. but happy lot fell upon few—at 9th Clock in the morning the attack begon—blind fortune not always keep pace with Curage and Good Cause—Colo Lee' upon our right took posesion of the smal redobt with very small loss.—but Colo. Campbell upon our left was unsuccesful in this attact—Capt Amstrong and 30 soldiers were killed of which Valor intrepidy left us Chearish their memory, regret the loss and bring the Example to posterity."

On the same day Greene, disappointed, ordered his army toward the Saluda River.

In Kosciuszko's own words, the siege of Ninety Six "will afford the Example what Fortitude, persevirence, Courage and exertions of the troops can perform." Warmly lauding the American forces

---

[17] Gibbes, *Documentary History*, II, 279.

[18] Remains of British trenches and of Kosciuszko's mine still may be seen near the present village of Ninety Six, S.C. A marker was erected on the site of the original village by D.A.R. According to a local legend, a girl, Kate Fowler, fearing that Kosciuszko's mine would kill the garrison of Ninety Six and her lover who belonged to it, betrayed the American cause (McCants, *History Stories,* 267-73).

[19] MS hardly legible.

"who exposed (themselves)Chearfuly to inavoided Denger," he also had a word of acknowledgement for the British "for their Vigilance, frequent judicious Sallies and proper means to counteract the assaliant measures."

Some historians accuse Kosciuszko of badly directing the siege, ascribing at least a part of the guilt to Greene.[20] The original source of this criticism was Henry Lee and his *Memoirs*. His objections may be summed up to two points:

a) That Kosciuszko "never regarded the importance which was attached to depriving the enemy of water, for which he entirely depended on the rivulet to his left," and

b) that "Koschiusko applied his undivided attention to the demolition of the star, the strongest point of the enemy's defence."[21]

"Gen. Greene," adds Lee, "much as he was beloved and respected, did not escape criticism, for permitting his engineer to direct the manner of approach. It was said, and with some justice too, that the general ought certainly to have listened to his opinion; but never ought to have permitted the pursuit of error, although supported by professional authority."

Alexander Garden, a Cornet of Lee's Legion, repeating these objections ventured an opinion that "had he (Lee) directed the operations of the besiegers at Ninety Six, instead of Koschiusko, different indeed would have been the result."[22]

As to the depriving the British of water Kosciuszko clearly states in his notes that the decision to concentrate all efforts of the small American army on the Star Redoubt was strengthened "very much by the Inteligence broud that the Enemys had Waills in every work and Could not be distresed been Cot of From the spring which could be effectued by takin possession of the smal redoubt." "A member of the general's family at the time" assured Judge William Johnson, the earliest biographer of Greene, that "the project of cutting off the water had been well weighed and considered, and rejected on mature deliberation. There was not a doubt entertained of the practicability of obtaining water by digging in almost

---

[20] The most vehement, perhaps, in this regard is G. G. White, *Life of Henry Lee*, 207; Channing regrets that Greene had no engineer "of the requisite ability," Winsor, *Narrative and Critical History*, VI, 491.

[21] Lee, *Memoirs*, II, 98, and 119 and note.

[22] Garden, *Anecdotes*, I, 54.

any part of the enemy's works. The country was so level and the crown of the hill so little elevated above the bed of the rivulet, that there was no room to doubt this."[23] There is only one contemporary testimony to the contrary, namely of Stedman, according to whom the rivulet was the only supply of water of Ninety Six, and the garrison, after unsuccessfully trying to get water by digging a well in the Star Redoubt, suffered much for want of it toward the end of the siege.[24] It is possible, therefore, that Greene had wrong intelligence on this point, and that Lee was right. But it was much easier for Lee to decide the question *post factum*, than for Greene to weigh it accurately before the attack.

It is an open question whether a concentrated assault upon the small redoubt would have been more successful, according to Lee's second objection, and it is superfluous to examine here such a theoretical proposition. However, it should be remembered that the Star Redoubt commanded all other fortifications.

Lee himself did not escape criticism for his actions at Ninety Six, and his general behaviour. He understood extremely well the partisan warfare, but had little patience for and knowledge of the engineering art, notwithstanding his captures of some small forts. Moreover "passion sometimes obscured his judgment,"[25] and, as historian, he was not too accurate.[26]

All authorities agree that Ninety Six was near capture and only Rawdon's arrival saved it. "A few Days more wo^d have reduced the garrison to the necessity of surrendering at discretion," said Williams.[27] Greene, to his mortification, also considered the garrison "on the eve of surrender."[28] Kosciuszko ascribed the slow progress of the siege to the very hard nature of the ground, to the inexperience of troops in the regular siege work[29] and to the alertness of the besieged. Greene cited additional causes: failure of "Sumter to collect all the force he could and throw himself in . . .

---

[23] Johnson, *Sketches*, II, 142.

[24] Stedman, *op. cit.*, II, 366, 370; Johnson puts to doubt his statement (*Sketches*, II, 142); McCrady, *History of So. Caro. in the Revol.*, 281-3, extensively, though inconclusively, examines the question of water at Ninety Six.

[25] Garden, *op. cit.*, I, addenda VIII, XV, XVII.

[26] Greene, *Life of Greene*, III, 188, 230, 235, 333; Boyd, *Light-horse Harry Lee*, 302; McCrady; *History of So. Caro. in the Rev.*, 505; Johnson, *Sketches*, II, 264, 279. 327.

[27] Williams, *loc. cit.*

[28] Greene to Joseph Reed, Aug. 6, 1781, Reed, *Life of J. Reed*, II, 363.

[29] Williams, *loc. cit.*, says that "the Troops were unused to this kind of duty."

front" of Rawdon,[30] and the failure of the Virginia militia to augment his forces.[31]

It is not clear how Kosciuszko might have been responsible for the repulse at Ninety Six. No decision of his was taken without the approval of Greene. Kosciuszko said in his notes that "we thought proper," that is the General and himself, to begin against the Star Redoubt. Johnson, on basis of a report of an eyewitness, states that "it was perfectly understood in camp, that the general himself directed the operations of the engineer."[32]

The most eloquent proof that the criticism of Kosciuszko by Lee and his successors was at least superficial, was Greene's order of the day of June 20, in which he very highly praised Kosciuszko. "The General presents his thanks," so ran the order, "to Colonel Kosciuzko chief Engineer for his Assiduity, preserverance and indefatigable exertions in planing and prosecuting the approaches which he is persuaded were judiciously design'd and would have infalliable gained Success if time had admitted of their being Compleated."[33] Williams, who also witnessed all events at Ninety Six, said this: "Coll Kosciuszko a young gentleman of distinction from Poland who left his native country to follow the banners of Liberty in america, superintended the operations, and by his Zeal, assiduity, perseverance and firmness promoted the business with . . . expedition."[34] Consequently to accuse Kosciuszko of inability at Ninety Six, is to give a lie to two Revolutionary heroes of irreproachable character, or to accuse them of partiality. There is also an additional testimony of Armstrong, according to whom Kosciuszko displayed at Ninety Six "the zeal, industry, perseverance and boldness, which though they could not increase the respect of his commanding General, entirely won his confidence."[35]

To what extent Greene's mistakes, if any, influenced the events at Ninety Six? Of all the Revolutionary leaders he, perhaps, most

---

[30] Greene to Lafayette, June 17, 1781, Greene, *op. cit.*, III, 311 n.
[31] Greene to the Pres. of Cong. June 20, 1781, *ibid.*, 318.
[32] Johnson, *Sketches*, II, 142.
[33] Huntington Library, Greene's Orderly Book.
[34] Williams, *loc. cit.* In a private letter to his brother, Elie, written immediately after the siege Williams declared that all deserved great credit (June 23, 1781, Williams Papers, no. 107).
[35] Sparks Papers, ser. 49, vol. I, p. 71; Ramsay also speaks with praise of Kosciuszko at Ninety Six (*History of the Revol.*, II, 242). William Gilmore Simms introduced Kosciuszko at Ninety Six in one of his historical novels, *The Scout, or the Black Riders of Congaree*, originally published in 1841 under the title of *The Kinsmen*.

carefully planned and weighed his every move. By the ultimate brilliant success of his Southern Campaign, attained in most disheartening circumstances, he paid with a surplus for all small inaccuracies and omissions. It was humanly impossible to expect anything more of him. Deciding on the transfer of the war to South Carolina, he wrote to Washington: "I shall take every measure to avoid misfortune; but necessity obliges me to commit myself to chance; and I trust my friends will do justice to my reputation if any accident attends me."[36]

In any event, by his further successful manoeuvres Greene forced Rawdon and Cruger to evacuate early Ninety Six and the whole upper country.[37] The British were now confined to their posts along the sea shore. The heats of summer began and Greene moved his weary army to the High Hills of Santee for a well deserved repose. Presumably the place was chosen by Kosciuszko who now had a chance for some rest, too. From this camp he wrote to Gates on July 29:

"It will be owing to a Fortunate Chance if this letter will Come safe to your hands; being not acquiented of your resident Place,[38] I could have not the Satisfaction of conveying it—This is the only reason of my being so Long Silent and as you promise (if I remember well) to acquiented me of your fixed home I expected it with great impatience.

"Any Circumstance in the World will never change my Esteem, Friendship and respect for you, but rather increase in it's perfection and maturity — Well grounded upon Sincerity Cannot suffer alteration . . .[39] military matters upon the Carpet. You had information so far as to our Blockade of Ninty six I supose, in which we were onlucky, the Ground was so hard that our aproaches Could not go but very slow, had Lord Roudon gave us four days more we should blow up Theirs Works and take Six Hundred men in it — however by our Maneuvres we have oblidged the Enemys to evacuate Ninty six."

---

36 March 29, 1781, Sparks, *Correspondence*, III, 277.

37 "An American Soldier" in the *N. Y. Packet*, Nov. 22, 1781, Moore, *Diary*, II, 525.

38 Gates visited Philadelphia in May, 1781, expecting a new assignment, but returned to Traveller's Rest after a month's absence.

39 One or two words torn out.

"Part of our Troops with the Militia," he continued, "attacked Monks Corner 22 mill from Charles Town, killed about one Hundred and took one Hundred and Fifty Prisoners, some of the same party came six mill near Charles town and caught twenty Prisoners, in all this Col. Lee's Legion bear the greatest Share. — We took at present this position very healthy and expect to be reinforced by North Carolina and Pensylvania Brygades who are in their march. If the Circumstances would not change their cours of affaires we will be able very Soon to confine the Enemys to Charles town.—

"I beg you would inform of the Northern Operations, had General Washington Blockad New York,[40] did they expect the Second Division of the French troops with hard money in it, etc. Peter Mulet and Istees (a justice)[41] are gon to the Enemys you have very just opinion of thos Rascals, Borek[42] made Governor, mercy upon us, you know the Genius of the creature and his facon de pensier. A propos we want Governor Rotledge her very much if you have uportunity to see him do intreat him to come, his real attachement to the Cause, the habilities of the Civilian, and his Conduct in every respect gained Him the General aplause of the Inhabitents and raise the warmest desire to see him, besides that the business of the Gouvernment and Thausand other maters wants to be Setled, and regulate. —

"My best respect to your Amiable Lady and good wish to you both, may Sucess attend you in every thing and without remembrance of the Ills past, you may Live Long happy with new always satisfaction and leave smal Corner for your Friend in your heart."[43]

---

[40] Because of slow and insecure communication between the North and South, it was firmly believed in the camp on the High Hills that Washington besieged New York (Greene, *Life of Greene*, III, 382).

[41] Peter Mallet, a justice of peace for County of Cumberland, prosecuted for treason (*Rec⋅ N. C.*, XII, 99; XXIII, 993).

[42] Thomas Burke. He had a dispute with Gates, while the latter commanded the Southern Army, on account of seizure of supplies for military purposes, and that is probably the reason of Kosciuszko's unfriendly attitude.

[43] Gates Papers, box 16, no. 57.

Chapter XIII

"MASTER OF HIS PROFESSION"

Only very meager reports of Kosciuszko's whereabouts reached Poland. In new surroundings, among new friends, in a new world, so entirely different from the old one, amid the ever changing historical scenery and new experiences, he somehow found little time to write to his relatives in his native country. His military tasks were often very exhausting, the distance from Poland and means of communication discouraging, and, if he longed for those whom he loved, he felt no disposition to return, even by letters to his old sorrows and disappointments.

Some reports about him found their way into Poland, it is true, but very much distorted. It was even reported that he found an early grave in the far-off country which he hoped to help to set free.[1] His friends, and above all, his beloved sister, Anna Estko, made several attempts to get some authentic news of him through Benjamin Franklin in Paris, or through their French friends.[2]

Still in 1778, Prince Czartoryski, Kosciuszko's former protector, asked his agent in Paris: "Will you kindly ask Franklin to inquire about Mr. Kosciuszko, one of those young officers who were sent to Paris by the King to complete their education; he is in the service of the United States in America; I had a letter from him two years ago, but no news about him since."[3]

In 1781, Princess Sapieha, at the request of Anna, who with her husband lived as tenants at Dołholiski, a village belonging to the Sapieha family,[4] renewed the inquiry in Paris through Count de Murinais, a Marechal de Camp of the French army, and well known in Poland whither he traveled as a French diplomatic agent during the Confederation of Bar. Murinais very gladly took up her re-

---

[1] Anna Estko to Benjamin Franklin, Oct. 19, 1783, Amer. Philosophical Soc., Franklin Papers, vol. 30, no. 140.

[2] Kosciuszko's correspondence with J. U. Niemcewicz in 1780 (Korzon, *op. cit.,* 172) and Ludwika Sosnowska's letter to him of 1781, given by Gordon, *Przechadzki,* 79-86, are undoubtedly spurious.

[3] Oct. 23, 1778, *Rocznik Tow. Hist. Lit.,* 279.

[4] Korzon, *op. cit.,* 97.

quest, and on December 8, was able to report that, according to a letter from Chevalier de Luzerne, Kosciuszko was alive and well. "Some of our officers," he wrote, "returned from America after the glorious York expedition, and they told me that they saw him and that at present he is with General Grasse in Virginia, that he performed functions of an engineer there, that he was occupied with building of a few small forts, and that, it seems, they are very well satisfied with him in the army, where he won recognition for his good conduct. I am very glad, Princess, to be able to give you much welcome news about a person in which you are evidently interested; in the near future he will return to his country with American laurels."[5]

Again on February 25, 1782, Murinais turned directly to Franklin in the same matter, asking him to make an official inquiry in America whether Kosciuszko was still alive. "This nobleman Cosciuscko by name" he wrote, "was still there after the York affair, and I could ask my French compatriots to assure his relatives that he enjoyed a good reputation. But it seems that at present a confirmation by Your Excellency of his being alive is absolutely necessary for the happiness and tranquility of his family."[6]

It was not only uneasiness about the whereabouts of her brother which induced Anna to all these exertions. The poor woman had legal troubles with the creditors of Joseph Kosciuszko; in view of rumors of Thaddeus' death, they now wanted to seize the remnants of his patrimony to which Joseph would have been entitled as heir. The loving sister strove to save them for her lost brother. The details sent by Murinais to Princess Sapieha were, indeed, very welcome tidings to her, still the courts demanded some official document to prove his being alive.[7] Unhappily Franklin either neglected to take care of the request of Murinais, or his correspondence became lost.

How did it happen, however, that Kosciuszko, attached to the staff of Greene, was seen by the French officers at York, or rather in its vicinity, during its siege? On August 12, from the camp on the High Hills, Greene at the request of Gov. Burke sent Kosciuszko to North Carolina to build "a number of small Posts judiciously dis-

---

[5] Franklin Papers, vol. 47, no. 209, a copy in French, wrongly giving the name of the author of the letter as "Murinet."
[6] Franklin Papers, vol. 31, no. 85, the original in French.
[7] Ibid., vol. 30, no. 140.

persed in different parts of the State" for the protection of military stores against the British who still occupied Wilmington and continuously threatened the State from Virginia. Greene wrote him: "I will send to your assistance Col. Kosciuszko, our principal Engineer, who is Master of his profession, and will afford you every aid you can wish."[8]

However, by the end of August the French fleet under Count de Grasse appeared at Chesapeake and Washington and Rochambeau were nearing Yorktown by rapid marches from the North. Cornwallis was nearly entrapped, but there were apprehensions that he would attempt to escape south through the State.

This changed the situation in North Carolina materially. The question of securing the stores became of secondary importance; the most pressing one was to close the avenue of possible escape of Cornwallis to the South. Gov. Burke set in motion the whole State in this emergency. He mobilized large numbers of militia; on his orders every boat on the Meherrin, Roanoke and Neuse was either destroyed or seized, and every crossing place was placed under guard and fortified by abatis.[9]

With the same purpose in view, Greene moved his army north of the Santee and assured Washington that "nothing shall be left unattempted in my power, to impede his (Cornwallis') march, so as to give your army time to get up with him."[10] In view of the lack of documentary evidence[11] it may be said with the utmost probability that it was Kosciuszko who chose the places in North Carolina to be so strengthened and that it was he who superintended the work. Most probably also it was during this action that he was seen and met by French officers; French detachments penetrated often far away from their camp, if for no other reason, than to draw supplies for their army.[12] The Frenchmen returning to their country reported his presence only generally, thus causing the inaccuracy as to the names of the state and of his commander in Murinais' letter.

---

[8] *Records N. C.*, XV, 606, the original in Kahanowicz, p. 35, no. 81.

[9] Johnson, *Sketches*, II, 244.

[10] Sept. 17, 1781, *ibid.*, II, 240.

[11] A search through *Thomas Burke Letter Book*, 1774-1781, and papers of Alexander Martin, who succeeded Burke as Governor, when the former was captured by the British on Sept. 12, 1781, in the North Carolina Historical Commission, Raleigh, did not bring out any details which might throw some light on Kosciuszko's activity in North Carolina at that time.

[12] Grasse to Washington, Sept. 25, 1781, *Correspondence of Washington and Grasse*, 49.

It seems hardly possible that Kosciuszko ventured as far north as Yorktown itself during the siege.[13] A part of Greene's army under Lafayette was active in Virginia, but he had no direct orders from Greene in this regard, and Duportail's and Gouvion's presence with Washington made his help unnecessary there. Personally, he had reasons rather to shun the unfriendly Duportail.

As to the forts which he originally was to help build in North Carolina, it seems that they were never actually constructed.[14] Unhappily, the Tories captured Gov. Burke in the midst of his action. Even if Kosciuszko started the work on these fortifications, they soon became unnecessary. Defeated at Yorktown, the British evacuated Wilmington on November 14, and Virginia and North Carolina became free.

Tradition linked Kosciuszko's name with the battle of Eutaw Springs (September 8), as savior of forty British prisoners who were said to be threatened with slaughter by the Americans,[15] but on that day he was undoubtedly still in North Carolina, and did not return to Greene's camp before November, if not later. The earliest positive proof of his being present again in South Carolina is Greene's order to him of early December, when the army encamped at Riddlesperger's plantation after the skirmish at Dorchester, to find a proper place for a new camp in the vicinity of Charleston. The order found Kosciuszko in poor physical condition. "Col. Kosciuszko is yet very much pained by an inflamation in his face", reported Col. Williams, "but will go forward tomorrow to look out a position."[16] In fact, notwithstanding his indisposition, he set out and selected Col. Saunders' plantation on the Round O.[17] It was in a fertile and rich region, full of rice farms and immense quantities of ducks. It abounded also in symptoms of civilization, so long unseen by the Southern Army; there were beautiful houses and gar-

---

[13] Many authors erroneously mention Kosciuszko as present at the surrender of Cornwallis. The source of this legend was most probably Falkenstein, *Kosciuszko*, 35. In 1834, a French firm, J. Zuber & Co., printed a series of wall paper composed of 24 scenes of the American Revolution. One of them showed the scene of the surrender and Kosciuszko next to Washington, in a Polish cap, red Polish coat, blue pants, yellow boots and long blue Polish cloak.

[14] Such is the opinion of the Secretary C. C. Crittenden of the North Carolina Historical Commission, as expressed to this author in a letter, April 15, 1942.

[15] Korzon, *Kosciuszko*, 165. There is no mention of Kosciuszko at Eutaw neither in Greene's orders pertaining to the battle, nor in its detailed account by Williams, Gibbes, *Documentary History*, III, 144-58.

[16] To Greene, Dec. 4, 1781, Kahanowicz, p. 35, no. 82.

[17] Johnson, *Sketches*, II, 268.

dens, the refinement of life, and, above all, handsome and cultured women. All this strongly contrasted with the chronically lamentable condition of the Southern Army. Throughout the campaign officers and soldiers alike were "literally naked,"[18] "without pay . . . and often with but a scanty portion of the plainest provisions;"[19] and on their long and exhaustive marches they "might be tracked by their bloody Feet"[20] Now, for the first time and at least for a while, the men could fill their stomachs full.

In order to cover the South Carolina legislature which was to be assembled at Jacksonborough, Greene tried to seize John's Island, but his plans went amiss, and on January 16, 1782, the army encamped at Skirring's plantation on the Pon-pon. Here Kosciuszko bade farewell to his warm friend, Col. Williams; the valiant Marylander lost his health in consequence of the hardships of the campaign and returned to Baltimore an invalid. But there were now many pleasant distractions; life smiled again on the weary soldiers of Greene. Their greatest care now seemed to be how to replenish their poor wardrobes. On March 12, Kosciuszko wrote to Dr. Brown:

"I received your favor, and according to your request I have made application, but it was arrangement made before that those who are not present should not have their share of Linen—I myself got only for four Shirts, this moment I received the good news that some Linen to be got at Camden. I will therefore if is true make application to the General, the Governor Rotledge will pass by your place going to Congress."[21]

While at Pon-pon Williams quartered at Mrs. Susan Hayne and, leaving for the North, took along with him her son, William, then a boy of sixteen years, in order to educate him.[22] Kosciuszko called her a "good Clever Sensible Woman", and it seems that he shared quarters with Williams at her house. Kosciuszko's few letters from the place give a glimpse of the comparatively care-free life of the army at this period, so different from the crude toils of the southern campaign. Enclosing a letter from Mrs. Hayne he wrote Williams on March 12:

---

18 Washington to Knox, Jan. 7, 1781, Fitzpatrick, XXI, 67.
19 Ramsay, *History of So. Caro.* I, 440.
20 James Lowell to Elbridge Gerry, March 5, 1781, Burnett, *Letters,* V, 6.
21 Gates Papers, box 14, no. 36. This letter is wrongly endorsed as of 1780. At that time Kosciuszko was still at West Point and in March, 1781, Camden was still in British hands.
22 Williams Papers, nos. 258 and 304.

"I would write very long letter but this moment I must set out upon some business, which deprave me of this pleasure, we have no news the report spread Yesterday that the Ennemys burn Quarter House.[23]—her every body is in love so far, that Colo. Moris fancy himself to be with Miss Nancy Eliot in love his displayed upon the occasion waste (vast) store not seen before of the humorous spritty disposition . . . Mr. Kean your good Friend send his Compliments."[24]

His next message, written about a week later, is the most frolicsome of his American letters. It shows us Kosciuszko joking and flirting with local belles with whom he evidently became popular not only because of his pleasant disposition, but also because of his skill in drawing. He liked to entertain his friends by sketching their portraits and several such drawings by him are still preserved.

"It is out of my resolution taken and Contrary to our Convention its self", he wrote Williams,[25] "that I should write before the reception of a letter from you, but as sometimes the best System is Changed with the view of obtaining more advantageous and, So I flatter my self that by importunities will at last receive a letter from you and Satisfie the eneasines and enxiaty which Friendly breast Comonly susceptible of the Alarme in the Absence of the person in whos happiness are interested. *stop here* Mrs. Hayne shoked head juste now at the vue of Dinning with me *tête atête* and made very Deep sigh you must resolve this, and make proper *Corolaire* for it, two days ago I was frightened out of my Soul, Mrs. Cedone bautiful Miss Stabow, Mrs. Frayer and our Good Elegant Miss Perry with mistress Haynes aid and the must (most) Charming of onaffected are[26] of Miss Hutchusons help, they Contrived the means to revenge them self as the(y) Call it upon me, on account of the expression that I made use of in the Company one day before wich they thought to reflect very high on them, you will judge (and I told them I will write to you, which is this) beeing importunet every day to make their pictures I said that I Cannot make them handsome judge pray without partiality wether was not Clock

23 A British post, 5 miles from Charleston.

24 Williams Papers, no. 145. John Kean of Charleston, member of Continental Congress in 1785, imprisoned by the British in 1781 (McCrady, *op. cit.*, 358) and now accompanying the army (Williams Papers, no. 146).

25 Some time before March 22, when the army started for Bacon's Bridge, mentioned at the end of this letter (Col. Harmar to Williams, April 10, 1782, Williams Papers, no. 147).

26 MS hardly legible.

(cloak) to exercise their natural propensity to the Cruel actes with more barefaced[27] . . . Soon they Came to Mistres Haynes they fluu (flew) immediatly at me one with Shovel and the other with tongues, this with Iron hook, that with fork and Charged me with great fury and barbarity, at the wiew of such cruel apparatus & instruments of death I finted (fainted) away. Some kind hand of my Sex broud me again to life but Soon renewed their Charge I beg them for explanation not one would listen to it, at last by accident Come to my mouth utered draw their pictures very handsome. immediatly they trow their tools down, approached me with very smiling Countenaces, kissed me half dousen times each, and beged I would instantly draw them but hansome—Such unexpected Change put me almost to extasy, I drew my pencil, paper Coulours and in a half hour time made perfectly like them, but unlocky for me they drinck more rum in the Closete as usuel, and found it unanimosly to be very ogly, they renuwed the Charge and realy would kill me if I should not ron away wich was very easy done as they could not follow me one step without fallen down so much rum affected their poor heads, tis is literaly true without omission or addition, blunders in my English narration and in speling, this will be overlocked (overlooked) by your superior Genious, your enswer perhaps will stop to the farther prosecution of your friend, we will move to the Bacons Bridge it is good and Strong position all your friends desired to be remembered by you—Moris felt in love. Burnet turn him self to be a Gallant. Pierce[28] beging (beginning) to Catch Sentymental Vissions. Pendleton propose to be a Priest, apropos a (I) was near to forget two Mrs. Wilikessons[29] lacked of their lovers (?) this is all news that Can afford this Country for you."[30]

In March Mrs. Greene joined the General and her arrival brightened still more the social atmosphere of the camp. But on March 22, the army moved to Bacon's Bridge on the Ashley River, and the old misery began to annoy it again. While there a letter from Gates reached Kosciuszko, the first one since their parting in 1780. The good General's star was in ascendency again and he now hoped to do something to save the Colonel from being so unjustly omitted

---

[27] One word illegible.

[28] Maj. Edmund Burnet and Capt. William Pierce, aides-de-camp to Gen. Greene.

[29] Most probably Eliza Wilkinson, "young, beautiful and witty widow" who lived at Young's Island, 30 miles south of Charleston (Ellet, *The Women of the Am. Revol.*, I, 255-70).

[30] Williams Papers, no. 171.

in distributions of promotions by Congress. Soon after Yorktown Duportail demanded new advances in ranks for himself and his colleagues. Washington warned him that this "could not be accomplished but at the expense of the tranquility of the Army."[31] Still Durportail persisted and by his impetuous, but clever solicitations carried his point completely with the Commander-in-Chief and Congress. He received the grade of Major General, Gouvion became Colonel, and both were granted a six months furlough. It was only logical, thought Gates, that Congress should now do something for Kosciuszko, too.

The Pole, however, did not want to hear anything about it. He answered Gates on April 8:

"Your kind letter I received by Major Pineknee,[32] you Cannot Conceive what Satisfaction I felt, as I had already given up all hope of ever happen to me such a favor, you will forgive me the Expression because Could I have more favorable Idea, when no enswer would Come to my Letters in the interval of two years time.

"The promotion General Do Portail I don't thing would be the Consequence of mine as the Congress latly resolved to make no more Brygadier—Generals, for my part nether Confidence I have enough to thing I deserve it nor resolution to ask, am extremly oblidged to you for your kind offers and think them of great weight of importence should you use your influence, but as to the other recommendation in my favor am entirely against, what I beg of you, will always denye to the others.—"

Thus cutting short the subject, he immediately turned to public affairs, continuing:

"The London Papers od December Leads me to think the Brytish policy will be to make the greatest afford (effort) in West India this sumer to Secure their Islands, and as they Cannot reinforce the Troops in America they must quit Charleston to suport New York in case of the Siedge or keep both towns in a passive maner, being not able to forme any Opperation.—

"The War will not last two years more I assure you, already the great debate was in Parlament wether they ought to carry the War in

[31] Washington to Duportail, Oct. 26, 1781, Fitzpatrick, XXIII, 269.
[32] Major Thomas Pinckney, who returned to South Carolina after the Yorktown campaign.

America or not, they lost even the shadow in imagenery vision of a distant perspective ever Conquered this Country. Our Army Encamp at Beckenbridge upon Ashlei river two and twenty mills from Charles Town, the Ennemys dare not move from the lines made at Quarter house.—I do not expect to go very soon to Philadelphia but if ever I should you may be sure that I will do me the honour to call on you, and would not Choose by no means to be depraved of the Satisfaction see you both in good health at Travellers rest.

"My best respect to Mrs. Gates and I beg her to believe that nor time or place will ever make me forgive her good heart and my Sentyments of gratitude."[33]

But the hero who so magnanimously spurned occasions for his promotions, had his Achilles' heel: he could not live without coffee. Ever since the British were confined to Charleston Neck and the adjacent islands, a contraband trade was carried on with Charleston and in this way both sides satisfied their daily needs. The delivery, however, met sometimes with unexpected obstacles, and Kosciuszko felt good for nothing if this happened to his shipment of coffee.

"I Expected Suply of Coffee from Charles Town", once he wrote to Dr. Read, "but Could not get, and this news was brod yesterday to my great mortification now you must return me as a sick because I Cannot live without Coffee and I propose to trouble you with it and to begin I beg you to Send me Six pound of Coffee, with Sugar in proportion, that surprise you I see but when I have the pleasure of Seeing you at my Quarters I Convince you of the necessity that I Should be well. God bless you and your family."[34]

Dr. Fayssoux, another surgeon of the Southern Army, was displeased with Kosciuszko for "having intruded himself" into the camp hospital while at the High Hills, when tea, coffee and sugar could scarcely be procured for the sick. But the good natured Dr. Read explained that it was a mutual accommodation. Kosciuszko "gave up all his rations to the hospital, never touching a drop of ardent spirits, but contenting himself with the slops and soups of that establishment, which fare was no luxury, and that he had invited him, as a companion, to do so."[35] As to his moderation in diet,

[33] Gates Papers, box 16, no. 28, wrongly endorsed as of 1781.

[34] N. Y. Public Library, Myers Collection, no. 1294, no date; reprinted in N. Y. Geneal. and Biogr. Record, II, (1871), 32.

[35] Johnson, Traditions, 415.

we have another contemporary testimony, that of Armstrong, according to whom Kosciuszko, though entitled as a Colonel to five rations, "declined taking more than a ration of bread and meat for himself and prevender for his horse during the two campaigns I served with him."[36]

[36] Armstrong to Sparks, Aug. 1837, Sparks Papers, ser. 49, vol. I, p. 72.

Chapter XIV

CHARLESTON

The warfare in South Carolina subsided. Though Greene changed his positions occasionally, he kept close to Charleston which became the last remaining stronghold of the waning British power between New York and Savannah. In July Savannah capitulated, too. The actions of the Southern Army were limited to manoeuvres and skirmishes. Under the impression of Yorktown the British parliament passed a resolution recognizing the reduction of colonies as impracticable and demanding the government to accelerate peace. At last the United States stood at the threshold of victory. But the enemy still occupied the American soil and it was impossible to lay down arms.

There was now little to do for an army engineer and Kosciuszko was only too glad to perform functions of an officer of the line, as long as it gave him an opportunity of escape from camp idleness. The army encamped at Ashley Hill, about fifteen miles above Charleston; the position, undoubtedly chosen by Kosciuszko, was "very good . . . ground high and dry, but it" was "now midsummer and sickly season. Men" died "very fast"; the army "lost several valuable officers."[1] The camp became a vast hospital; there was not enough men even for the relief of guards[2] and "the air was so affected with the stench . . . that" one "could scarcely bear the smell."[3] The littoral parts of the state were deadly to men not acclimatized to these malaria-breeding regions. Greene himself became seriously ill. Kosciuszko kept comparatively well under the rigors of the campaign. Though of small stature, he had a shapely and strong physique; agile and always active, muscular and inured to hardships,[4] he was able to out-distance his colleagues in physical endurance.

---

[1] "Military journal of Maj. E. Denny," *Memoirs of the Hist. Soc. of Pa.*, VII (1860), 250.

[2] "Journal of Lt. Wm. McDowell," *Penna. Archives*, ser. 2, vol. XV, p. 314.

[3] Moultrie, *Memoirs*, II, 357.

[4] Askenazy, *Kosciuszko*, 11.

On the death of the gallant Lieut. Col. Laurens, Greene entrusted him with a command of an advanced post at Ashley Ferry,[5] about six miles down the Ashley River, "where the great road from Charleston to the upper county crosses."[6] His primary task was to observe the enemy, to report all his suspicious movements, and to keep his roving detachments in check. His command consisted of a squad or two of dragoons of the former Lee's Legion and some infantry from the Delaware and of the Pennsylvania Continentals who under St. Clair reinforced Greene after the Yorktown campaign.

Judge Johnson attests that Kosciuszko's "innumerable" letters to Greene written at this period, "exhibit the industry and intelligence" with which he discharged his new duties.[7] Pleading for relief of Lieut. Foster[8] of his command, he acknowledged that "it is true the duty is harder than in the Army,"[9] but he evidently enjoyed his constant activity on patrols, reconnaissances and ambushes. He was always on the alert and anxious to search after opportunities for enterprise. "One word from you instantly I will go", he wrote to Greene on one occasion, urging him to allow him to attack the British on James Island.[10] At the head of his small force he harassed the enemy, dispersing and destroying his detachments;[11] whenever he saw a chance of harming him, he was ready to attack his ships,[12] or to carry off his cattle,[13] to cut off his delivery of provisions or his lines of communication. No move of the enemy escaped his at-

---

[5] Now Bee's Ferry.
[6] "Journal of Denny," *loc. cit.*
[7] Johnson, *Sketches, II,* 344. For most of these letters see Kahanowicz, *passim.* Additional letters appear here and there; one of Sept. 18, advising Greene of a large party of British troops having gone up the Cooper River, was quoted for sale by C. Tyborowski of New York in 1941; another of Sept. 28, mentioning Col. Harmar, is in the Archives and Museum of the Polish R. C. Union, Chicago; still another of Oct. 3, 1782, is quoted by J. W. Barnwell, "Letters to Gen. Greene," *So. Caro. Hist. and Geneal. Mag.,* XVI (1915), 147.
[8] Lt. Foster of Virginia, served in Lee's Legion.
[9] To Greene, Aug. 30, 1782, Kahanowicz, p. 3, no. 6.
[10] Sept. 20, 1782, Kahanowicz, p. 8, no. 17.
[11] Capt. John Markland of Pennsylvania records a victorious engagement at Quarter House, "Revolutionary services of J. M.," *Penna. Mag.,* IX (1885), 109; most probably it was the one which Armstrong mentioned in his letter to Gen. Sumner, July 27, 1782, *Records N. C.,* XVI, 631; together with Capt. Wilmot, Kosciuszko made an expedition against a party of the British who landed at Dill's Bluff, on James Island, on Oct. 23, Wilmot to Greene, Oct. 24, 1782, Johnson, *Sketches, II,* postscript, 10; William Seymour, Sergeant-Major of the Delaware Regiment, recalls another successful skirmish on Nov. 4, 1782, "A Journal of the Southern Expedition," *Papers of the Hist. Soc. of Dela.,* vol. II, no. XV (1896), 40.
[12] John Laurens to Greene, Aug. 6, 1782, Kahanowicz, p. 36, no. 83.
[13] Kosciuszko to Greene, Sept. 15, and Dec. 4, 1782, *ibid.,* p. 6, no. 14, and p. 11, no. 25.

tention. He was now the ever wakeful watchdog of Greene's army. Early in September, Gov. Mathews, at the request of Greene, issued orders for mobilization of the St. Andrew's Company of militia "to wait on Col. Kosciuszko for his particular orders."[14] Quite famous became his incursion on James Island in which he succeeded in carrying off about sixty fine horses.[15] Some of them were originally the property of citizens of the state and the seizure evoked a conflict between the federal and state rights. According to a law passed by Congress, the horses should have been sold at auction and the proceeds paid into the federal treasury. However, Gov. Mathews and the Council of South Carolina championed the rights of the citizens, claiming "that original owners are entitled to restitution of all re-captured property". Greene, recognizing "that the sufferings and losses of the people of this State have claim to a genenerous attention,"[16] had, however, his hands tied up by the federal law. In his dilemma, he called a council of war at which Kosciuszko was also present. All officers decided against the validity of the state claim. Eventually Greene referred the matter to Congress and ordered Lt. Col. Carrington to "dispose of the horses taken by Colonel Kosciuszko . . . In the sale you will notify the purchasers that should any of the horses prove to be formerly the property of inhabitants of this State and they should lay claim to them, and Congress determine that their rights of post liminium shall extend to property under such circumstances, they must be given up to them, and the purchase money will be returned them by the public Agents."[17] The committee of Congress which ultimately decided the question in favor of the original owners, on December 23, was composed of James Madison, Alexander Hamilton and Thomas McKean.[18]

Kosciuszko's "highly confidential and important"[19] duty was the intelligence service between the Whigs at Charleston and the command of the army. Frequent mentions of and several enclosures from these "inteligencers" appear in Kosciuszko's correspondence;

14 Maj. Burnet to Gov. Mathews, Sept. 5, and Mathews to Burnet, Sept. 6, 1782, *ibid.*, p. 36, nos. 84 and 85.

15 Markland, *loc. cit.*, 109.

16 Greene to Gov. Mathews, Oct. 22, 1782, Library of Congress, Papers Cont. Cong., ser. 155, vol. II, p. 587; this volume contains many other pertinent documents.

17 Oct. 19, 1782, *ibid.*, p. 595; the original in the Kahanowicz Coll., p. 37, no. 86.

18 *Journals Cont. Cong.*, XXIII, 825-7; McGrady, *op. cit.*, 662-66, examines the matter from the juridical point of view at great length; his work, however, is marred by a strong aversion toward Greene and a sectional feeling.

19 Johnson, *Sketches*, II, 339.

only one, Edmund Petrie, is identified by name, others are only known by initials W., P., and X. A negro, Prince, often served Kosciuszko as messenger in this service.

Highly unpleasant to him was the duty of suppressing contraband trade with Charleston. Provisions and other supplies were again so scarce in the army that it subsisted on carrion. Greene complained of the bad situation constantly, but it was of little avail. On July 8, he wrote to Col. Horry: "We have hundreds of men as naked as they were born." A few weeks later he informed Gen. Barnwell: "Our troops are more than one third of their time without provision."[20] In November Gen. Wayne, who rejoined Greene after the surrender of Savannah, asserted that the army was "experiencing every possible distress for want of provision, even of the meanest kind."[21] Greene wondered "what charms keeps them together" in such circumstances: "I believe nothing but the pride of the army, and the severity of discipline, support them under their sufferings."[22]

Nevertheless, while the army suffered hunger and nakedness, large quantities of fresh food passed continually into the beleaguered city. Gov. Mathews branded this as "infamous traffic carried on by persons who will contribute nothing for the army, because they can get an enormous price, and the cash, for what they send to town."[23] Kosciuszko did not mind to pass a "few small articles to buy sugar and coffee for the family use", as he was allowed by Greene, but relentlessly tried to stop all larger loads.[24] "Let be young or old Blood, it is very bad one to furnish such quantity of catle for the Enemys", he wrote to Greene after having caught some contraband cattle which belonged to a Mr. Youngblood.[25]

The dashing hero of Stony Point was not careful enough in granting permits to inhabitants for their boats to pass to Charleston. Kosciuszko was obliged to look through his fingers at heavily laden boats which cruised immune from seizure under Wayne's passes. "It will appear in my opinion as a jock," he remonstrated

---

[20] Johnson, *Sketches*, II, 351.
[21] Hist. Soc. of Pa., Wayne MSS, XVIII, 93.
[22] To the Pres. of Congress, March 9, 1782, Johnson, *Sketches*, II, 317.
[23] To Greene, *ibid.*, II, 353.
[24] Kosciuszko to Greene, Sept. 5, 1782. Kahanowicz, p. 4, no. 8.
[25] Dec. 4, 1782, Kahanowicz, p. 11, no. 25. Most probably the remark pertained to Capt. Youngblood of Edisto, who negotiated a local truce with Tories in the summer of 1782.

to Greene, "and serve only to expose me to the hatred of the inhabitants, if I stop according to your orders every provision Boat and General Waine will have exclusif power to gives passes. Every one will suppose that my ill natured disposition rather or interested wue governe me and favorise one more than the other, the people will be apte to think so and I would of the other too in the same circumstances."[26]

On September 27, Kosciuszko received information that "some persons from camp have send quantity of beeff to town". This looked like a scandal and he immediately reported it to Greene: "I hope we can discover what persons are, but at the same time I should be sorry because it would (cast) great Reflection upon Poor our Army".[27] Most probably to this affair pertains his curt and peremptory order to one of the officers of the Quartermaster Department: "You must thing self as in the arrest and I will ask the General for the Court Martial."[28] Eventually, suspicions fell on Wayne who indignantly denied any guilt "upon the honor of a Gentleman and a soldier." However, he was not able to deny that he had issued passes which might have been abused and that he himself obtained wine and porter from the city.[29] Wayne, brave as he was, liked high life and at least in one instance before was not scrupulous enough to abstain from commercial dealing with the enemy, if it served his comfort or his love affairs.[30]

For the most part Kosciuszko's letters to Greene pertaining to this period are strictly military, but occasionally exhibit trends of his character. His contact with the southern black slaves taught him compassion for their misery which he perhaps compared with the wretched social position of Polish peasants. A few days after Laurens' death he wrote to Greene in the matter of disposing of his effects, and took the ocassion, in a plain but very eloquent term, to intercede in behalf of his slaves: "The Bearer Le Bresseur desire me to write to you that (he) could have the Linen and Clothg belong (ing) to the late L Col. Laurence, it is a Costum in Europe and he expect it as his due—but he may take more liberty as it would necessary. I think somebody ought to inspect when the Bagage come to

---

26 Sept. 11, 1782, *ibid.*, p. 6, no. 13.
27 Undated and unaddressed, *ibid.*, p. 9, no. 20.
28 Undated and unaddressed, *ibid.*, p. 9, no. 19.
29 Greene to Wayne, Nov. 1, and Wayne to Greene, Nov. 2, 1782, Wayne MSS, XVIII, 92 and 93.
30 Wildes, *Anthony Wayne*, 202 and 295.

your Quarters. I recomend to you two negroes belong(ing) to L C Laurence that they may have part with Le Bresseur they are nacked they want shirts & jackets Breeches and their skin can bear as well as ours good things."[31]

With equal sympathy he cared for his soldiers; urging Greene to avail himself of a chance to barter some arms for rum, he wrote him: "as the time is sickly it would be of great service to them."[32] At another occasion he interposed for his overworked dragoons, explaining to the General: "you will not blame me if I confind to the security of the Post only, as (it) would be very hard for men and horses to do duty day and night and after to go upon other imergency."[33] He regretted when he had to part with his officer colleagues; but he became equally attached to common soldiers, as in the case of some men from the Delaware Regiment. "They was great times with me", he wrote of them to Greene, "and I should be very unhappy should thos men was taken away who are realy attached and I can have Confidence in them."[34] He cared for "Bark in powder" as an anti-fever remedy for Gen. Wayne[35] and for minor comforts of Mrs. Greene to whom he sent "sweet oranges and Figs"[36] and little notes, equally full of imperfect spelling, as well as gratitude for her acts of kindness.[37]

When there appeared more persons who thought themselves entitled to the effects of Laurens, Kosciuszko felt indignant at this display of human cupidity. He wrote of one of them, a Mr. Fuller, that "the Devil himself would not take from him, you know the World we see some of mean, low thinking some very interested." He spurned a proposition to participate in their distribution: "As to my part I wanted to be clear of intierely and to have nothing to do with any article whatsoever belong(ing) to L Col Laurence."[38]

Fate preserved for Kosciuszko the honor to fire the last shot in the Revolutionary War. "On the 14th of November", as related by Markland, "Colonel Kosciusko, Capt. Wilmot, Lt. Markland, and

---

[31] Sept. 2, 1782, Kahanowicz, p. 3, no. 7.
[32] *Ibid.*
[33] Dec. 4, 1782, *ibid.,* p. 11, no. 25.
[34] Sept. 28, 1782, Archives and Museum of the Polish R.C. Union, Kosciuszko Papers, no. 5.
[35] Kahanowicz, p. 5, no. 11.
[36] To Greene, Sept. 11, 1782, original quoted for sale by C. Tyborowski of New York.
[37] Ellet, *Women of the Am. Revol.,* II, 80.
[38] Undated and unaddressed, Kahanowicz, p. 5, no. 10.

other officers, with some fifty to sixty men, attempted to surprise a British party engaged in cutting wood on James Island, near Fort Johnson. Withdrawing every evening to near the fort, the British would again commence their labors by daylight in the morning. Kosciusko gained their working ground about 2 o'clock in the morning, and remained undiscovered until their advance, consisting of British dragoons, were within striking distance, when the Americans gave them a fire, on which they retreated with some loss. Kosciusko then forming his men, attacked their advanced corps of infantry, already drawn up to receive them. A severe action ensued; the British advance retreated, warmly pressed by the Americans, but being continually reinforced until they numbered about 300 men, with a field piece, the Americans were compelled to retire, which they did in good order, bringing one prisoner. In this affair Capt. Wilmot of the Maryland line was killed and Lt. Moore was mortally wounded. Lt. Markland lost three men of his platoon. This was the last action and . . . the last gun fired in the war for Independence."[39] "Kosciuszko, although a spontoon was shattered in his hand, and his coat pierced by four balls, escaped unhurt. A British dragoon was in the act of cutting him down, when he was killed by Mr. William Fuller, a very young and gallant volunteer, who had joined the expedition."[40]

Already in the beginning of August the British began preparations for the evacuation of the city. Greene's feint against James Island compelled them to abandon their exposed post Quarter House. On August 8, Kosciuszko wrote to Williams:[41]

"I recv'd yours with great pleasure as you Could expect from the person who have reall friendship not intervowing with the interested wue—The Ennemys will leave Charlestown in two month time at farthest they embark the Canon and the Bagage — the Quarter House is Evacuated four days ago, hoever they made advance post near Shubrick house three mill from the Town, and

---

[39] Markland, *loc. cit.*

[40] Garden, *Anecdotes*, I, 79; he criticizes this expedition as "very rash" and generally exhibits a dislike toward Kosciuszko. His objections were answered by T. W. Field, *ibid.*, I, addenda VIII. The objections of James, author of the *Life of Marion*, also pertaining to this affair, were examined by Johnson, *Sketches*, II, postscript, 9-11. It is to be regretted that McGrady, *History of So. Caro.*, 662, saw fit to use the evidently prejudiced stories of Garden and James and a letter of Marion of questionable authenticity as a basis for his narrative of the skirmish and to brand Kosciuszko as a "soldier of fortune."

[41] This letter is undated; however, the evacuation of Quarter House by the British, mentioned in the letter, took place on Aug. 4, 1782 ("Journal of Lt. McDowell," *loc. cit.*, 327).

have made redoubt as is usuel to them every step they go backward, it is reported her that Nyork will be Evacueted also, Great terror and Confusion among the Tories and the Inhabitence of the Town, they Send the Ambasadors to the Governor to Sound what terms they Can expect, Part of them goes with the Ennemys and greater number would Chouse to stay, every day four or six deserters we have of every denomination and as to Distingvish the faces of great rascals from thos of a Honest men, I wish ve had Adisson Glass to see the Sincerity of their Hearts, but fewe would like pass the examen to let the others know the inmost inward Corner and recesse, from which flow the Sentyments and established principle of a mortal."

With the evacuation of Charleston and New York imminent, Kosciuszko still believed that an expedition to expel the British from Canada would be unavoidable. He evidently was ready to join it. "I believe," he continued, "we will have the satisfaction sooner to see you at Baltimore then you us in this Country nothing to do after the Ennemys leave the Place but to go to Canada, you will be of the party I hope more field for you to Show your meryt but safter passion than Ambition perhaps kreaped in your heart and find her Impire—Apropos Colo. Moris pay peculiar Courtship and attention to get Miss Nancy Elliot.[42] I do not thing you will have Chance he was one Month sick at her house in which time I believe he gained her affection."[43]

But the British were very slow with the evacuation which did not contribute to the pacification of the country. "The Inhabitants upon the Neck and in Charles Town," Kosciuszko wrote to Greene on November 14, "very much allarmed and affraid to be plundered by the Ennemys and by our people. I assured them of our Army that they will Loose not a pin but I cannot say of the militia if they go first. I mentioned that you will pay particular attention so far as will be in your power to prevent any desorder of any Troops."[44]

Kosciuszko himself became impatient with the British slowness. "I wish I was mistaken in my opinion that if the enemys not goes today or tomorow they will not go till next spring but not of the

---

[42] Elliott. According to Ellet, *The Women of the Am. Revol.*, II, 100, Kosciuszko greatly admired the future Mrs. Morris and kept up a Platonic correspondence with her.
[43] Williams Papers, no. 172.
[44] Kahanowicz Coll.; this letter not included in the printed catalogue.

tide but of the year," he wrote to Greene on December 6.[45] In a post-script to the same letter, however, he was able to add with exultation: "Hura and again Hura. Just now I recive intelligence from James Island that all are going to morow but I will know more sure this day wich I will comunicate to you immediately."

At last the evacuation took place on December 14,[45a] and Gen. Wayne marched in at the head of the victorious American troops. Kosciuszko took part in the triumphal procession, leading his detachment[46] among the throngs of enthusiastic citizens. He caught a bad cold in consequence of "swiming over the cut"[47] shortly before the historical day, but evidently got rid of it quickly and now had an opportunity to fully share the joy of the Americans. The celebration was closed with a grandiose ball at the instigation of Mrs. Greene, and Kosciuszko decorated the hall with magnolia leaves hung up in festoons, and pieces of paper curiously cut in imitation of the flowers.[48]

But still the military toils of Kosciuszko were not ended. Almost immediately after the occupation he had to organize, on orders of Greene, an armed expedition by water for the transportation of rice for the army. In trying to gather some vessels he met with ill-will on the part of inhabitants, and indifference on the part of the state government. "The former not willing to go," he complained, "the later not taken proper measure. . . . The Public affaires seames to be not very much at heart, reluctance in spit(e) of many shows her impire."[49] The fact was that the Southern Army became an unwelcome guest to those for whom it fought and bled. The people considered the war as ended for a long time, and the maintenance of the army, always a very troublesome burden, now became doubly disagreeable to them. The very presence of an armed body of

---

[45] Kahanowicz, p. 12, no. 26.

[45a] On December 13, 1782, Col. Lewis Morris wrote to Miss Ann Elliott: "Never was there such a thirst for news. Headquarters is crowded with inquisition. Every ear is open, and every horse that gallops at a distance, is an Express. Have you heard from Gen. Wayne, or has Colonel Kosciusko returned from below? I am told he says the fleet is in motion, and that he saw a man who heard another say, that the troops would embark this night" (Rutherfurd, "Letters from Col. Lewis Morris," *So. Caro. Hist. and Geneal. Mag.*, XLI, 1940, 12).

[46] Markland, *loc. cit.*, III.

[47] Kosciuszko to Greene, Dec. 4, 1782, Kahanowicz, p. 11, no. 25; the canal dividing John's Island from the continent, between the Stono and Edisto Rivers, was called New-Cut.

[48] Garden, *Anecdotes*, III, 168.

[49] To Greene, Dec. 26, 1782, N. Y. Public Libr., MSS Mics.

hungry and half naked men among them was looked upon as a threat of possible disorders. "The people regarded them as little else than the last enemy to get rid of," wrote an early biographer of Greene.[50] Observing this change of hearts with regret, Kosciuszko wrote to his friend, Williams: "it is said that hospitality in this Country was in alliance in many parishes with the interested wue wich after the Evacuation of Charles Town by the Britysh, died and to wich was erected very pompeus Thomb with the butifull inscription *Never rise again.*"[51] In the first half of February, 1783, the Southern Army was still in poor circumstances. "Money money money it is the Echo in every place of our officers and Soldiers," continued Kosciuszko. "Cry prompted by wants—the calamity is more keen wich sugest more distresfull sitiuation as well as speedy need of relieve."

Thanks to the efforts of Greene, who even impaired his fortune by them, conditions in the camp soon improved, however. The last cantonment of the army was on James Island, a "butifull and healthy place," according to Kosciuszko. Soldiers were delighted with it; it seemed to them "a little paradise." Perhaps for the first time in the whole campaign all had comfortable quarters. Provisions improved in quantity and quality. The winter was "delightful" and so warm, that there was little occasion for fire. All this greatly improved the health of the troops. Soldiers received new clothing and officers some cash to outfit themselves decently.[52] For the first time, too, the army began to "make a very fine appearance." Officers went often to the city, invited in rotation by the General to dine with him[53] and Kosciuszko was a frequent and one of the most welcome guests at his house.

Somehow, however, at that time he suffered an attack of fever. Quartering then at the house of Mr. and Mrs. Scott, he many years later remembered with gratitude how they treated him "wyth afection, friendship and nursed" him "like their one (own) Child."[54]

---

[50] Johnson, *Sketches*, II, 391.
[51] Feb. 11, 1783, Williams Papers, no. 192.
[52] The uniform of Kosciuszko, as Colonel of the Corps of Engineers, consisted of "a blue coat with buff facings, red lining, buff under cloaks and" two "epaulettes," as regulated by the General Order of the Commander-in-Chief, June 18, 1780 (Fitzpatrick, XIX, 22).
[53] "Journal of Maj. E. Denny," *loc. cit.*, 255.
[54] Kosciuszko to Evan Edwards, Nov. 5, 1797, Etting Papers, Hist. Soc. of Pa.; Kosciuszko to Alexander Garden, Dec. 17, 1797, So. Caro. Hist. Soc., reprinted in the *So. Caro. Hist. and Geneal. Mag.*, II (1900), 126.

Not only the General, but also Mrs. Greene, became concerned for the health of their faithful friend. Fortunately, the attack was a light one. Greene wrote him a sympathizing letter, to which Kosciuszko gratefully replied, repaying the General's kindness with a current joke and his wife's compassion with a separate letter and an elegant compliment: "Your the lest uneasiness for my health would be to make me more sick."[55]

To the General he wrote:

"I am sorry that I was the object of uneasiness in your breast, your generous attention of your Friends health, make me more alarming of yours, of wich all care ought to be taken, I had fears of the fever but today I am prety well and expect to come over tomorow very early. Major Edvards[56] was at my Quarters and left the house on acccount of his fever, just before arival of your Letter, I Cannot numberd the Epithetes he give to this state, that was the ocasion of the fever tyrant to his precious health, and I doubt not that he will beg Leave to go to Philadelphia the first uportunity he have, he is impressed with the idea that the world would sustined the greatest Loss by the accident to one of the three, viz. Colo. Carington *Julie* and himself—I afraid that your Monk should be of Such disposition, and well known efficece of his prayers as this whom the Neybouring inhabitents beged him to pray for rain that they had great want of, his enswer was as follow, is I will pray if you choose but I be D-md if will rain until the Moon Change."[57]

Gradually the officers' corps of the Southern Army became much reduced; "all the Gentlemen of" Greene's official family were "going into civil life;"[58] those who remained yet, awaited eagerly their chance. Kosciuszko diligently reported all these events to Williams: "Moris is maried 25th January to Miss Nancy Elliot—the Cack I tasted wich was send upon the occasion to their Friends I thought had bitterish Savour—our Friend Kean have left the Army and propose to be rice Planter and have the means also to be great one—the Speculation in mariges is stop'd for Some time to give

[55] Huntington Libr., Greene Papers, HM 22728; undated, except for "Thursday Evening."
[56] Major Evan Edwards of the Fourth Pennsylvania Regiment, the Adjutant-General in lieu of Williams.
[57] Huntington Libr., Greene Papers, HM 8055; undated except for "Thursday Evening."
[58] Greene to Williams, April 11, 1783, Williams Papers, no. 200.

leasure and times to go to the Country, and hear of the riche girls and Widows, as all of riche of the first Class are maried already except Miss Mott[59] who is reserved I suppose for to be admired and that South Carolina Gintilman Could boast that they have also the prodigy in Nature as Mrs. Charles Elliott who thoght to be one is maried to Beresford.[60] The Pirates from Augustine make very on easy the Inhabitents upon the Cost as they plunder very often—Lord Charles Montague[61] is taken with the ship and broght to Willmington he is now our Prisoner on parol. Pendleton give you hearty Compliments."[62]

The last known official duty of Kosciuszko in the South was an inspection with Gen. Greene of Fort Moultrie, on April 11.[63]

Five days later the welcome news of preliminaries of peace reached Charleston. There followed "great rejoicing—grand review —dinner" in the city; on April 23, there was a great display of fireworks, most probably made under the direction of Kosciuszko, and a *feu de joie* in the camp at James Island, attended by ladies and gentlemen from Charleston.[64] Then came the sad moments for Kosciuszko of taking leave of the General and Mrs. Greene, of his colleagues, of all who became near and dear to him. Most probably sometime in May Kosciuszko left Charleston by vessel for Philadelphia, accompanied by Maj. Pierce and a Mr. Godin.[65]

---

[59] Motte.

[60] Richard Beresford, at that time Lieut. Governor of South Carolina.

[61] British officer, accused of impressing American prisoners into the British service and of sending them to West Indies.

[62] Feb. 11, 1783, Williams Papers, no. 192.

[63] Greene to Williams, April 11, 1783, *ibid.*, no. 200.

[64] Denny, "Military journal," *loc. cit.*, 256.

[65] Greene to Kosciuszko, July 10, 1783, Kahanowicz; this letter not included in the printed catalogue. It acknowledges the receipt of a letter of Kosciuszko dated Philadelphia, June 18. As the passage by vessel from Charleston to Philadelphia took about ten days, Kosciuszko must have embarked not later than in the first days of June. Godin, a little known personality; he visited Washington on Jan. 14, 1784 (Fitzpatrick, XXVII, 301).

Chapter XV

BACK TO THE NORTH

Kosciuszko's long career in the South, lasting two and a half years, added new laurels to his achievements in the North. From the military point of view, "his personal bravery in action," while in the South, "secured to him the high commendations of his commanding officers, and the confidence of the whole army."[1] Col. David Humphreys attested that he was "Expert to change the front, retreat, advance, And judge of ground with military glance."[2] "To Greene," according to Armstrong, "he rendered the most important services to the last moment of the war, and which were such as drew from that officer the most lively, ardent, repeated acknowledgments."[3] One may agree with Lee and Col. Troup that he was not a military genius "of the first order;"[4] his greatness was of different character; but few Revolutionary officers had earned such splendid testimony of their services from their superiors, as that which Greene gave to Kosciuszko in a letter to Gen. William Irvine shortly after the former's departure from Charleston:

"Among the most useful and agreeable of my companions in arms, was Colonel Kosciuszko. Nothing could exceed his zeal for the public service, nor in the prosecution of various objects that presented themselves in our small but active warfare, could any thing be more useful than his attention, vigilance and industry. In promoting my views to whatever department of the service directed, he was at all times, a ready and able assistant. One in a word whom no pleasure could seduce, no labor fatigue and no danger deter. What besides greatly distinguished him was an unparalleled modesty and entire unconsciousness of having done anything extraordinary. Never making a claim or pretention for himself and never omitting to distinguish and commend the merits of others. This able and gallant soldier has now left us for the North;

---

1 Johnson, *Traditions*, 415.

2 Humphreys, "A Poem on the Love of Country," *Miscellaneous Works*, 147.

3 Washington, ed., *Writings of Jefferson*, VIII, 497.

4 Lee, *Campaign*, 402-6; Troup to Timothy Pickering, Oct. 12, 1824, Mass. Hist. Soc., Pickering Papers, vol. 32, no. 110, p. 8.

intending to return directly to his own country, where he cannot fail to be soon and greatly distinguished."[5]

Not only Greene, but also other officers liked the amiable "Count of Poland," as he was jestingly nicknamed by the Southern Army,[6] and there were few of those who came into contact with him, who did not succumb to the charm of his character. Throughout their life "the noble conduct of this brave Pole was the fond theme of their admiration and praise" and even their gravestones became eloquent witnesses of their admiring feelings.[7] "Light Horse Harry" Lee himself, so critically disposed toward his action at Ninety Six and blind to that "spark of the etherial in his composition" which Byron saw like "Hecla's flame,"[8] had to acknowledge that "Koschiusko was extremely amiable, and I believe, a truly good man, nor was he deficient in his professional knowledge."[9] Williams idolized him and extolled his virtues in his letters to his friends with such an ardor that Kosciuszko himself tried to discourage him. "Major Edwards," he wrote to him, "told me that you speak of me in such terms that even he who knows me well and very well acquiented of my Pictor in the world, could not distinguish. . . . I advise you not to put your Colory upon my pictor for fear that should resamble more to yourself than to me. Original not worth taken pains to Copy it."[10]

In turn, Kosciuszko became strongly attached to his companions of the Southern Campaign and throughout his life he cherished their memory, from Greene down through the rank and file, even to Billy, Dr. Read's black servant boy, who shaved and dressed the hair of officers.[11]

As he now stood upon the deck of the vessel bringing him to Philadelphia, he undoubtedly understood that an important chapter in his life was nearing its close. His self-imposed task was done, and he could conscientiously say that it was done in a very honorable and upright way.

---

[5] Armstrong MS, Sparks Papers, ser. 49, vol. I, p. 72.

[6] Tarleton, *History*, 147.

[7] Quotation from the gravestone of Col. William Lamar, at the Vale, a farm near Frostburg, Alleghany County, Md., Ridgeley, *Historic Graves*, 169.

[8] Byron, *Don Juan*, canto X.

[9] Lee, *Memoirs*, 119 n.

[10] March 17, 1783, Williams Papers, no. 196.

[11] Gibbes, *Documentary History*, II, 267.

He had behind him seven years of unintermitted service. Other officers enjoyed furloughs, some even frequent and long ones; he was one of the few who had stuck to their stations without any rest, except perhaps his brief digression to Traveller's Rest in 1780, and to the very end. Many battlefields and posts, from Ticonderoga down to Charleston, throughout the whole length of the then United States, marked his long road of duty. His talents and industry more than once helped to gain success for the American arms, sometimes very decisively, as in the case of Saratoga. His enthusiasm helped to inspire others with patriotic fervor. His human sympathy dictated his care for rum for his artificers and soldiers, for shoes for his carpenters, for uniforms for his colleagues, for clothes for the naked Negroes. Even his good humor contributed to the morale of the army. His loyalty to the cause never faltered and even in the worst conditions he never uttered a word of complaint; it is true that once an impatient word slipped out from under his pen when to obey the order of Washington meant to be separated from a dear friend, but he put up quickly with his personal pain. However, he was always absolutely loyal to his superiors, ready to risk his life for their safety and honor. In one point he was perhaps unique in the whole Continental Army: in his modesty and disinterestedness. Revolutionary documents are full of struggle and intrigues and importunities of American and foreign officers for higher ranks. Soldiers of the eighteenth century were extremely sensitive to honors. Not willing to be a cause of envy of his colleagues or of inconvenience to Washington and Congress, he spurned all thoughts of a promotion for himself, even if it could be had through efforts of others. He contented himself with the satisfaction of a well done duty. Evidently in a rare moment of utmost openness, he expressed his feelings in this regard in a letter to Williams:

"O! how happy we think our Self when Conscious of our deeds, that were started from principle of rectitude, from conviction of the goodness of the thing itself, from motive of the good that will Come to Human Kind."[12]

Here is the whole story of his part in the American Revolution; here are motives which impulsed him to cross half of the globe to lift his sword for freedom; here is his broad humanitarian view

---

[12] Feb. 11, 1783, Williams Papers, no. 192.

of the Revolution, which he saw as the harbinger of a new era in the human struggle for the highest ideals. Revealing further his heart before the friend, he disclosed the wonderful association of his thought of humanity with his thoughts of his own country and friends:

"Let be this said by some the Self interest and mere dilusion. O! Charming Delusion, do Candle my breast with it for ever, to you I owe the memory of my Country, to your influence belong to let drop a tear inpession (impassioned) by seeing only a wreched,[13] you open the arms with warm transports, to meet a Friend—." As if he was ashamed of his openness, he stopped abruptly his musing at this point and concluded it apologetically: "so much upon Philosophie my mind wanted a vent let it be here or in any other place or time no matter."

Just about the same time Anna Estko, again begging Franklin for some official news of Thaddeus, paid the American sage a tribute, also with the ultimate thought on Poland. "Though we inhabit a very distant and a very little known country in the rest of the universe," she wrote him, "we do not neglect to partake in the admiration of whole Europe in this regard. O, that we have a Franklin who would deliver us from oppression."[14]

The mention in Greene's letter that Kosciuszko intended to return "directly" to Poland permits the assumption that, in fact, he left Charleston in that hope. Before his final departure, however, he had to settle two matters with Congress; the first one was to ask for promotion; the war was over, the army was near disbandment, and in no way it could displease anyone; the other was to adjust his accounts which was all important to him.

It is impossible to explain exactly his financial position during the Revolution. On the whole, the lot of most of the officers of the Continental Army was lamentable. They were paid very irregularly and depreciation of money annoyed them doubly. In the spring of 1780, Continental money was worth nearly two percent of its nominal value. Many times Washington called the attention of Congress that "an officer instead of gaining any thing, is impoverished by his commission."[15] "Unable . . . to support themselves,"[16]

---

13 Here follow two words: "in distress," crossed out.
14 Oct. 19, 1783, Franklin Papers, vol. XXX, no. 140, p. 3.
15 To the Committee of Congress, Jan. 29, 1778, Fitzpatrick, X, 364.
16 Washington to John Armstrong (the father), May 18, 1779, *ibid.*, XV, 98.

they were "obliged to anticipate their pay, or participate their Estates."[17] "No officer can live upon his pay," complained Greene.[18] In December, 1782, the officers, petitioning Congress for help, pointed out their "extreme poverty."[19]

There were several acts of Congress providing for the remuneration of officers after the war. An Act of 1778 promised them half-pay for seven years and in 1780 Congress extended it for life. These acts, however, were of little practical meaning, as Congress made no provision for financing them, making it dependent upon the good will of the States. In fact, Continental Congress had no power to impose taxes.

With arrival of the actual, if not the formal, peace, the question of liquidation of officers' accounts became a burning one. The problem was one of the knottiest to solve and full of political dynamite. Congress procrastinated; the impatience of the army grew from day to day. Most probably, before leaving the South, Kosciuszko had a chance to read the famous Newburgh Addresses which so eloquently and strongly expressed the exasperation of the army. Personally, and out of regard for his colleagues, he deeply sympathized with these stirring appeals. He too "had long shared in their toils, and mingled with their dangers,"—he, too, "felt the cold hand of poverty, without a murmur." But under no condition he could acquiesce in the purpose of the addresses. Therefore with a sigh of relief he read the moving reply of Washington of March 15, to the meeting of officers of the main army at New Windsor, and their resolutions. His old commander, Gen. Gates, presided at the meeting and Kosciuszko undoubtedly felt satisfaction that it was he who helped to thwart off the threatening storm.

Under the pressure of the Newburgh affair Congress, on March 22, 1783, resolved, "that such officers as are now in service . . . shall be entitled to receive the amount of five years full pay in money or securities, on interest at six per cent per annum . . . instead of the half-pay,"[20] which had many opponents even in the army. But the treasury was empty; the actual meaning of the act was that officers were to receive certificates "that money is due to

17 Washington to Joseph Jones, March 18, 1783, *ibid.*, XXVI, 233.
18 To Joseph Reed, Aug. 1780, Greene, *Life of Greene*, II, 335.
19 *Journals Cont. Cong.*, XXIV, 291.
20 *A Collection of Papers*, 30.

them,"[21] payable at some better, perhaps very distant future. The army, mollified by thanks of Congress and grants of western lands, accepted this settlement without further murmurs thus giving "one more distinguished proof of unexampled patriotism and patient virtue."[22] However, many officers were in such a pressing need that they were forced to sell these certificates to speculators at a usurious discount.[23]

Foreign officers of the Revolutionary army were even in a worse position financially; a memorial submitted to Congress late in 1783, by some Frenchmen of the Corps of Engineers, Armand's Legion and a few others, gives some notion in this regard: "Foreign officers lately in the service of the United States, who were not attached to the line of any particular State, complain of great and singular hardships under which they have laboured during the late war. The pay which they received for a considerable time in depreciated money, was very unequal to their actual expences, nor could they be profited by the recommendations of Congress on the subject of depreciation, which afforded immediate relief to the rest of the army, because there was no State to which they could look for the balance of their pay; hence it followed, that some of them have depended in a great measure for their support, on remittances from their friends in France, while others less fortunate, have contracted considerable debts in America. . . . In their present situation, they neither have the means of subsisting in America, nor of returning to their native country."[24]

Kosciuszko's situation was, undoubtedly, not much better than that of the Frenchmen, if, perhaps, not worse in view of his very long service. Armstrong who made two campaigns with him, stated that he declined to draw his monthly pay, most probably out of patriotic motive, in order not to be a burden to the federal treasury, and out of thriftiness, in order to save money for the time of his discharge; again, according to Armstrong, all expenses, except provisions, to which he in common with other officers was exposed during the war, were paid from his own funds.[25] Evidently he lived on the money he borrowed from the Estkos before his de-

---

21 Hill, *Narrative*, 16.
22 Washington at the meeting of officers, March 15, 1783.
23 Hatch, *Administration*, 194.
24 *Journals Cont. Cong.*, XXVI, 43.
25 Sparks Papers, ser. 49, vol. I, p. 72.

parture for America. His intercourse with Europe was cut off, consequently there is little likelihood that he received any other funds from his family or his friends. He lived very frugally, but it is doubtful whether he managed to support himself for seven years without some additional income. At least occasionally he drew some money.[26] Perhaps he also incurred some debts.

Besides his regular pay there were due to him some amounts for deficiencies of rations and clothing. Altogether his unpaid emoluments reached a rather large sum. Now he needed money to cover the cost of his long return voyage to Poland, for his first expenses there, and to settle the debt with the Estkos; if anything would be left to pay mortgages burdening his paternal estate, he certainly would be very happy. Not very intimately acquainted with the state of Continental affairs, he therefore intended to ask Congress that all his dues would be paid to him in ready cash.

Kosciuszko had a pleasant trip in a very agreeable company. Even his health, somewhat impaired by the southern climate, improved much, as was the case with other members of the party, except Mr. Godin.[27] They landed in Philadelphia some time before June 18.

---

[26] There is a receipt for $371, as for his pay for five months and thirteen days, signed by Kosciuszko and dated March 31, 1783, Polish R.C. Union Archives and Museum, Kosciuszko Papers, no. 3.

[27] Greene to Kosciuszko, July 10, 1783, Kahanowicz, p. 37, no. 87.

Chapter XVI

PHILADELPHIA — PRINCETON — NEW YORK

If Kosciuszko thought that his affairs could be settled in a comparatively easy way and in a brief time, he was destined for disappointment. Immediately after his arrival, he found out that modesty is the worst policy in dealing with politicians. He lacked completely that boldness, ingeniousness and persistency in personal matters which so easily gained for Lafayette, Duportail and for some others anything they wanted from the American authorities. Moreover, still early in 1784, members of Congress did not know exactly "what has and what has not been promised or done for the Foreign Officers who have been in our Service."[1]

He felt helpless and all he could devise in his situation was to turn to Greene with a request that he intercede in his behalf. The General very gladly promised to write the necessary letters to Boudinot, the then President of Congress, and to Morris, the Superintendent of Finance, trying at the same time to inject into Kosciuszko a dose of egotism.

"Repeated application may obtain what no influence can effect," he warned him. "I know your modesty and feel your difficulty on this head, but unless you persist I am apprehensive nothing will be done in the matter. For once you must force nature and get the better of that independent pride which is our best support in many situations, and urge your suit from the necessity of the case." If Kosciuszko would not insist that the arranging of his affairs is indispensable, he will be disappointed, he continued. "Political bodies act not from feeling so much as policy but if they find there is no other way of getting rid of an application which has become troublesome, they will grant the thing although against policy. . . . In human life we are in a state of probation, and for the trial of our virtues mortification is sometimes necessary."

Greene expected to be in Philadelphia in September and assured Kosciuszko that he would gladly try to be of more help to him then

---

[1] Hugh Williamson to the Paymaster General, Jan. 1, 1784, Burnett, *Letters*, VII, 406.

if he were still in America and if his matters were not settled by that time. However, were he to leave the country meanwhile, his most sincere wishes will accompany him always, either on thorny roads or flowery fields, wherever fate will lead him.

Asking that Kosciuszko would write to him regardless in whatever part of the world he would find himself, Greene closed the letter with renewed acknowledgment of his "zeal with which you served the public under my command and for your friendly disposition towards me. My warmest approbation is due to you as an officer and my particular acknowledgments as a friend."[2]

Kosciuszko acknowledged the wisdom of Greene's advice, but still was not able to muster any aggressiveness. To his ill-luck, Congress was now preoccupied with the mutiny of the Pennsylvania troops, who, too, demanded settlement of their accounts, but in a noisy way and with arms in their hands. With disgust he saw and heard "their disorderly and menacing appearance . . . about the place within which Congress was assembled" and their "insulting the authority of the United States."[3] These incidents rather restrained him from pressing his case.

Because of the mutiny, Congress left Philadelphia and renewed their sessions at Princeton on June 30. Kosciuszko meekly followed them. At any rate, he expected to meet Williams, already promoted to the rank of Brigadier General, at Elizabethtown on July 4. Congress, however, thwarted his designs; at their request he had to remain at Princeton and prepare fireworks for the celebration of the seventh anniversary of the national independence.

Explaining to Williams the unforeseen obstacle, he wrote him on July 2:

"Congress having intention to make Illumination on the forth of July, they have made Choise of me as nobody is beter for the execution of it, it was in vain to say that I was ingaged to go to Elisabeth Town, to join my friend. They insisted upon, judge but favorably that is not my fault, that I will be not able to see you onles (unless) you Come her and join to celebrate the festivity. I (am) afraid you condemn in your self my disposition or rather fickle temper, but you will do wrong if you think so, the witness

---

[2] July 10, 1783, Kahanowicz, p. 37, no. 87.

[3] Proclamation of Boudinot, June 24, 1783, Burnett, *Letters,* VII, 196.

is Jackson[4] that my write (right) foot was forward as to the left foot is is true she was behand (behind). I do not know how Philosopher will argue upon the occasion and will decide wether the heart was with the write foot and the reason with the left, true it is that I was overpowered with Thousand stoffs (stuffs) and promised them to stay, did you think that Jacksons head was strockd with Electrick fire, this morning the Clouds ware (were) very havy (heavy)—famous Heroe of Savana[5] made his apearence and gon to Philadelphia. Give my Compliments to all my acquientence at west point particularly to General Washington, Colo Nicolas,[6] Colo Jackson,[7] Colo Brooks[8] and Mrs. Brooks, tell her that I come (to) see her when ever she will be able to receive me in a Silk Gown."[9]

Kosciuszko was "extremely concerned" with this unexpected "breach of rendezvous" with Williams, but he undoubtedly agreed with the "glossary" of Maj. Jackson to his letter that "Liberty is nothing without a Pole." Jackson, writing simultaneously to their common friend, still amplified his statement: "His presence here is essential — The illumination — the rockets — and the racket are lost without him."[10]

The Fourth of July passed in a gay atmosphere and still "Kosci," as Jackson nicknamed him, waited patiently and silently what Congress would be pleased to decide in his matter. All the exhortations of Greene were fruitless; Kosciuszko remained too modest to demand, too proud to ask; he evidently decided to stake everything on the outcome of Greene's intercession and then let the matter take its own course. In fact, the General's letter reached Congress on July 26.[11]

"Col. Kosciuszko," wrote Greene to Boudinot, "who has been our chief engineer in the Southern department and with the Northern army at the taking Burgoyne; and whose zeal and activity have been equalled by few, and exceeded by none, has it in contempla-

---

[4] Major William Jackson, later Secretary to Washington.
[5] Gen. Robert Howe passed Princeton on July 2, with his troops to Philadelphia.
[6] Perhaps Col. Wilson Cary Nicholas, commander of Washington's bodyguard.
[7] Perhaps Col. Michael Jackson of the 8th Mass., who was with the Northern Army in 1777 (Heath, *Memoirs*, 131) and served at West Point in 1779 (*Mass. Soldiers*, VIII, 681). He corresponded with Kosciuszko in 1797.
[8] Col. John Brooks, future Governor of Massachusetts, who fought with Kosciuszko at Saratoga.
[9] Williams Papers, no. 216.
[10] *Ibid.*, no. 215.
[11] *Journals Cont. Cong.*, XXIV, 447.

tion to return to Europe. To enable him to do this and bring his affairs with the Public to a close in this Country, he wishes to have such pay and emoluments, as he is entitled to from the rank he holds in the Army, and the service he has performed for the accomplishing our independence, put on such a footing, as to enable him to reduce it all to ready money. From his peculiar situation, I beg leave to recommend his case to Congress, and, if the thing be practicable, that the financier be desired to settle and accomodate the matter with him.

"My friendship for the Colonel must apologize for the singularity of this recomendation. My feelings are warmly interested in his favor, but I pressume not to judge of the difficulties attending the business."[12]

Congress referred the letter to the Superintendent of Finance for his opinion. The request was hopeless. Above all, there was the danger of a precedent, especially at a time when the whole army clamored for money. Morris, well-disposed toward Kosciuszko, as he was, made it clear to Greene.

"That young Gentleman's acknowledged merit and services," he answered him on August 1, "joined to your warm interposition in his favor, excite my sincerest wish to render the adjustment of his affairs equal to his most sanguine Expectations. Your Letter to Congress on the same Subject, having been referred to me to report, I have (consistently with my Duty) stated at the same Time my Conviction of his Talents and Zeal and the Danger of excepting Individuals out of the general Rules. This my Dear Sir, is a thing which I cannot do, but Congress may. Should they think proper to make a special Order on the Occasion I shall be very happy to carry it into Execution."[13]

Basing his opinion on a law of 1781, providing as a recompense for the depreciation of pay, that foreign officers shall be paid one fifth of the balance of their arrearages and that the remaining four fifths shall be placed on interest, Morris submitted to Congress the following:

"That the merit of Col. Kosciuszko is great and acknowledged, his Talents brilliant, his zeal unquestioned, and of Consequence his

---

[12] Papers Cont. Cong., ser. 137, vol. II, f. 747; the original in Kahanowicz Coll., p. 38, no. 88.
[13] Bancroft's Revol. Papers, vol. II, f. 463.

application must be placed among those which are not to be declined unless for the most cogent Reasons and even insurmountable obstacles. But that if it be complied with other officers of Merit Talents and Zeal will doubtless make similar applications.

"That it is the Exclusive Priviledge of the Sovereign with discerning Eye to mark and distinguish the Degrees of Activity Knowledge and Enthusiasm which their Different Servants are endowed with.

"That it is equally their priviledge to declare the Rewards to be bestowed on the most eminent, But that in claims for Justice, all must stand on equal Ground, and distressed as they are will naturally conceive that the duties of Justice must preceed those of Generosity."[14]

Without any debate and with no further action Congress accepted the report on August 5, and so the question of complete refunding of Kosciuszko's arrearages was irrevocably buried *ad calendas Graecas*. Evidently, he could not even immediately receive that small part of his dues in cash to which he was entitled; at that moment the Superintendent of Finance was unable to pay even interest on public debts. Kosciuszko had to await a more favorable turn of events. His plans for an early departure were thwarted for the present; but seeing his comrades now "turned loose on the world to starve,"[15] he would not demand a better treatment for himself under any circumstances.

With what promptness Congress acted, however, when a few weeks later Duportail asked that the accounts of Gouvion, Laumoy and his own be settled. On October 6 he wrote to the President of Congress in this regard, on October 10 Congress resolved that the accounts be "immediately" adjusted, and on October 16 it provided them with passage to Europe at the expense of the United States.[16]

In the same modest, unobtrusive way Kosciuszko undertook now his endeavors for a promotion. It seems that he contented himself with a personal interview with Gen. Lincoln, Secretary at War, who wrote the following letter to Congress on this subject on August 8:

---

[14] *Journals Cont. Cong.*, XXIV, 488-9.
[15] Thacher, *Military Journal*, 346.
[16] *Journals Cont. Cong.*, XXV, 668-9, 695.

"At the close of the Campaign of 1781, Congress, from a conviction of the services and merits of General Du Portail, and of the other Gentlemen, officers in the Engineering department, gave them promotions, in the army of the United States.—At that time Colonel Kosciuszko, who is among the oldest Colonels in our service (his Commission is dated 18 October 1776) was with General Greene, who has made the most honorable mention of his services to Congress, they have been such from his first entering into our service, as to gain the notice and applause of all under whom he has served. —I beg leave therefore to mention him to Congress as a highly deserving officer and hope that the same regard to merit which procured the promotion of the greatest part, if not all, of his brother officers in the Engineering department will operate in his favor so far that he may be promoted to the rank of Brigadier General."[17]

This letter was read in Congress on the next day and referred to a committee composed of Richard Peters, James McHenry and James Duane.[18] Kosciuszko was not even willing to wait for their decision. He returned to Philadelphia, perhaps to await the arrival of Gen. Greene. From there he again wrote to Williams on August 25:

"Your situation in every circumstances of your life is very interesting to your friends, not to give them news of you, they are realy enxious to see you happy——do not deny them their wish—so Long as you find opportunity to convey your Letters, you most write— few words will suffice Like that you are well, and will afford more satisfaction, as it is pointed to the heart, then your Common Elegenc of Style in the description of different Subjects, which force our admiration, or delit our Curiosity—

"The moral faculties of human nature have greater share in contributing towards real happiness, because their invard progress from first Conception of Idea to the last stage of enjoyment, pass throu different steps. Like that, of emotion, Sensation, which every one give new kind of pleasure and redouble in us the effect—

"Colo Lemoy[19] requested me to beg you for your journal of the Southern Campain, if you can spare him for a few days you will oblidge us both — I wish to know how I could direct my letters to

---

[17] Papers Cont. Congr., Letters and reports from B. Lincoln, ser. 149, vol. III, ff. 123-5.

[18] *Journals Cont. Cong.*, XXIV, 498.

[19] Jean Baptiste Joseph, Chevalier de Laumoy, of the Corps of Engineers.

General Gates, his place is so ill situated that nobody can give me proper information, if you see him tell him that I will not move from Philadelphia before October—

"You Cannot conceive how many Persons are here inquiring after you, I will grow Jealous very Soon, the Ladies make you the most Amieable and the Gentilmen made you the most Sinsible and All in concert they Esteem you and Love you—

"General Washington is arriv'd to Princeton yesterday where I am sure will stay many Weeks to Setled different Claims of officers as well as on many other Accounts . . . General Carlton wrote to Congress that he had received orders to evacuat New York 16th of October—"[20]

There seems to be no doubt that Kosciuszko returned north with the hope of meeting once more his beloved Gen. Gates. It was nearly two years since they parted at Camden, and the Pole sincerely desired to take personal leave of him before his departure for Europe. But Gates left the camp soon after the historical meeting at Temple Hill in consequence of the Newburgh Addresses, and hurried to the bedside of his dying wife. Once more a heavy cross fell on his shoulders. In a short period of two years the Traveller's Rest became an empty home.

Most probably while in Philadelphia Kosciuszko met Thomas Cajetan Wengierski, a prominent Polish poet who just about that time reached the city. Exiled from Poland at the order of the Russian Empress, Catherine II, for a satire ridiculing her, he came to America, eager to become acquainted with the heroes of the Revolution and with the country which inspired him with admiration. Philadelphia entertained him "hospitably, kindly and politely."[21] From Wengierski Kosciuszko was able to receive first hand accounts of conditions in Poland, and the news was by no means consoling.

By the end of September Greene came, and Kosciuszko left again for Princeton soon, most probably in company with him and his suite. At Trenton, Greene met Washington and they made the rest of the way together. No doubt, Greene took the occasion to relate personally to the Commander-in-Chief Kosciuszko's achievements

---

[20] Hist. Soc. of Pa., Dreer Papers, vol. II, no. 10; reproduced by B. J. Lossing in the *Amer. Histor. Record*, I (1872), 82.

[21] Cf. Haiman, *Poland and the Am. Revol. War.*, 119.

in the South and his desiderata as to his pay and promotion. At Princeton, President of Congress, Boudinot, entertained both commanders and their suites with a dinner. Garden relates that Boudinot himself ushered Washington and Greene into the room, then a member of Congress invited all the members of the body, but Kosciuszko, Col. Maitland, Maj. Edwards, and the aides of Gen. Greene were left to find their own way to the table, and this lack of manners which they suspected to be intentional to show the dislike of civil officers for the military, affected all of them disagreeably.[22]

On October 8, Wengierski overtook them at Princeton and here he was introduced to Gen. Greene, perhaps by Kosciuszko. The poet was well satisfied with his new acquaintance. "His modesty equals his merits," he said of Greene, "and the mildness of his character and a very careful education, which the majority of the American generals lack, made him a very agreeable man."[23] On the same day Wengierski visited Washington at his headquarters at Rocky Hill[24] and on the next day set out toward New York and the Highlands. He never met Kosciuszko again.

At last, long and faithful services of Kosciuszko met with some, however slight, recognition by Congress. The letter of Gen. Lincoln passed through it without effect. Still before leaving Philadelphia Kosciuszko, disappointed again at his fruitless waiting, wrote to Washington:

"General Lincoln was pleased to recommend me to Congress and requested them to promote me to the Ranck of Brygadier General, which by the date of the Commission I hold he thought I was intitled to long ago.

"Your Excellency will forgive me the Liberty I take in troubling you in this affair—Unacquiented as Congress may be out of my Services—by the different promotions already granted to many, Made me fearfull of puting me at last in the oblivion List of a General promotion.

"One word from your Excellency to Congress in my favor (if I can flater my self to obtain it) will Clear the doubt and rise my hope to certainty."[25]

22 Garden, *Anecdotes,* II, 430.
23 Haiman, *op. cit.,* 120.
24 Fitzpatrick, XXVII, 180.
25 Aug. 26, 1783, Washington Papers, vol. 225 (1783, Sept. 5-Oct. 9).

Assuring Kosciuszko: "I heartily wish your application to meet with success,"[26] Washington wrote to the President of Congress:

"I do myself the honor to transmit your Excellency copy of a Letter I have received from Colonel Kosciuszko—on the subject of his promotion.

"The General promotion now before Congress, should it take place, would have included him—but this does not seem to be his wish—as a Foreigner—I suppose a particular promotion would be more consonant to his views and interest—and from my knowledge of his merit and service and the concurrt. testimony of all who knew him I cannot but recommend him as deserving the favor of Congress."[27]

However, the endeavor of Kosciuszko and the letter of Washington were too late. A general promotion of one grade by brevet to all officers who received no promotion since January 1, 1777, was passed by Congress on September 20. This "oblivion List" included also Kosciuszko. However, in consequence of Washington's letter, Congress tried to sugar for him their forgetfulness which, it would seem, was not accidental. The same committee, composed of Peters, Duane and McHenry examined the matter and on October 13, brought the following report:

"That the vote of the 30th day of September last past has already effected the promotion of Col. Kosciosko to the Rank of Brigadier General; nothing further on that subject can with propriety be done at this time; but as your Committee are deeply impressed with the great merit and beneficial services of that officer, they submit the following Resolve:

"Resolved, That the Secretary at War transmit to Colonel Kosciosko the brevet commission of brigadier general; and signify to that officer, that Congress entertain an high sense of his long, faithful and meritorious service."[28]

Even this modest recognition seemed still too dangerous to some members. In the final reading they stroke out "great" before "merit,"

26 Oct. 2, 1783, Fitzpatrick, XXVII, 174.

27 Oct. 3, 1783, ibid.

28 Journals Cont. Congr. XXV, 673. In 1933, the United States Government issued a commemorative stamp, showing Kosciuszko's monument at Washington, D. C., to honor the sesquicentennial anniversary of his promotion to Brigadier-Generalship.

and "beneficial" before "services," and in this form the report was accepted. That was all Congress found in their hearts to do for Kosciuszko and he accepted it without murmur.

At last formal peace became a fact. On November 2, Washington issued his Farewell Orders to "those he held most dear," though already the army became merely a skeleton force through furloughs and dissolution. Most probably Kosciuszko remained near headquarters at that time and the gift of Washington to him, a sword and a pair of pistols, might pertain to this period.[29] Still another gift to Kosciuszko ascribed to Washington was connected with their membership in the Society of the Cincinnati. It was an antique cameo mounted in a ring which Washington himself received as a souvenir from the Cincinnati.[30] It cannot be ascertained when Kosciuszko was admitted to this military Order, the purpose of which was "to perpetuate those friendships which have been formed during a time of common danger and distress."[31] However, his signature appears on the "Parchment Roll,"[32] and it is known that he contributed a month's pay to the treasury of the Order, as required by its "Institution."[33] Perhaps he joined it through the intermediary of Lafayette whom Washington asked to invite the foreign officers.[34]

On November 25, Kosciuszko took part in the triumphal entry of Washington into New York.[35] Most authorities agree that he was present in the "long room" of Fraunces' Tavern, on December

---

[29] The sword, preserved in the National Museum in Warsaw, had an engraved Latin inscription: "America cum Vashington suo Amico T. Kosciusconi," on the reverse another Latin legend: "Mater Dei ora pro nobis," and Polish: "With God, all together and boldly"; the two latter inscriptions evidently added afterwards. According to a story attached to the sword, it was carried by Kosciuszko during his Insurrection of 1794. The pistols, property of the National Museum in Cracow, were richly ornamented with gold and bronze; their wooden parts were of mahogany; their barrels were engraved: "G. Washington 17 E Pluribus Unum 83 Th. Kosciuszko" (Buczkowski, "Bezcenne pamiątki," Światowid, IX, no. 9, p. 21).

[30] Girardot, L'Ordre Américain, 50; Mag. of Am. History, IV (1880), 158; Keim, Rochambeau, 601.

[31] Washington to Conrad Alexandre Gérard, Oct. 29, 1783, Fitzpatrick, XXVII, 210.

[32] Roster signed by original members of the Cincinnati who were not then members of any State Societies.

[33] Hume, Poland and the Society of the Cincinnati, 7; Thomas, Members of the Soc. of the Cin., 90; Metcalf, Original Members, 188. It was not necessary to pay the initiation fee in cash; officers only signed an assignment on the Paymaster General for one month's pay to be deducted from the balance after the liquidation of their accounts (Saffell, Records, 478).

[34] Oct. 20, 1783, Fitzpatrick, XXVII, 202.

[35] He is shown in the suite of Washington, in Polish coat, on a contemporary engraving reproduced in Ellis' and Horne's The Story of the Greatest Nations, IX, 1586.

4, "when the principal officers of the army assembled . . . to take a final leave of their much-beloved commander-in-chief. Soon after, his excellency entered the room. His emotions were too strong to be concealed. Filling a glass, he turned to them, and said, 'With a heart full of love and gratitude, I now take leave of you. I most devoutly wish that your latter days may be as prosperous and happy as your former ones have been glorious and honorable.' Having drank, he added, 'I cannot come to each of you to take my leave, but shall be obliged to you, if each of you will come and take me by the hand.' General Knox, being nearest, turned to him. Incapable of utterance, Washington, in tears, grasped his hand, embraced and kissed him. In the same affectionate manner he took leave of each succeeding officer. In every eye was the tear of dignified sensibility; and not a word was articulated to interrupt the eloquent silence and tenderness of the scene. Leaving the room, he passed through a corps of light-infantry, and walked to White Hall, where a barge waited to convey him to Paulus' Hook. The whole company followed in mute and solemn procession."[36]

And so in tears of deep emotion the military career of Kosciuszko in the American Revolution was closed forever.

---

[36] Thacher, *Military Journal,* 346.

Chapter XVII

DEPARTURE FOR POLAND

Instead of returning from New York to Baltimore, as he promised Gen. Williams, Kosciuszko availed himself of an invitation of General and Mrs. Greene and visited them in their Newport home. His stay there prolonged itself. The hosts were hospitable and old colleagues-in-arms quite readily gathered around them to retell their stories of common experiences. There "Lafayette passed pleasant days, talking hopefully of the future of his France, . . . Steuben told entertaining stories of the Great Frederick, . . . Kosciusko painted in imperfect English the wrongs of Poland, and Gordon questioned the actors in the scenes which his homely but honest pen was busily recording for posterity."[1] In some of the families of Newport the memory of Kosciuszko's sojourn in the town remained alive almost to this day.[2] He evidently visited his other friends in the vicinity, among them Col. Jeremiah Wadsworth at Hartford,[3] former Commissary General, whom he knew from his Northern Campaign.

Meanwhile Gen. Williams, awaiting his friend in vain, was becoming patient. Informing Gen. Greene on January 14, that a Sophia refused him her hand, he added: "Kosciuszko will be petrified at all this if he hears it, but where he is, or how to let him know it (if I would make A Statue of him) I cannot imagine, for in his last he promised to be here a month ago."[4]

It is very probable that Kosciuszko was in Philadelphia at the time of the general meeting of the Society of the Cincinnati, from May 1 to 18, 1784. Generals Greene and Williams were there as state delegates, as well as Lt. Col. Morris, Col. White[5] and many

---

[1] Greene, *Life of Greene*, III, 522. The Rev. Gordon evidently took a liking to Kosciuszko. On April 5, 1784, writing to Greene, he mentioned him alone of all the guests of the General and asked to express to him "his best regards." (Gordon, "Letters," *Mass. Hist. Soc. Proceedings*, LXIII, 1931, 504).

[2] Mason, *Reminiscences*, 391, records that during his stay in Newport, Kosciuszko presented his grandmother with a beautifully carved ivory box which was preserved in the family. Kosciuszko was a fine turner, and possibly the box was made by himself.

[3] Wansey, *Journal*, 60.

[4] Rough copy in the Williams Papers, no. 236; the original in the Kahanowicz Coll., p. 38, no. 89.

[5] Anthony Walton White, Kosciuszko's companion of the Southern Campaign.

others of his friends.[6] If the supposition were true, it was there that he met Gen. Washington for the last time. Though their common relations never were so intimate, as for instance, of Washington and Lafayette, there is nothing in documents which would affirm the assertion of some writers that Washington purposely kept Kosciuszko at a distance because of his known friendship for Gates.[7] Because of their political prestige, Washington preferred to keep the Frenchmen on his staff, and there was no room for more engineers, but it is pure injustice to accuse him of some imagined dislike toward the modest and zealous Polish officer, whom he himself publicly praised and of whom all his superiors always spoke in warm terms. There is not a word of censure of him in Washington's letters; on the contrary, several times their correspondence strikes a note of cordiality. Circumstances kept them mostly at distant fields of action and Kosciuszko's unobtrusive modesty acted rather as a restraint, but, the least which may be said in this respect is that Washington's attitude toward the Pole was always very correct and openly friendly and that the latter evidently strove to repay it with loyalty and respect.

His presence in Philadelphia in May was all the more probable as he had still to settle his accounts. Evidently that was done sometime in June, perhaps even in the first days of July, though Greene still in December tried to interpose again with Morris in behalf of Kosciuszko.[8] On May 4, 1783, Duportail and the majority of the officers of the Corps of Engineers signed an agreement to accept the commutation of the half-pay, as required by the law.[9] At that time Kosciuszko was still in the South, or on his way to Philadelphia, and though he did not sign the paper, it was binding him as well. The accounts of the remaining French engineers were ultimately adjusted early in 1784, most probably on the basis of the settlement with Duportail. On the same principle, Kosciuszko received a certificate for $12,280.49, bearing interest at six per cent, from January 1, 1784,[10] which was to be paid to him annually by drafts on Paris.[11] He was also entitled to five hundred acres of public land, but at that

---

[6] Sargent, "Journal," Hist. Soc. of Pa., *Contributions*, VI, *passim*.

[7] The most extreme on this point seems to be Kite, "Gen. Washington," *Records Am. Cath. Hist. Soc.*, XLIV (1933), 275.

[8] Morris to Greene, Dec. 19, 1783, Kahanowicz, p. 38, no. 90; the catalogue wrongly dates the letter as of 1787; evidently it pertains to 1783; Greene died in 1786.

[9] Papers Cont. Cong., no. 149, vol. 31, f. 393.

[10] *Amer. State Papers*, XIX, 207.

[11] According to a law of Feb. 3, 1784, *Journals Cont. Cong.*, XXVI, 65.

time the grant had still little practical value to him. Morris tried to be as liberal in providing Kosciuszko with cash, as the letter of the law and the state of the treasury allowed, as is evidenced by a letter written by the Pole just before his departure from New York: "Your generous behavior towards me, so intirely took hold of my heart that forgeting your uncommon delicat feelings, I am force, by a great uneasiness of my mind, to present my warmest thanks to you, before I quit this country; and to assure you that your kindness will be always fresh in my memory with the gratitude I owe you, and shall endeavour to put in practice what susceptibility now sugest the means to adopt."[12] Most probably, however, the money in cash which Kosciuszko received, amounted comparatively to very little.

Contrary to the common belief, Kosciuszko was never accorded American citizenship. Aptly said an author[13] that his deeds naturalized him as an American, but he never passed through the formality of naturalization.[14] Throughout the war he served with the intention of returning to Poland after its end.

When at last he was free to go, he parted with America with sincere regret and with a hope that, perhaps if affairs in Poland would not be very propitious for him, he would return to the new country with which he grew so familiar. On July 9, the day of his departure from Philadelphia for New York, where he was to board a vessel for Europe, he wrote to Williams:

"At last the necessity force me to quit this Country, you may be sure with great reluctance, as I have so many acquiantence amongst

---

12 Bancroft's Revol. Papers, vol. II, f. 479. This copy is wrongly dated as of July 17; on that day Kosciuszko was already at sea, and most probably the correct date of the letter is July 14, when he wrote his other farewell letters. On the basis of this letter Kozlowski ventured a supposition that Morris loaned his own money to Kosciuszko for his return trip to Europe ("Ostatnie Lata," *Przegląd Hist.*, X, 366), which is hardly plausible. There is an entirely fantastic Polish account of an American lady who fell in love with Kosciuszko and gave him funds for his passage to Poland (Kraszewski, *Pamiętnik*, 121-2). That Kosciuszko received little cash may be assumed from the fact that still in January, 1784, Col. Pickering complained that officers received no pay for six months and just a few dollars cash "to enable them to travel home without begging." (to Mr. Hodgdon, Jan. 12, 1784, Pickering, *Life of Pickering*, I, 493).

13 Armstrong, *Heroes.*

14 There are no references in this regard in the *Journals Cont. Cong.;* the laws of thirteen colonies have been examined by the Superintendent of the Library of Congress in 1933, to determine the possibility of Kosciuszko's having been accorded the privilege of state citizenship, but no such references have been found (Report of the Superintendent, June 9, 1933, to Congressman J. Lesinski).

the number, some are very valuable friends, for whom no boundary can be afixed of my affection.

"You thought I believe to this time that my friendship for you was always of *torrid Zone* warmth, but you are mistaken and I forgive you without retaliation, as I keep no Looking glace (glass) in my bossom to anable you to see the inward emotion of my heart.

"Believe me hoever few person are in the world for whom I have equal regard, or that their happiness was more at my heart as yours —it is not my method to make parade of, and the circumstances not allow me to put in practice Conformable to my desire.

"I would be happy to convince you of one thing, that your friendship and kindness for me, never shall be vipe of (wiped off) out of my memory, by an circumstanc whatsoever.

"Of the Lottery of Chance I am prety well acquianted, for this reason I would Choose to make ample provision; that I might not be so much exposed to her Ladyship's caprice, you have in your power to oblidge me and, I ask you with the same Confidence I expect you will act with me, and this is— If Congress should make a peace establishment, that you would interest your self with the delegates of your state to apoint me a Chieff Ingenier with the rank of Brygadier General—

"You are one of the number (:and not the Last *N B:*) with whom I would be happy to correspond with, in Consequence your Letters must be very particular that not one thing should be omited as to your own private affairs and those of public nature.

"Already my feelings anticipate the pleasure I shall have one days in reading letters wrote by the hand, which, friendship unite(d) to me for ever — this you may say somthing of very romantic style — no — The mind fixing an object with Conviction have hard task to be separate with, and if the *necessity,* bad word (:I wish it was out of Dictionary in all languages:) force to the abscence, the imagination still find(s) the pleasure even in the shadow of that dear object . . . I must stop, am cal(l)ed to go in the stage to New York from whence I am to embark in French packet to L'orient and I have time only to wish you happiness, adieu, once more adieu."[15]

---

[15] Williams Papers, no. 262.

Reaching New York, Kosciuszko repeated his request as to his appointment as Chief Engineer in a letter to Greene, and in heartfelt words took leave of the General: "The principal of propryety inculcated in my early age, have so strong hold of my feelings, that, to act against inward Conviction makes me very unhappy indeed.— As I must part, give me leave to present my sincere thanks to you both, for so generous hospitality I experienced in your house, for so much interesting your self in my favor, and for your friendship for me, — your delicat feeling forbids me to express of my Greatitude, and the wishes of my heart—I leave to the strogle of my inward emotion; and the practice to time; whenever opportunity will present its self without knowledge to you. — The separation must be very sensible to a Person of susceptible mind and more so when the affection with Esteem links to the person of Merit."—He begged the General that he would write to him and give him a "very minutely an account" of all events of personal and public nature, "as by long staying here I have form a partiality for this Country and for its Inhabitants, and would equally within (where ever I should be) feel the sentiment of good patriot upon every occasion.— Farewell my dear General, once more farewell, be as happy as my Bosom augur for you, Let me shook here you by the hand by my delusive Imagination, as you should be present in Person, and Seal our friendship for each other for ever."[16]

Most probably Kosciuszko had a chance to take leave of Gen. Gates personally, either in Philadelphia or in New York; turning his back upon the now empty Traveller's Rest after the death of his wife, he was at that time in the North. Major Jackson,[17] Gen. Paterson and other comrades flocked to New York to shake Kosciuszko's hand for the last time; there must have been quite a numerous gathering of officers at the wharf, inasmuch as Col. Humphreys, his companion of the Northern Campaign, recently appointed secretary to a commission which was to conclude commercial treaties with European powers, was to sail aboard the same vessel. Still another veteran of the Revolution to accompany them was Col. Christian Senf, "an honest German,"[18] who made the Southern campaign together with Kosciuszko. Good-byes and presents were exchanged; Paterson presented Kosciuszko with what was perhaps

---

16 July 14, 1784, Kahanowicz, p. 13, no. 28.
17 Jackson to Williams, July 20, 1784, Williams Papers, no. 265.
18 Humphreys, "An Epistle to Dr. Dwight," *Miscellaneous Works,* 213.

the most original gift; he gave him his faithful black servant Grippy, whom Kosciuszko learned to like so well during his West Point days; but Grippy unable to decide on so long a voyage and a separation from his master, disappeared somewhere just before the departure of the ship.[19]

On Thursday, July 15, 1784, the Courier de l'Europe with Kosciuszko aboard set her sails eastward.[20] Almost full eight years of his life, spent on the American soil, were now behind him; though all the contemporary letters speak of him as young man, he was already in his thirty-ninth year of life; evidently he looked much younger than he was in fact. What were his feelings at that moment, when his ship began to retire from the land and when the outlines of New York and of the New World began to melt with the horizon?

The American Revolution ultimately shaped Kosciuszko's character. It deepened and widened his thoughts. It taught him the practical meaning of these ideas which were inborn in him and which he tried to fathom in theory in his youth. He was returning to Poland with an important military experience, but, above all, with a new political and social vision. His American experiences became the foundation of his future rôle in Poland which so strongly influenced all her subsequent history.

"When I think, Sir, that with three million people, and without money you have shaken off the yoke of such a power as England, and have acquired such an extensive territory, — and that Poland has suffered herself to be robbed of five million souls and a vast country, — I acknowledge, I do not understand the cause of such a difference."

So wrote Wengierski in his farewell letter to John Dickinson not long before,[21] and undoubtedly Kosciuszko also often made similar comparisons in his yearning thoughts; but if Wengierski could find no answer to his doubts, there were no doubts in Kosciuszko's mind

---

[19] Lee, "Address," N. Y. Geneal. and Biogr. Record, XXI (1890), 109.

[20] Humphreys, Life of David Humphreys, I, 307.

[21] This letter was often reproduced in America as written by Kosciuszko, Niles Register, XIII (1817-8), 383-4. Even Kozlowski did not perceive the error, quoting excerpts from it in his article "A Visit," Century Mag., LXIII (1901-2), 512; however he made the proper correction in his later article "Ostatnie Lata," loc. cit., 374.

as to the causes of the different lots of both countries. His later career was his reply to the question, so painful to his patriotic heart.

* * *

Kosciuszko and his colleagues had a very agreeable journey. The vessel was comfortable, the weather exceptionally fine, the passengers "well-bred, discreet and free." There were "pleasant liquors and well-flavour'd food." Col. Humphreys, in a poetic vent, described the journey quite punctiliously in an "epistle" to Dr. Timothy Dwight and, of course, did not omit to introduce all his companions to him:

> "Him first, known in war full well,
> Our Polish friend,[22] whose name still sounds so hard,
> To make it rhyme would puzzle any bard;
> That youth, whose bays and laurels early crown'd,
> For virtue, science, arts and arms renown'd.[23]

They arrived at L'Orient, France, on August 8, after a "most delightful" passage of twenty-four days.[24] Advising Washington of the fact, Humphreys wrote him on August 12:

"General Kosciusko and myself are to set off in a Carriage together for Paris tomorrow."

In a post-script he added: "Gen'l Kosciusko desires his best respects may be presented to your Ex^y"[25]

The comrades spent a few days together at Paris. Most probably Kosciuszko, who knew the city well, served as cicerone to Col. Humphreys. But his joy of his being so near to his country again, was already dimmed by that peculiar feeling experienced by many who return to Europe after a prolonged stay in America. While in the New World they yearn for their native country, but when they reach it, their hankering turns into disappointment. They find new conditions, so different from those which they left and which they carried in their memory. They begin to feel themselves strangers in their own homes and among their kindred. They begin to pine for America. This unhappy state of mind of Kosciuszko, augmented

---

22 Kosciuszko knew Dwight from the Northern Campaign and, most probably met him in Connecticut during his stay with Gen. Greene, Cuningham, *Dwight,* 69.

23 Humphreys, "Epistle," *loc. cit.,* 213.

24 Humphreys, *Life of Humphreys,* I, 307.

25 *Ibid.,* I, 314.

by the pre-revolutionary atmosphere of France and by bad news about Poland and his family affairs, which reached him soon after landing, is clearly shown in his letter to Gen. Williams written on the eve of his departure from Paris:

"I will not entertain you with the Eligency or afluence of Paris and the other places; because it will (not) give any real pleasure to me or to you. We require more solid food to our unbiased sentyment, and we are sensible of the strict conexion which nature assigned to peace the innocence, the riches to industry, to tranquility the valour, and the enjoiment of Liberty — dear Word — I wish my Country feel its influence. — Can you believe I am very unhappy been absent from your Country it seems to me the other world her, in which every person finds great pleasure in cheating himself out of common sense. The time may have some power to preposses my mind in your Countrys favour and adopt the opinion of greater number of men, but Nature more, it is in every breast, here they take great pains to subside the Charmes which constitute real happiness, but you folow with full speed the marked road, and you fined (find) by experience that domestic Life with liberty to be the best gift, that nature had to bestow for the human specie.—To morow I am going to Poland and with some reluctance as am informed by one of my countrymen that the affairs of the republick as well as mine are in a very horrid situation, you shall know it in my next. — I must prepare for the worst, perhaps you will see me again in your country, for this reason you must use your influence in Congress in my favor, and write me as soon as you can."[26]

About the middle of September, exactly nine years after he left Poland, he returned to her, far from being happy, undecided as to his future, with little money and with meager prospects for a chance "to be of use to his country."

[26] Kahanowicz, p. 14, no. 29.

BIBLIOGRAPHY

Kościuszko, Biografia z Dokumentów Wysnuta (Kraków, 1894), by Thaddeus Korzon (1839-1917), a prominent Polish historian, still remains the best full-fledged biography of Kosciuszko.

No other author attempted to cover the subject on such a grandiose scale, and though hundreds of books, pamphlets and articles have been published about the hero during the many decades since his death, to Korzon's work still belongs the distinction of being the most exhaustive and the best documented biography, at least as far as it covers the European career of Kosciuszko. Indeed, the weakest part in Korzon's efforts was Kosciuszko's role in the American Revolution and his connections with America. He had no chance to make a research in the American archives and in this regard had to rely almost entirely on a few secondary sources which he was able to find in Europe.

His omissions—and his errors which were inevitable in such conditions, were subsequently supplemented and corrected by two authors who, though both working about the same time, had no knowledge of the other, or any mutual contact. The first one was Władysław Mieczysław Kozłowski (1858-1935), a Polish naturalist, philosopher and historian, and the other Martin I. J. Griffin (1842-1911), an American Catholic historian. Kozłowski made a lecturing visit to the United States at the end of the last century and utilized this as an occasion for research into the documents pertaining to the participation of Poles in the American Revolution. He was the first to look at the Gates Papers and other important manuscript material as sources for a biography of Kosciuszko. He published the fruit of his labors in a series of monographs on Pulaski, Kosciuszko, Beniowski and others, which, however, hidden in Polish literary or historical magazines, became hardly accessible to the general public. The American career of Kosciuszko was described by him in three articles on the Revolution: "Pierwszy rok służby amerykańskiej Kościuszki," "Kościuszko w West Point," and "Ostatnie lata amerykańskiej służby Kościuszki," which all appeared in the *Przegląd Historyczny* (Warszawa), in 1909, 1915 and 1918 respectively: his fourth article of the series, "Washington and Kosciuszko," has been published posthummously as vol. VII of the *Annals of the Polish Roman Catholic Union Archives and Museum* (Chicago, 1942). The second visit of Kosciuszko in America has been covered by Kozlowski in his essay: "Pobyt Kościuszki i Niemcewicza w Ameryce (w latach 1797 i 1798)," which appeared in the *Biblioteka Warszawska* in 1906. These five articles by him constituted hitherto the most reliable and complete story of Kosciuszko in America.

Griffin who also made quite an exhaustive research into the manuscript material, published its results in an extensive chapter "General Thaddeus Kościuszko," forming a part of his three-volumed work *Catholics and the*

American Revolution (Philadelphia, 1907-11) ; it appeared also in *The American Catholic Historical Researches* (new series, vol. VII, April, 1910, no. 2). Though perhaps less exact than Kozlowski's, Griffin's monograph still is a valuable and quite a reliable account of Kosciuszko in America.

Of other biographers of Kosciuszko only two more deserve our attention. One was Prof. Adam Skałkowski (1877-) of the University of Poznań who published a pamphlet *Kościuszko w Świetle Nowszych Badań* (Poznań, 1924) in which he was the first one to try to supplement Korzon and Kozłowski with the Kosciuszko papers collected in this country by the late Dr. Alexander Kahanowicz of Brooklyn and Detroit, and brought to Poland shortly before that year for a temporary exhibit. Skałkowski's pamphlet became, however, an iconoclastic attempt at the nimbus surrounding the memory of Kosciuszko. The attempt was ineffective; it was refuted by most prominent Polish historians; the author tried to write authoritatively on the subject without regard to a possibility that many more documents pertaining to Kosciuszko might still be hidden in the American archives; his additional error was an incomplete knowledge of the American background and a general misconception of Kosciuszko's character.

The other biographer to deserve mention was Monica Gardner (-1941), an English writer, who published *Kosciuszko, a Biography* (London and New York, 1920). This work may be considered as an abstract of Korzon. Written in a popular style, the chief value of the book consists of being the only extant biography of the Polish-American hero in the English language. However, the work is entirely too superficial; the author encompassed Kosciuszko's services in the Revolution in a single chapter of 16 pages, and his second visit to America in 6 pages.

Most of the innumerable other books, pamphlets and articles on Kosciuszko in Polish, English and other languages are based on secondary sources, sometimes entirely legendary, in regard to his connections with America, and are, for the most part, of little consequence. Works of Korzon, Kozłowski and Griffin are out of print and rather rare. Gardner's work is insufficient. Since the original researches of Kozłowski and Griffin many new documents came to light; the access to others was made easier. Many manuscript sources are used here for the first time in connection of a biography of Kosciuszko. The author supposes that he was able to collect a quite complete material, of primary importance, on the subject, and that only some scattered documents, of minor importance, escaped his attention.

Because of the present emergency he was obliged to omit one letter of Kosciuszko, Fogg Collection, ALS, 2 pages, undated, preserved by the Maine Historical Society, Portland, Me.; together with other documents it was removed to a place of safety before the author was able to get a copy of it.

MANUSCRIPT SOURCES

American Antiquarian Society, Worcester, Mass., Orderly books of Philip Schuyler and Henry B. Livingston.

American Philosophical Society, Philadelphia, Pa., Franklin Papers, Correspondence relating to the American Revolution of Maj. Gen. N. Greene.

Archives and Museum of the Polish Roman Catholic Union, Chicago, Kosciuszko Papers.

Connecticut State Library, Hartford, Conn., Letter book of John Fitch, Orderly books of Nathan Savage.

Harvard College Library, Cambridge, Mass., Jared Sparks Papers.

Historical Society of Pennsylvania, Philadelphia, Pa., Dreer Collection, Etting Papers, Gratz Collection, Wayne Papers.

Henry E. Huntington Library and Art Gallery, San Marino, Cal., Greene Papers.

Library of Congress, Washington, D. C., Letter book of Nathanael Greene (1781), Papers of the Continental Congress, Washington Papers and miscellaneous documents.

Maryland Historical Society, Baltimore, Md., Otho Holland Williams Papers.

Massachusetts Historical Society, Boston, Mass., Heath and Pickering Papers.

The National Archives, Washington, D. C., Revolutionary War Papers.

New York Historical Society, New York, N. Y., Gates and McDougall Papers.

New York Public Library, Bancroft's Revolutionary Papers, Emmet Collection and miscellaneous papers.

South Carolina Historical Society, Charleston, S. C., one letter of Kosciuszko.

William L. Clements Library, Ann Arbor, Mich., Greene Papers.

Several letters of Kosciuszko quoted for sale by autograph dealers.

The Kahanowicz-Wachowski collection of Kosciuszko's papers. Its history is as follows: A collection of Greene's correspondence in the possession of his family contained 26 letters of Kosciuszko, mostly pertaining to his service in the South. This collection was sold to a dealer in autographs in New York (J. F. Jameson, "Papers of Major-Gen. Nathanael Greene," *Publications of the R. I. Hist. Soc.,* new ser., III, 1895, 164). In the course of time most of the letters reappeared in the collection of Kosciuszko papers of the late Dr. Alexander Kahanowicz of Brooklyn and Detroit. In 1927, Dr. Kahanowicz exhibited the collection at the Anderson Galleries in New York and at that time published a catalogue *Memorial Exhibition—Thaddeus Kosciuszko, etc.* containing excerpts from the letters. Thereafter he was still able to enlarge the collection by a few letters, but about 1930 the whole collection became the property of the late Rev. Joseph P. Wachowski of Toledo, O. At the present moment the estate of the latter is under the care of probate courts.

PRIMARY PRINTED SOURCES

American State Papers, Documents, Legislative and Executive of the Congress of the United States, Washington, 1834, Claims, vol. XIX.

(Angell, Israel.) Diary of Colonel Israel Angell, Commanding the Second Rhode Island Continental Regiment during the American Revolution, 1778-1781, transcribed from the Original Manuscript together with a Biographical Sketch of the Author and Illustrative Notes, by Edward Field, Providence, 1899.

(Baldwin, Jeduthan.) "Baldwin Letters," *American Monthly Magazine*, Washington, vol. VI (1895), pp. 193-200.

——"The Revolutionary Diary of Jeduthan Baldwin," *The Bulletin of the Fort Ticonderoga Museum*, Ticonderoga, vol. IV (1938).

——The Revolutionary Diary of Col. Jeduthan Baldwin, 1775-1778, ed. by Thomas William Baldwin, Bangor, 1906.

Baxter, James Phinney. The British Invasion from the North. The Campaigns of Generals Carleton and Burgoyne from Canada, 1776-1777, with the Journal of Lieut. William Digby, of the 53d, or Shropshire Regiment of Foot, Albany, 1887.

(Blanchard, Claude.) The Journal of Claude Blanchard, Commissary of the French Auxiliary Army sent to the United States during the American Revolution, 1780-1783, translated by William Duane, edited by Thomas Balch, Albany, 1876.

Chastellux, Marquis de. Travels in North-America in the Years 1780, 1781 and 1782, London, 1787, 2 vols.

A Collection of Papers Relative to Half-pay and Commutation of Half-pay, granted by Congress to the Officers of the Army, compiled by Permission of His Excellency General Washington, from the Original Papers in his Possession, Fish-Kill, 1783.

(Clinton, George.) Public Papers of George Clinton, ed. by Hugh Hastings and J. A. Holden, Albany, 1899-1914, 10 vols.

(Deane, Silas.) The Deane Papers, *Collections of the New York Historical Society,* New York, vols. 19-23 (1887-91).

(Dearborn, Henry.) Revolutionary War Journals of Henry Dearborn, 1775-1783, Caxton Club, Chicago, 1939.

(Denny, Ebenezer.) "Military Journal of Major Ebenezer Denny," *Memoirs of the Historical Society of Pennsylvania,* Philadelphia, vol. VII (1860).

(Du Roi, the Elder.) "Journal of Du Roi the Elder," *German American Annals,* Philadelphia, vol. XIII (1911).

The (Boston) *Evening Post and General Advertiser,* Oct. 17 and 24, 1778.

Force, Peter. American Archives, consisting of a Collection of Authentic Records, State Papers, Debates and Letters, Washington, 1837-53, fifth series, vols. I-III.

Garden, Alexander. Anecdotes of the American Revolution with Sketches of Character of Persons the Most Distinguished, in the Southern States, for Civil and Military Services, second edition, edited by T. W. Field, Brooklyn, 1865, 3 vols.

(Gérard, Conrad Alexandre.) Despatches and Instructions of Conrad Alexandre Gérard, 1778-1780, Correspondence of the First French Minister to the United States with the Comte de Vergennes, ed. by John J. Meng, Baltimore, 1939.

Gibbes, R. W., M.D. Documentary History of the American Revolution, consisting of Letters and Papers, relating to the Contest for Liberty, chiefly in South Carolina, Columbia and New York, 1853-1857, 3 vols.

(Glover, John.) Memoir of General John Glover of Marblehead; ed. by William Upham, (from the *Historical Collections of the Essex Institute*) Salem, 1863.

(Gordon, William.) "Letters of the Rev. William Gordon, Historian of the American Revolution, 1770-1799," *Massachusetts Historical Society Proceedings,* Boston, vol. LXIII (1931).

(Greene, Nathaniel.) "Letters to General Greene and Others," ed. by Joseph W. Barnwell, *The South Carolina Historical and Genealogical Magazine,* Charleston, vol. XVI (1915).

(Heath, William.) Heath's Memoirs of the American War, ed. by Rufus Rockwell Wilson, New York, 1904.

——"The Heath Papers," *Massachusetts Historical Society Collections,* Boston, ser. 5, vol. IV (1878), and ser. 7, vols. IV and V (1904-05).

Humphreys, David. The Miscellaneous Works, New York, 1804.

(Jefferson, Thomas.) The Writings of Thomas Jefferson, ed. by Andrew A. Lipscomb, Washington, 1903-05, 20 vols.

——The Writings of Thomas Jefferson, ed. by Henry A. Washington, Washington, 1853-4, 9 vols.

Jordan, John W. "Bethlehem during the Revolution, Extracts from the diaries in the Moravian Archives at Bethlehem, Pa.," *Pennsylvania Magazine of History and Biography,* Philadelphia, vol. XIII (1889).

(Kosciuszko, Thaddeus.) Memorial Exhibition, Thaddeus Kosciuszko, the Revered Polish and American Hero, His Patriotism, Vision and Zeal Revealed in a Collection of Autograph Letters . . . the Collection formed by Dr. and Mrs. Alexander Kahanowicz, New York, n. d.

——"Kosciuszko to Gen. Williams," ed. by B. J. Lossing, *American Historical Record,* Philadelphia, vol. I (1872).

——Kosciuszko to Maj. Alexander Garden," *The South Carolina Historical and Genealogical Magazine,* Charleston, vol. II (1900), pp. 126-7.

——"Listy Kościuszki do Przyjaciół Amerykańskich i Inne," ed. by Adam Skałkowski, *Przegląd Historyczny,* Warszawa, vol. VI, second series (1924).

——"Original Letters," *New York Genealogical and Biographical Record,* New York, vol. II, 1871, No. 1. (Kościuszko's letter to Dr. Read).

(Lafayette, Marquis de.) "Letters from the Marquis de Lafayette to Hon. Henry Laurens, 1777-1780," *The South Carolina Historical and Genealogical Magazine*, Charleston, vols. VII-VIII (1906-07).

(Laurens, John.) The Army Correspondence of Colonel John Laurens in the Years 1777-8, now first printed from Original Letters addressed to his Father, Henry Laurens, President of Congress, ed. by William Gilmore Simms, New York, 1867.

(Lee, Charles.) The Lee Papers, *Collections of the New York Historical Society*, vols. IV-VII (1872-75).

Lee, Henry. The Campaign in the Carolinas; with the Remarks Historical and Critical on Johnson's Life of Greene, Philadelphia, 1824.

——Memoirs of the War in the Southern Department, Philadelphia, 1812, 2 vols.

(McDowell, William.) "Journal of Lt. William McDowell, of the First Pennsylvania Regiment in the Southern Campaign, 1781-1782," Pennsylvania Archives, Harrisburg, 1890, ser. 2, vol. XV.

Mackenzie, Roderick, late Lieutenant in the 71st Regt., Strictures on Lt. Col. Tarleton's History of the Campaigns of 1780-1781 in the Southern Provinces of North America, London, 1787.

(Markland, John.) "Revolutionary services of Captain John Markland," *Pennsylvania Magazine of History and Biography*, Philadelphia, vol. IX (1885), pp. 109-11.

Moore, Frank. Diary of the American Revolution, from Newspapers and Original Documents, New York and London, 1860, 2 vols.

(Morris, Lewis.) "Letters to General Lewis Morris," *Collections of the New York Historical Society*, New York, VIII (1875).

——"Letters from Col. Lewis Morris to Miss Ann Elliot," ed. by Morris Rutherford, *The South Carolina Historical and Genealogical Magazine*, Charleston, vol. XLI (1940).

(Morris, Robert.) The Confidential Correspondence of Robert Morris, ed. by Stanislaus V. Henkels, Philadelphia, n. d.

Moultrie, William. Memoirs of the American Revolution, New York, 1802, 2 vols.

The (Fishkill) *New York Packet,* Sept. 17, 24; Oct. 8, 29, 1778.

Niles' Register, Baltimore, vol. XIII (1817-8).

North Carolina Historical Commission, The State Records of North Carolina, Goldsboro, 1886-1914, 30 vols.

Pennsylvania Archives, Harrisburg and Philadelphia, ser. 5, vol. III; ser. 2, vol. XV.

Pennsylvania Colonial Records, Harrisburg and Philadelphia, 1852, vol. X.

(Putnam, Rufus.) The Memoirs of Rufus Putnam and Certain Official Papers and Correspondence, comp. by Rowena Buell, Boston and New York, 1903.

(Richards, Samuel.) Diary of Samuel Richards, Captain of Connecticut Line, War of the Revolution, 1775-1781, Philadelphia, 1909.

(Riedesel, General.) Memoirs, and Letters and Journals, of Major General Riedesel, during his Residence in America. Transl. from the original German of Max von Eelking, by William L. Stone, Albany, 1868.

Saffell, William T. R. Records of the Revolutionary War, Baltimore, 1894.

(St. Clair, Arthur.) "Proceedings of a General Court Martial, held at White Plains in the State of New York, by Order of His Excellency General Washington, for the Trial of Arthur St. Clair, August 25, 1778, Philadelphia 1778, *Collections of the New York Historical Society,* New York, vol. XIII (1880).

Sargent, Major Winthrop. Journal of the General Meeting of the Cincinnati in 1784, ed. by Winthrop Sargent, Contributions to American History, Historical Society of Pennsylvania, Philadelphia, 1858.

(Seymour, William.) "A Journal of the Southern Expedition by William Seymour, Sergeant-Major of the Delaware Regiment," *Papers of the Historical Society of Delaware,* Wilmington, vol. XV (1896).

(Shaw, Samuel.) The Journals of Major Samuel Shaw, the First American Consul at Canton, with a Life of the Author, by Josiah Quincy, Boston, 1847.

Stevens, Benjamin Franklin. Facsimiles of Manuscripts in European Archives Relating to America, 1773-1783, London, 1889-98, 25 vols.

Tarleton, (Banastre), Lt. Col. A History of the Campaigns of 1780 and 1781 in the Southern Provinces of North America, London, 1787.

Thacher, James, M.D. Military Journal during the American Revolutionary War, from 1775 to 1783, Hartford, 1862.

(Towarzystwo Historyczno-Literackie w Paryżu). *Rocznik Towarzystwa Historyczno-Literackiego w Paryżu za rok 1866,* Paris, 1867.

Trumbull, John. Autobiography, Reminiscences and Letters of, from 1756 to 1841, New York and London, 1841.

(U. S. Continental Congress.) Journals of the Continental Congress, 1774-1789, ed. by W. C. Ford, G. Hunt, J. C. Fitzpatrick and R. R. Hill, Washington, 1904-37, 34 vols.

——Letters of Members of the Continental Congress, ed. by Edmund C. Burnett, Washington, 1921-36, 8 vols.

Wansey, Henry. The Journal of an Excursion to the United States in 1794, Salisbury, 1796.

(Washington, George.) The Writings of George Washington, from the Original Manuscript Sources, 1745-1799, ed. by John C. Fitzpatrick, Washington, 1931-40, 33 vols.

——The Writings of George Washington, ed. by Jared Sparks, Boston, 1834-37, 12 vols.

——*Annual Report and List of Members of the New York Historical Society for the Year 1941,* New York 1942, p. 17 (reproduction of a letter of Washington to McDougall pertaining to Kosciuszko).

————Correspondence of General Washington and Comte de Grasse, 1781, August 17-November 4, 71st Congress, 2nd Session, Senate Document No. 21, Washington, 1931.

————Correspondence of the American Revolution, being Letters of Eminent Men to George Washington, ed. by Jared Sparks, Boston, 1853, 4 vols.

(Webb, Samuel Blachley.) Correspondence and Journals of Samuel Blachley Webb, ed. by Washington Chauncey Ford, New York, 1893-4, 3 vols.

Wilkinson, James. Memoirs of My Own Times, Philadelphia, 1816, 3 vols.

SECONDARY SOURCES

Armstrong, William Jackson. The Heroes of Defeat, Cincinnati, 1905.

Askenazy, Prof. Szymon. Thaddeus Kosciuszko, London, n. d.

Baker, William S. Itinerary of General Washington from June 15, 1775, to December 23, 1783, Philadelphia, 1892.

Barlow, Joel. Columbiad, London, 1809.

Bellas, Henry Hobart. "The Defences of the Delaware River in the Revolution," Proceedings and Collections of the Wyoming Historical and Geological Society, Wilkes Barre, Pa., vol. V (1900).

Boyd, Thomas. Light-horse Harry Lee, New York and London, 1931.

Boynton, Major Edward C. History of West Point, New York, 1871.

Brandow, John Henry. The Story of Old Saratoga and History of Schuylerville, Saratoga Springs, 1906.

Brigham, Clarence S. "Bibliography of American newspapers, 1690-1820," part VII, New York, Proceedings of the American Antiquarian Society, Worcester, new series, vol. XXVII (1917).

Bryant, C. B. "General J. E. B. Stuart," The Virginia Magazine of History and Biography, Richmond, vol. XII (1905).

Buczkowski, K. "Bezcenne Pamiątki po Waszyngtonie i Kosciuszce," Swiatowid, Kraków, vol. IX, no. 9.

Campbell, Mrs. Maria. Revolutionary Services and Civil Life of General William Hull, New York and Philadelphia, 1848.

Carrington, Henry B. Battles of the American Revolution, 1775-1781, New York, Chicago and New Orleans, 1876.

Cuningham, Charles E. Timothy Dwight, 1752-1817, A Biography, New York, 1942.

Dzwonkowski, Włodzimierz A. "Młode Lata Kościuszki." Biblioteka Warszawska, Warszawa, vol. CCLXXXIV (1911).

Egleston, Thomas, LL.D. The Life of John Paterson, Major-General in the Revolutionary Army, New York and London, 1898.

————"Major Azariah Egleston of the Revolutionary Army," The New York Genealogical and Biographical Record, New York, vol. XXIII (1892).

Ellet, Elizabeth F. The Women of the American Revolution, Philadelphia, 1900, 2 vols.

Ellis, Edward S., A.M. and Horne, Charles F., Ph.D. The Story of the Greatest Nations . . . and the World's Famous Events, New York, 1921, vol. IX.

Falkenstein, Karol. Tadeusz Kosciuszko czyli Dokładny Rys Jego Życia, Wrocław (Breslau), 1827.

Freeman, Douglas Southall. R. E. Lee, A Biography, New York and London, 1934-5, 4 vols.

Girardot, M. le Baron de. L'Ordre Americain de Cincinnatus en France, Nantes, n. d.

Goodrich, S. G., ed. "The Fur Coat," The Token and Atlantic Souvenir. Boston, 1833.

Gordon, Jakób. Przechadzki po Ameryce, Berlin and Poznań, 1866.

Gordon, William, D.D., The History of the Rise, Progress, and Establishment, of the Independence of the United States of America: including an Account of the Late War; and of the Thirteen Colonies, from their Origin to that Period, London, 1788, 4 vols.

Gottschalk, Louis. Lafayette joins the American army, Chicago, 1937.

Greene, George W. Life of Nathanael Greene, Major General in the Army of the Revolution, Boston, 1871, 3 vols.

Griffin, Martin, I. J. "General Thaddeus Kosciuszko," Catholics and the American Revolution. Ridley Park, Pa., 1907-11, vol. III.

Haiman, Miecislaus. Poland and the American Revolutionary War, Chicago, 1932.

——Z Przeszłości Polskiej w Ameryce, Buffalo, N. Y., 1927.

Hall, Charles S. Life and Letters of Samuel Holden Parsons, Major-General in the Continental Army and Chief Judge of the Northwestern Territory, Binghamton, 1905.

Hatch, Louis Clinton. The Administration of the American Revolutionary Army, New York, 1904.

Hayner, Rutherford. Troy and Rensselaer County, N. Y., New York and Chicago, 1925, 3 vols.

Heitman, Francis B. Historical Register of Officers of the Continental Army during the War of the Revolution, Washington, 1914.

Hildreth, Samuel P. Biographical and Historical Memoirs of the Early Pioneer Settlers of Ohio, Cincinnati, 1852.

(Hill, M. L.). A Narrative shewing the Promises made to the Officers of the Line of the Continental Army, for their Services in the Revolutionary War, and, the Manner in which, and how far, these Promises have been fulfilled, Elizabeth Town, N. J., 1826.

Hume, Edgar Erskine. Poland and the Society of the Cincinnati, reprinted from the Polish-American Review, Chicago, vol. I (1935).

Humphreys, Frank Landon. Life and Times of David Humphreys, Soldier-Statesman-Poet, "Belov'd of Washington," New York, London, 1917, 2 vols.

Humphreys, Mary Gay. Catherine Schuyler, New York, 1897.

James, W. D. Sketch of the Life of Brig. Gen. Francis Marion, Charleston, 1821.

Jameson, J. F. "Papers of Major-General Nathanael Greene," *Publications of the Rhode Island Historical Society*, Providence, new series, vol. III (1895).

Johnson, Allen and Malone, Dumas, ed. Dictionary of American Biography. New York, 1928-36, 20 vols.

Johnson, Joseph. Traditions and Reminiscences chiefly of the American Revolution, Charleston, S. C., 1851.

Johnson, William. Sketches of the Life and Correspondence of Nathanael Greene, Charleston, 1822, 2 vols.

Jones, Mrs. William F. "Catherine Schuyler," *The American Monthly Magazine*, Washington, XIV (1899), pp. 164-8.

Jordan, John W. A History of Delaware County, Pa., and its People, New York, 1914, vol. I.

Kain, Henry C. The Military and Naval Operations on the Delaware in 1777, Publications of the City History Society of Philadelphia, no. 8, 1910.

Keim, D. Randolph. Rochambeau, 59th Congress, 1st Session, Senate Documents, no. 537, Washington, 1907.

Kite, Elizabeth S. "General Washington and the French Engineers: Duportail and companions," *Records of the American Catholic Historical Society of Philadelphia*, Philadelphia, vols. XLIII-XLV; also a reprint: Brigadier-General Louis Lebégne Duportail, Commandant of Engineers in the Continental Army, 1777-1783, Baltimore, 1933.

Knapp, Samuel L. Tales of the Garden of Kosciuszko, New York, 1834.

Knollenberg, Bernhard. Washington and the Revolution, a Reappraisal, New York, 1940.

Korzon, Tadeusz. Kosciuszko, Życiorys z Dokumentów Wysnuty, Kraków, 1894.

Kozlowski, Władysław M. "A Visit to Mt. Vernon a Century Ago," introduction by Worthington C. Ford, *Century Illustrated Monthly Magazine*, New York, vol. LXIII (1901-2) pp. 510-522.

——"Kosciuszko w West Point," *Przegląd Historyczny*, Warszawa, vol. X (1915).

——"Ostatnie Lata Amerykańskiej Służby Kościuszki," *Przegląd Historyczny*, vol. XIII (1918).

——"Pierwszy Rok Służby Amerykańskiej Kościuszki," *Przegląd Historyczny*, Warszawa, vol. IV (1909).

——Washington and Kosciuszko, Annals of the Polish R.C. Union Archives and Museum, vol. VII. Chicago, 1942.

Kraszewski, J. I. Pamiętnik Anegdotyczny z Czasów Stanisława Augusta, Poznań, 1867.

Lasseray, Commandant André. Les Français sous les Treize Etoiles, 1775-1783, Macon, 1935, 2 vols.

Lee, William Henry. "An Address on the Life and Character of Major General John Paterson, of the Revolutionary Army," *The New York Genealogical and Biographical Record*, New York, vol. XXI (1890).

Lodge, Henry Cabot. The Story of the Revolution, New York, 1898, 2 vols.

Lossing, Benson J. The Pictorial Field Book of the Revolution. New York, 1860, 2 vols.

McCants, E. C. History Stories and Legends of South Carolina, Dallas, 1929.

McCrady, Edward. The History of South Carolina in the Revolution, 1780-83, New York and London, 1902.

"Washington Cincinnatus," *Magazine of American History*, New York and Chicago, vol. IV (1880), p. 158.

Martineau, Harriet. Retrospect of Western Travel, London and New York, 1838, 2 vols.

Mason, George Champlin. Reminiscences of Newport, Newport, 1884.

Metcalf, Bryce. Original Members and Other Officers eligible to the Society of the Cincinnati, 1783-1939, Strasburg, Va., 1938.

Munsell, Joel. The Annals of Albany, 1850-59, 10 vols.

Neilson, Charles. An Original, Compiled and Corrected Account of Burgoyne's Campaign, and the Memorable Battles of Bemis' Heights, Sept. 19 and Oct. 7, 1777, Albany, 1844.

Nickerson, Hoffman. The Turning Point of the Revolution, or Burgoyne in America, Boston and New York, 1928.

Patterson, Samuel White. Horatio Gates, Defender of American Liberties, New York, 1941.

Petigru, Charles. An Oration, prepared for Delivery on the Occasion of Laying the Corner Stone of a Monument Erected to the Memory of Kosciuszko at West Point by the Corps of Cadets, July 4, 1828, Newburgh, 1828.

Pickering, Octavius. The Life of Timothy Pickering, Boston, 1867-73, 4 vols.

Polk, William M. Leonidas Polk, Bishop and General, New York, 1893, 2 vols.

Race, Henry. The two Colonels John Taylor, Flemington, N. J., 1892, Hunterdon Historical Series, no. 2.

Ramsay, David. History of the Revolution in South Carolina, Trenton, 1785, 2 vols.

——The History of South Carolina from its earliest Settlement in 1670 to the year 1808, Charleston, 1809, 2 vols.

Reed, William B. Life and Correspondence of Joseph Reed, Philadelphia, 1847, 2 vols.

Ridgely, Helen W. Historic Graves of Maryland and the District of Columbia, New York, 1908.

Roberts, Kenneth. Rabble in Arms, A Chronicle of Arundel and the Burgoyne Invasion, New York, 1933.

Sass, Ks. Józef, T. J. "Narodowość Tadeusza Kościuszki," *Przegląd Katolicki*, Milwaukee, vol. V (1930).

Schuyler, George L. Correspondence and Remarks upon Bancroft's History of the Northern Campaign of 1777, and the Character of Major-Gen. Philip Schuyler, New York, 1867.

Secretary of the Commonwealth, Massachusetts Soldiers and Sailors of the Revolutionary War, Boston, 17 vols, 1869-1908.

Simms, William Gilmore. The Scout, or the Black Riders of Congaree, New York, 1854.

Skałkowski, A. M. Kosciuszko w Świetle Nowszych Badań. Poznań, 1924.

Smith, William Henry. The St. Clair Papers. The Life and Public Servies of Arthur St. Clair, Cincinnati, 1882, 2 vols.

Stedman, Charles. The History of the Origin, Progress, and Termination of the American War, London, 1794, 3 vols.

Superintendent of the Library of Congress, report of, to Congressman John Lesinski, dated June 9, 1933, concerning Kosciuszko's American citizenship.

(Thomas, Frederick William.) The Polish Chiefs, an Historical Romance, New York, 1832, 2 vols.

Thomas, William S. Members of the Society of the Cincinnati, Original, Hereditary and Honorary, New York, 1929.

Trevelyan, Sir George Otto. The American Revolution, London and New York, 1899-1914, 4 vols.

Van Rensselaer, William K. Annals of the Van Rennsselaers in the United States, Albany, 1888.

Walworth, Mrs. Ellen Hardin. "Value of National Archives." *Annual Report of the American Historical Association for the year 1893*, Washington, 1894.

White, G. G. Life of Major General Henry Lee, Commander of Lee's Legion in the Revolutionary War, New York, 1859.

Wildes, Harry Emerson. Anthony Wayne, Trouble Shooter of the American Revolution, New York, 1941.

Wilson, Woodrow. A History of the American People, New York and London, 1902, 5 vols.

Winsor, Justin, ed. Narrative and Critical History of America, Boston and New York, 1884-1889, 8 vols.

ICONOGRAPHIC NOTES

Portrait of Kosciuszko by Joseph Grassi, belonging to the Polish Embassy at Washington, D. C., and reproduced here as frontispiece is one of the best portraits of Kosciuszko by this painter and one of the least known.

Kosciuszko's talent as an artist was rather meager. In fact, he never considered himself an artist, and treated art as his hobby. The chief value of his drawings is historical.

The author strove to collect and reproduce here all drawings by Kosciuszko pertaining to his part in the American Revolution; he was only partly successful.

The original caricature of Gen. Charles Lee is in the Historical Society of Pennsylvania, Peters Collection, vol. IX, p. 14. It was reproduced in the *Pennsylvania Magazine of History and Biography*, vol. XV (1891), p. 26. The drawing pertains to Lee's capture by the British in 1776.

The plan of the battlefield of Saratoga is said to have been drawn by Kosciuszko for his sister Anna Estko, after his return from America to Poland. The original drawing is in water-colors and till the present war was in the Zamoyski Library in Warsaw. It is reproduced here from Thaddeus Korzon's *Kim i Czem Był Kościuszko*, Warszawa, n.d., p. 48.

Portrait of Gen. Enoch Poor, now hanging in the State House at Concord, N. H., was painted by U. D. Tenney from a miniature made by Kosciuszko. According to the *New Hampshire Manual* for 1893, "the original painting was in an oval locket about two by one and one half inches. It was sketched in church, one Sunday, on the blank leaf of a copy of the New Testament, and was afterwards colored and presented by the artist to Colonel Poor, his personal friend. Col. Bradbury Poor Cilley inherited this locket from his mother, a daughter of Colonel Poor, who wore it as a breast pin until her death." For a description of this miniature see also: "Kosciuszko as an Artist," *Magazine of American History*, vol. VIII (1882), p. 440; Amos T. Akerman's *Sketch of the Military Career of Enoch Poor, Brig. Gen. in the Revolutionary War*, Manchester, 1878, p. 4; and B. F. Prescott's "Portraits of New Hampshire Governors, Judges, Senators," *The New England Historical and Genealogical Register*, vol. XXVIII (1874), p. 444. The present whereabouts of the original are unknown. Most probably Kosciuszko drew it either during the Northern Campaign of 1777, or while at West Point, sometime in 1780, when Poor was stationed there. According to J. T.'s "Kosciuszko as an Artist," *Mag. of Am. History*, VIII, 854, Kosciuszko also made a similar sketch of the Rev. John Mason, Chaplain of the New York line, which still at that time (1882) was preserved by his descendants as a faithful portrait.

The pen and ink sketch of Captain Judah Alden of Massachusetts is reproduced here from *The Memorial History of Boston, including Suffolk County, Mass.,* 1630-1830, ed. by Justin Winsor, Boston, 1880-1, 4 vols., vol. III, p. 99. According to a tradition, this drawing was made by Kosciuszko at Valley Forge in 1777, which does not agree with historical facts; most probably it was drawn during the Northern Campaign of 1777. The present possessor of the picture is unknown; in 1883, it was owned by Alden's descendants, according to W. G. A. and Charles Henry Stuart's "Kosciusko again," *Magazine of American History,* vol. IX (1883), p. 144.

The original map of West Point is in the New York Historical Society, McDougall Papers, book IV; it evidently pertains to Kosciuszko's letter to McDougall of April 25, 1779.

Two sketches of fortifications reproduced on page 75 are from the same source, book V. This book also contains a third sketch, similar to the upper drawing. All are marked as made by Kosciuszko, and evidently all three pertain to one of the redoubts at West Point. They are in black, gray and yellow ink, on heavy drawing paper. One of the sketches shows a hill in the extreme left, designated as "Putnam Heel."

The letter to Gen. Heath of April 24, 1780, is from the Massachusetts Historical Society, Heath Papers, vol. IX, p. 286. It is typical of Kosciuszko's candor.

The letter to Washington of July 30, 1780, is from the Historical Society of Pennsylvania, Gratz Collection, case 4, box 12. It shows Kosciuszko's penmanship at its best, which reflects his respect for the Commander-in-Chief.

The plan of Traveller's Rest is from the New York Historical Society, Gates Papers, box 21, no. 81.

The plan of Halifax accompanied Kosciuszko's letter to Greene of February 19, 1781, and the original is in the Huntington Library, Greene Papers, HM 8054.

The catalogue *Memorial Exhibition, Thaddeus Kosciuszko etc.* contains a reproduction of an oil portrait of Kosciuszko, attributed to John Trumbull.

Incidentally, the Archives and Museum of the Polish Roman Catholic Union, Chicago, has what is probably the largest collection of Kosciuszko's portraits in this country. It contains over one hundred prints, the oldest dating since 1792.

36; to Timothy Pickering, 29-30 and 30n., 142.

Trumbull, John, Lt. Col., 20n.

Trumbull, Jonathan, letters from George Clinton, 48; from Sherman, 13.

Turgot, Anne Robert Jacques, 3.

United States Military Academy, 98n.

United States of America, III, 5, 29, 52, 56, 69, 82, 120, 121, 127, 128, 130, 144, 147, 148, 149, 150, 155, 157n., 162, 166; sympathies of Stanislaus Augustus for, 9.

Vale, Md., 143n.

Valley Forge, Pa., Pulaski at 42; possible visit of Kosciuszko, 42; Radière at, 44.

Van Rensselaer, Philip, Col., letter from Kosciuszko, 97 and n.

Van Schaick's Island, N. Y., 21, 25; fortified by Kosciuszko, 22.

Varick, Richard, Capt., letter from Schuyler, 17.

Vergennes, Charles Gravier, Comte de, letters to Noailles, 5; from Gérard, 70n.

Verplanck's Point, N. Y., captured by Clinton, 82; evacuated, 84.

Villefranche, ——, Maj., at West Point, 95.

Virginia, 100, 106, 109, 110, 121, 122, 123; Line, 86; militia, 117.

W., "intelligencer," 133.

Wade, Francis, Col., 106.

Wadsworth, Jeremiah, Col., visited by Kosciuszko, 160.

Warren, ——, Mrs., 95.

Warsaw, Poland, 1, 9n., 158n.

Washington, George, Gen., 6, 17, 29, 34, 44, 51, 66, 73n., 78n., 81, 86, 87, 119 and n., 141n., 144, 151 and n.; has no engineers, 9; retreats through New Jersey, 10; hears of Kosciuszko for the first time, 11; orders Radière to West Point, 44; and "Conway Cabal," 39; loyalty of Kosciuszko to, 41, 161; at West Point, 51-3, 55, 78, 81-4; defends Kosciuszko against claims of the French engineers, 52, 78; and invasion of Canada, 69; refuses Kosciuszko permission to join Gates, 70-72, 144; inquires of whereabouts of Kosciuszko, 77-8; at New Windsor, 82; expects attack on West Point, 90; allows Kosciuszko to go south,

92; meets Kosciuszko at Orange, 99; refuses any infringement of Kosciuszko's authority, 110; at Yorktown, 122, 123 and n.; calls attention of Congress to distress of officers, 145; at Newburg, 146; at Princeton, 155-6; at Trenton, 11, 155; Farewell Orders, 158; gifts to Kosciuszko, 158 and n.; enters New York, 158; at Fraunces' Tavern, 158-9; supposed last meeting with Kosciuszko, 161; review of his relations with Kosciuszko, 161; his opinions of Kosciuszko, 11, 30, 47, 49, 52, 54-5, 81, 99, 157; letters to Armstrong, Sr., 145; to Boudinot, 157; to the Committee of Congress, 145; to Duportail, 54, 127; to Estaing, 70; to Gates, 71, 72, 95, 99; to Gérard, 158; to Gordon, 17; to Hancock, 10, 11; to Heath, 82, 85, 95; to Howe, 90; to Huntington, 85, 89-90; to Jay, 70, 71, 82; to Jones, 146; to Knox, 124; to Kosciuszko, 83, 92, 95, 157; to Lafayette, 110, 158; to Henry Laurens, 30, 42, 48, 52, 69; to Malcolm, 49, 53; to McDougall, 44-7, 77, 81, 83; to the Pennsylvania Council of Safety, 9-10; to Israel Putnam, 43; to John A. Washington, 10; from George Clinton, 48; from the Committee of Conference, 41; from Duportail, 30, 52; from Gates, 70-1, 91, 95; from Grasse, 122; from Greene, 103-6, 109, 118, 122; from Heath, 95-6; from Humphreys, 166; from Huntington, 99n.; from Kosciuszko, 83, 91-2, 156; from Henry Laurens, 30; from McDougall, 44, 47-8, 78; from the Pennsylvania Council of Safety, 9-10; from St. Clair, 23.

Washington, John Augustine, letter from George Washington, 10.

Washington, William, Lt. Col., 103.

Waxhaws, S. C., 103.

Wayne, Anthony, Gen., 135, 138n.; joins Greene, 133; not careful with contraband, 134; enters Charleston, 138; letters to Greene, 134; from Greene, 134.

Wells, ——, letter from Kosciuszko, 80 and n.

Wengierski, Thomas Cajetan, 155-6, 165; his opinion of Greene, 156; meets Washington, 156; letter to Dickinson, 165.

Westchester County, N. Y., 51n.

West Indies, 73 and n., 127, 141n.

ADDENDUM

The following letter comes from the private collection of Lt. Col. Cabell Gwathmey, temporarily deposited with the Alderman Library, University of Virginia. Owing to the present conditions the permission of the owner could not be obtained in time to include the letter in the text.

Albany 17 January 1778.

Sir

I begin my Letter to beg your Protection for me and my Countryman Mr. Zielinski if his side is right as he informed me: But if it is not, tell him Sir that he had better return to his Country than make confusion to me and others. I should be very sorry to see him Conduct bad in this Country.—

I beg more of your favour Sir to have me always under your Command and believe my Sincere attachement to you and that

I am Sir with respect

your Most Humble Servent

Thad: Kosciuszko

To Gen. Washington—

The letter is important not only on account of expression of Kosciuszko's sentiments, but also as the only documentary evidence of his relations with other Poles in America during the Revolution. John Zielinski, a relative of Gen. Pulaski, came to America in 1777, eager to join the Continental Army. At first he served as a volunteer, attached to Pulaski, then Commander of Cavalry, and it was in that capacity that he became involved in a dispute with Col. Stephen Moylan in the Fall of 1777 (Library of Congress, MSS Cont. Cong., II, 341, and XXI, 215 and 275). The adversaries came to blows, however it was Moylan who struck Zielinski first. It seems that the Pole acted out of his attachment to Pulaski. On April 18, 1778, Zielinski was commissioned Lieutenant of Lancers, Pulaski Legion. He advanced to the rank of Captain and died of wounds received in action on September 25, 1779, in a hospital in Charleston, S. C. He endeared himself to Gen. William R. Davie who was confined to the same hospital, "for his noble qualities and long suffering" (*Niles Register,* LXXIII, 68).

The author expresses his thanks to Lt. Col. Gwathmey for permission to print this letter. Mrs. Gwathmey and Mr. Harris H. Williams, in charge of Manuscripts, Alderman Library, kindly aided the author in this regard.